# Colloquial
# Italian

## The Complete Course for Beginners

Sylvia Lymbery

ROUTLEDGE

London and New York

First published 1996
by Routledge
11 New Fetter Lane, London EC4P 4EE

Simultaneously published in the USA and Canada
by Routledge
29 West 35th Street, New York, NY 10001

Typeset in Times Ten by Florencetype Ltd, Stoodleigh, Devon
Printed and bound in England by Clays Ltd, St Ives plc
Illustrations by Carmen Gennari (people) and Andrea Ravarino (maps, buildings)

*British Library Cataloguing in Publication Data*
A catalogue record for this book is available from the British Library

*Library of Congress Cataloguing in Publication Data*
A catalogue record for this book is available from the Library of Congress

ISBN 0–415–12086–1 (book)
ISBN 0–415–12087–X (cassettes)
ISBN 0–415–12088–8 (book and cassettes course)

Colloquial
# Italian

# The Colloquial Series

The following languages are available in the Colloquial series:

| | |
|---|---|
| Albanian | Japanese |
| Amharic | Korean |
| Arabic (Levantine) | Latvian |
| Arabic of Egypt | Lithuanian |
| Arabic of the Gulf and Saudi | Malay |
|   Arabia | Norwegian |
| Basque | Panjabi |
| Bulgarian | Persian |
| * Cambodian | Polish |
| * Cantonese | Portuguese |
| * Chinese | Romanian |
| Czech | * Russian |
| Danish | Serbo-Croat |
| Dutch | Slovak |
| English | Slovene |
| Estonian | Somali |
| French | * Spanish |
| German | Spanish of Latin America |
| * Greek | Swedish |
| Gujarati | * Thai |
| Hindi | Turkish |
| Hungarian | Ukranian |
| Indonesian | * Vietnamese |
| Italian | Welsh |

Accompanying cassette(s) are available for the above titles.
* Accompanying CDs are also available.

**This book is dedicated to Charlotte**

# Contents

# Acknowledgments

Warmest thanks to: Cinzia Buono, Luigi Mazzucco and Sandra Silipo who read the text as it evolved; to Carmen Gennari for her delightful drawings of people and to Andrea Ravarino for his plans, maps, and drawings of buildings. Also to Norberto Bastia, Gabriella Dal Fior, Piera Morino Craveia, Mariella Stagi Scarpa; to the Editor of *La Stampa*, Torino, for permission to use various extracts; to Lietta Tornabuoni for permission to use part of her article; to Ristoranti Brek; and to many friends and my colleagues at the International School of Turin. Finally to the editorial staff of Routledge.

Permission to use the extracts from *Anna* was sought but no reply received.

# About this book

So you are thinking of learning Italian? Or perhaps you are already learning and want more food for thought, another approach to help you on your way? Read on and you will see why *Colloquial Italian* is perhaps just what you are looking for.

## Why Italian?

Italian is the language of Italy and it is also one of the four official languages of Switzerland. Small though Italy is, its inhabitants over recorded history have had very significant effects on civilization and the land of Italy has been a source of pleasure and interest to travellers for centuries. Today it still offers the tourist many and varied delights: scenery, artistic treasures, music, good food and wine, snow, sun and sea. Italy is, of course, one of the founder members of the European Community and for businesses it holds many challenges and opportunities. This in spite of problems of a political, economic and environmental nature which mean that there is also much to frustrate and annoy the traveller. These problems and their background also however make Italy a fascinating subject of study.

The language is possibly the easiest European language for English speakers to learn. The pronunciation seems easier for English speakers than French, the grammar less tricky than that of German or Russian and there is the great plus point that the spelling of the words reflects the way they are said and the meaning of many is guessable.

Italian has its origins in Latin, the language spoken in Ancient Rome. For anyone who has studied Latin or one of the Romance languages (languages derived closely from Latin such as Spanish, French, Portuguese), it is particularly approachable for not only will many more words be guessable but the structure too will be similar to that of the language they know. This is not to say it is trouble-free, but you, the learner, can feel optimistic as you start the task.

As a nation state Italy is young. It was united between 1860 and 1870 after centuries of division into a number of smaller states. At the time of unification Italian was essentially a written language used by poets, playwrights and other writers. Only a small percentage of the population spoke it. Most communicated in their local dialect. Today universal education, military service, population mobility and TV and radio mean that most people speak and understand Italian although many also continue to speak their local dialect as well.

## *Colloquial Italian*

The aim has been to write a book in which the language learner, who may not have experience of learning foreign languages, is helped with the difficulties, particularly in the early and potentially confusing stages. At the same time we have tried not to insult the learner's intelligence. As has been said, many Italian words are guessable and we have deliberately challenged the learner by introducing a wide vocabulary, confident that he/she will find it manageable. We have tried too to entertain and stimulate.

As a language learner you need to be aware that different people learn languages in different ways and to try to find the way that works for you. There are few people who can sit down with a grammar book, read the rules, do a few exercises and start speaking the language. Many people find it helpful to become familiar with chunks of language, for instance the dialogues and texts in *Colloquial Italian*. This does not mean trying to learn by rote but rather reading them, ideally aloud, several times, becoming thoroughly familiar with them; going back over them after a break and, even better, listening to the recordings. Why not put the recording in your walkman while you are doing something which does not engage your mind, jogging, perhaps, or washing the dishes? Or play it on your car stereo as you sit in traffic jams? Gradually the language becomes part of you and you find you can adapt it to say what you want to say.

Learning a language takes patience and determination. You will have your ups and downs, your moments of frustration but moments of satisfaction too. We recommend you try a 'little and often' routine: work at your Italian regularly but not necessarily for long periods of time.

Many people find it helpful to back up their learning in every way available to them: exchanging a few words with a friendly waiter in an Italian restaurant, or watching Italian films. Treat yourself to an Italian magazine or newspaper occasionally. The biggest aid of all is a trip to Italy. Don't, however, expect too much from the first visit. Much will depend on the extent to which you are able to be with Italians and 'have a go'. 'Having a go' is probably the key to success. And beware: you will always understand more than you can say. Make the most of each opportunity and above all don't worry about making mistakes. Italians are usually delighted when foreigners try to speak their language. We can almost guarantee they won't laugh at you.

# Getting started

You almost certainly already know a number of Italian words. Stop reading and write down those that come into your mind. Add too the names of places or of famous Italians which come to mind.

Did your list include greetings such as **ciao**, **arrivederci**? Or perhaps words relating to food and drink such as: **pasta**, **spaghetti**, **pesto**, **pizza**, **gelato**, **vino**, **cappuccino**, **gorgonzola**, **Chianti**, **Asti spumante**. Maybe you know some words from the field of music such as: **orchestra**, **cello**, **piccolo**, **trombone**, **pianoforte**, **solo**, **soprano**, **aria**. Or words like: **chiaroscuro**, **viva voce**, **tuttifrutti** – or maybe single words like **ghetto**, **piazza**.

How about the names of people and places? Did you have **Gucci**, **Ferragamo**, **Armani**? Or **Giotto**, **Botticelli**, **Piero della Francesca**? Or maybe **Vivaldi**, **Puccini**, **Verdi**, **Palestrina**. Or perhaps **Sofia Loren**, **Marcello Mastroianni**, **Federico Fellini**, **Giulietta Masina**; Or again **Maserati**, **Ferrari**, **Lamborghini**, **Fiat**, **Lancia** . . . Oh, we nearly forgot **Luciano Pavarotti**! But maybe you had some other list we have not foreseen? It all depends on your own personal interests. Place names are more difficult, unless you have already visited Italy, as we anglicize so many names of parts of Italy: Rome, Venice, Milan, Tuscany, Sicily . . . But you may know **Palermo**, **Cattolica**, **Rimini**, **Como**, **Garda**, **Brindisi** . . .

So already you have an idea of how Italian looks and sounds. One immediately noticeable feature is that words mostly end with vowels. You will gradually learn that these final vowels often carry meaning. That is perhaps the most difficult aspect of Italian: it is an *inflected* language. This means the endings of words vary to express grammatical information. To a certain extent this happens in English: 'book/books' – the 's' expresses the plural. It is more developed in Italian but you, the learner, should not worry too much: in the heat of a conversation, if you are unsure, your meaning will usually be clear even if you slur the word ending to cover your uncertainty. Gradually, with practice, this aspect of the language slots into place.

So, you're ready to go. Good luck! **In bocca al lupo!**

# The sounds of Italian

What follows does not pretend to be a full academic treatment of Italian pronunciation but rather a practical guide to help the foreign learner speak in a way that is reasonably comprehensible and acceptable. It should also be viewed as a reference section, which will be difficult to absorb in one reading but can be returned to from time to time.

Italian spelling reflects the sounds of the Italian language on a more regular and simpler basis than English spelling does for English. There are however some cases where the spelling conventions of Italian conflict with those of English and it is important that students get these clear in their mind from the start. They are explained below.

Since the letters represent sounds, we are starting from the sounds using phonetic symbols (those of the International Phonetic Association) enclosed in square brackets: [ ]. If you have the recordings they will help you grasp what these sounds are, especially if you are unfamiliar with the system. We give rough English equivalents but they are a poor substitute for hearing the sounds spoken by an Italian.

## Vowels 🔲

| Phonetic symbol | Letter | English equivalent (approximate) | Italian examples |
|---|---|---|---|
| [a] | a | band | **casa**, **grande**, **fantastico** |
| [e][1] | e | bed, case | **tè**, **bello**, **vedo** |
| [i] | i | feet | **vino**, **Pisa** |
| [o][1] | o | not | **cosa**, **rosso**, **porta**, **come** |
| [u] | u | soon | **fumo**, **cupola** |

Many words contain two vowels; both are pronounced: **bu***o***no**, **p***ae***se**, **fi***u***me**, **si***a***mo**, **p***au***ra**, etc.

1 In some regions of Italy there is a distinction between a closed [e] and an open [ɛ], but this usage varies from region to region and it is a distinction the learner can safely ignore. The same is true of the distinction between closed [o] and an open [ɔ].

## Consonants 🔊

In the notes we refer to *voiced* and *unvoiced* consonants. In English *t*, *p*, *k*, are *unvoiced* and *d*, *b*, *g*, are *voiced*. Say them aloud and you should understand that the second group have a voice sound to them.

| | | | |
|---|---|---|---|
| [b][2] | b | *boy* | **b***uono*, a***b***itare |
| [d] | d | *dog* | ***d***ata, i***d***ea |
| [f] | f | *form* | ***f***avore, ***f***ame |
| – | h | – | initial *h* is not pronounced: ***h***o, ***h***ote***l***[3] |
| [l] | l | *leg* | ***l***ira, a***l***to |
| [m] | m | *m*ood | ***m***adre, a***m***ore |
| [n] | n | *n*ice | ***n***aso, u***n***o |
| [p] | p | *p*ot | ***p***era, cu***p***ola |
| [kw] | qu | *qu*estion | ***qu***estione[4] |
| [r][5] | r | – | ***r***iso, r***a***dio, ***R***oma, a***r***te, po***r***ta, bi***rr***a |
| [s][6] | s, ss | *s*ong, | ***s***era, s***p***e***ss***o, ro***ss***o, cor***s***o |
| [z][7] | s | ro*s*e | ro***s***a, ***s***viluppo, ***s***b***a***glio |
| [t] | t | *t*all | ***t***empo, ***t***reno |
| [ts][8] | z, zz | – | ***z***ucchero, a***z***ienda, raga***zz***o |
| [dz][8] | z, zz | – | ***z***ero, a***zz***urro. |

2 The learner will sound more genuinely Italian if he/she can make [b], [d], [k], [p], [t], less 'breathy', harder. But it is not crucial. The most easily done is [t].

3 For the other use of *h* see below under [k].

4 The letter *q* is always followed by *u* and pronounced as in English.

5 The Italian [r] is rolled. There is no real English equivalent. The letter appears only when the [r] is pronounced: **porta**, **arte**. Note the difference between **cane** 'dog' and **carne** 'meat'. Some Italians make their **r** in their throats but it is always audible and more prominent that in standard southern English.

6 [s] as in *s*ong or hi*ss*, occurs: (1) at the beginning of a word before a vowel: **sera**, **sempre**; (2) when double s (ss): **rosso**, **cassa**; (3) after a consonant: **corso**; (4) before an unvoiced consonant: **scarpa**, **spaghetti**, **stare**, **posto**, **Tosca**. Some people also pronounce **s** between vowels [s]. See note 7.

7 [z] is spelled with the letter s and occurs: (1) between vowels: **casa**, **riso**, **rosa**; (2) when followed by a voiced consonant: *s*bagliare, *s*viluppo. As with the vowel sounds [e] and [o] (see footnote 1) there are regional variations (e.g. [casa] for [caza]) but the foreign learner can safely stick to [z], which is probably what comes naturally.

8 There are also regional differences in pronouncing the letter(s) z, zz. The learner need not worry about whether they should be voiced or unvoiced; in practice it is not crucial.

So far, so good. The remaining sounds are, however, those where the spelling conventions of English and Italian differ significantly and learners should pay particular attention to them. Using the recordings and imitating them throughout the course will also help you avoid errors. The first two are a little difficult to pronounce:

| | | | |
|---|---|---|---|
| [ʎ] | gl(i) | mi*lli*on | **fig*li*o, mag*li*a, g*li*** |
| [ɲ] | gn | o*ni*on | **bag*n*o, ag*n*ello** |

With the sounds [k] and [g] there is no pronunciation problem but the spelling depends on which vowel follows. The vowels divide into two groups:

(1) **a, o, u**

| | | | |
|---|---|---|---|
| [k] | c | *c*at | **cane, campo, caffè, casa, Canada, cosa, costa, comune, cortesia, Como, curioso, cuore, cultura, Cuneo** |
| [g] | g | *g*old | **galleria, gamba, gallese, Garda, gondola, golf, gorgonzola, Goldoni, Gonzaga, guidare, guardare, Gubbio, Guttuso** |

(2) **e, i**

| | | | |
|---|---|---|---|
| [k] | ch | *c*at | **che, orchestra, Cherubino, Michelangelo, chi, chilo, Chianti, Chiusi, Chioggia** |
| [g] | gh | *g*old | **ghetto, spaghetti, Ghiberti, Ghirlandaio, Lamborghini** |

The same grouping of vowels is also important in the spelling conventions for the sound pairs [t] and [d]:

(1) **a, o, u**

| | | | |
|---|---|---|---|
| [tʃ] | ci | *ch*urch | **ciao, ciò, Luciano, Lancia** |
| [dʒ] | gi | *G*eorge | **giapponese, giallo, giorno, giovedì, Giotto, giù, giusto, Giulia, Giuseppe** |

(2) **e, i**

| | | | |
|---|---|---|---|
| [tʃ] | c | *ch*urch | **cento, cena, certo, violoncello, San Francesco,** |

Botticelli, *ci*bo, *ci*nema, cappu*cci*no, Pu*cci*ni, Gu*cci*

[dʒ] g *George* **gente, generalmente, gelato, geografia, Germania, gita, girare, Gino, Gilda, Gigli**

Finally the spelling of the sound [ʃ]:

(1) **a, o, u**

[ʃ] sci *sh*arp *sci*arpa, *sci*opero, *sci*upare
[ʃ] sc *sh*ip *sc*endere, pe*sc*e, *sci*, Gram*sci*

## Double consonants

When a word is spelled with a double consonant, it is because the sound is different from the same consonant written as a single. It takes practice to get this right but it is important. Try to linger on the double consonant or pause before it. The preceding vowel becomes shorter:

**ecco, freddo, bello, mamma, anno, cappuccino, terra, stesso, fatto, pazzo**

(Note the contrast: **eco, ecco; fata, fatta.**)

## Stress

The most common place for an Italian word to be stressed is on the syllable before the last (the *penultimate* syllable, as underlined):

**italiano, aeroporto, interessante, il mondo moderno, la stazione della ferrovia**

Some words are stressed on the *final* vowel. In that case the vowel is written with an accent:

**città, possibilità, perciò, può, tivù, lunedì**

The most problematic for the foreign learner are the words where the *antepenultimate* (the third from the end) syllable is stressed:

**sabato, domenica, albero, cinema, chilometro, lettera, libero, macchina**

Occasionally, for instance, in the third person plural of some verbs, the stress may fall on the *fourth* syllable from the end: **telefonano.**

Dictionaries always give help with stress and so does our Italian–English glossary, which uses underlining to show irregular stress. We have also done this in the pronunciation section of the book. But in print or in writing, it is not normally indicated. The best you can do is *listen* to Italians speaking and try to build up a sound memory. However, stress *is* important. The wrong stress is more likely than a generally not very Italian-sounding accent to obscure your meaning.

Related to stress is *intonation*, the 'tune of the phrase'. This is also best acquired by imitation and should not constitute a big problem.

## The Italian alphabet

The Italian language uses an alphabet of 21 letters. The other letters of our familiar 26-letter alphabet are used in writing foreign words. When spelling something out for someone, especially over the telephone, it is usual to use the names of towns to make the letter clear (see examples below). Below is a list of letters, with their pronunciation and the town name usually used:

| | | | | | |
|---|---|---|---|---|---|
| a | **a** | Ancona | m | **emme** | Milano |
| b | **bi** | Bologna/Bari | n | **enne** | Napoli |
| c | **ci** | Como | o | **o** | Otranto |
| d | **di** | Domodossola | p | **pi** | Pisa |
| e | **e** | Empoli | q | **cu** | cu |
| f | **effe** | Firenze | r | **erre** | Roma |
| g | **gi** | Genova | s | **esse** | Savona |
| h | **acca** | hotel | t | **ti** | Torino |
| i | **i** | Imola | u | **u** | Udine |
| l | **elle** | Livorno | v | **vi/vu** | Venezia |
| | | | z | **zeta** | Zara |

The following are not considered Italian letters and are used mainly in foreign words.

| | | | | |
|---|---|---|---|---|
| j | **i lungo/a** | | x | **ics** |
| k | **cappa** | | y | **i greco/a**, **ipsilon** |
| w | **vi/vu doppio/a** | | | |

Examples of how a name can be spelt out, especially over the telephone:

Roma, Otranto, Savona, Savona, Imola = *Rossi*

Savona, Milano, Imola, Torino, hotel = *Smith*
Livorno, i greco, Milano, Bologna, Empoli, Roma, i greco = *Lymbery*

The letters are considered either masculine or feminine: some people will say **i greca** rather than **i greco**. They are not usually made plural, so **ss** is: **due esse**; also: **doppio esse** or **doppia esse**.

## Accents

An accent is used to indicate the stress when it falls on the final vowel of a word. There is some discussion in Italy about using acute (´) or grave (`) accents, particularly over the letter e, where some people like to show the open/closed distinction mentioned in footnote 1. In practice, when writing, Italians write something which could be either: (⌣). You are advised to do the same.

In a very few cases an accent is used to distinguish one word from another:

| | | | |
|---|---|---|---|
| **e** | and | **è** | is |
| **da** | from | **dà** | gives |
| **ne** | of it, of them *etc.* | **nè** | neither, nor |
| **si** | oneself | **sì** | yes |
| **la** | the, *also a pronoun* | **là** | there |
| **li** | *pronoun* | **lì** | there |

Did you find all this difficult to absorb? Of course you did. Don't worry. It will gradually make sense.

# 1 Buongiorno, un caffè per favore

## Good morning, a coffee please

First things first, let's get a drink. In Italy the bar (**bar** or **caffè**) is a popular meeting place as well as being a place to drop in for a coffee, a glass of water on a hot day, a snack or an ice cream. Although alcohol is served, you rarely see drunkenness and bars are used by people of all ages, including young people and families. Many bars have terraces where, in the summer, people sit outside chatting, reading the newspaper or watching everyone else go by. Of course there are bars of all sorts, from the very elegant to the simple and down to earth. The prices of **caffè** and **cappuccino**, consumed standing at the counter (**al banco**), are regulated but otherwise what you pay is likely to be directly related to the smartness of the décor and even more to the position of the bar. In St Mark's Square in Venice, for instance, expect to pay a lot. Popular drinks are:

**caffè** a small very strong black coffee, also called '**espresso**'
**cappuccino** a small, very strong, black coffee with frothy milk added, often sprinkled with powdered chocolate
**vino, bianco o rosso** wine, red or white
**acqua minerale, naturale o gassata** mineral (bottled) water, still or fizzy

**tè, con latte o con limone** tea, with milk or with lemon
**tè freddo** iced tea, a refreshing drink in hot weather
**birra** beer
**succo di frutta** fruit juice
**succo di pera, di mela, di arancia** pear, apple, orange juice
**spremuta** freshly squeezed citrus fruit
**arancia**, **limone** or **pompelmo** orange, lemon or grapefruit

You can also order **un panino**, a roll with some sort of filling, ham, egg and tomato, for instance; or **un toast**, a toasted ham and cheese sandwich; or for the sweet-toothed, **una pasta**, a pastry, or **una brioche**, a currant bun, or **gelato**, ice cream.

The following conversations take place in a bar. If you have the recording, listen first without the book and try to understand. See if you can answer the question below. It may take more than one hearing before you understand but persevere. (See advice on studying in 'About this book'.)

# Dialogue 1 ▢▢

## *Al bar*

*A group of friends order drinks*

> Among the drinks ordered are some not explained above. Can you pick them out and guess what they are?

| | |
|---|---|
| CAMERIERE: | Buongiorno. Prego. |
| PAOLO: | Una birra, per favore. |
| ANNA: | Per me, un caffè. |
| TOMMASO: | Un vino bianco. |
| MARISA: | Un'aranciata. |
| FILIPPO: | Una Coca-Cola. |
| CAMERIERE: | Una birra, un caffè, un vino bianco, un'aranciata e una Coca-Cola. Va bene. |

> The drinks not explained were **un'aranciata**, 'an orangeade (fizzy)', and **una Coca-Cola**. No prizes for guessing that! You will find answers to questions and exercises in the Key at the back of the book.

## Vocabulary notes

**prego** *lit.* 'I pray, I beg'. *Here it is an invitation to order.* ***Prego*** *is also used to reply when someone thanks you for something and then means 'don't mention it, not at all, you're welcome'*
**per favore** please. *The words 'please' and 'thank you' are not as necessary in Italian as they are in English. When you are shopping or ordering in a bar or restaurant, you need not keep repeating them*
**per me** for me
**va bene** fine, OK. *Va **bene** is not, however, just for casual speech, as is OK. It is perfectly acceptable in a formal context too*

# Language point

## Introducing Italian nouns and indefinite articles

Italian nouns are either *masculine* or *feminine*. This is sometimes related to sex, in the case of people or animals for instance, but mostly not. The word for '*a, an*' is **un** with a masculine noun and **una** with a feminine noun.

|  | Masculine |  | Feminine |
|---|---|---|---|
| un | vino<br>caffè<br>gelato<br>succo di frutta<br>panino<br>tè<br>toast | una | birra<br>aranciata<br>spremuta<br>pasta<br>brioche<br>Coca-Cola |

*Note:* When **una** comes before a noun beginning with a vowel, such as **acqua**, it is usual to drop the **a** of **una** and just say **un'**. When speaking, it comes naturally to run one vowel into another. When writing this, you put an apostrophe (') to show something has been left out: **un'aranciata, un'acqua minerale**.

**Un, una** also mean 'one'. When the word 'one' is not with a noun, the masculine form is **uno**. See below.

Many masculine Italian nouns end in **-o**, and many feminine nouns end in **-a**. This makes it easy to guess the gender of a noun in very many cases. In the above list there are some foreign words adopted by Italian which do not fit this pattern: **caffè**, **Coca-Cola**, **tè**, **toast** and **brioche**. Mostly foreign words adopted into Italian are masculine. **Brioche** and **Coca-Cola** which are feminine are exceptions. Try to learn the gender of a noun with the noun.

# Dialogue 2 📼

## *Prima colazione*

*It's the early morning rush hour in a busy bar, when Italians pop in for a quick breakfast on the way to work. In most bars, particularly in cities, you go to the cash desk first and say what you want. You pay and are given a receipt (**scontrino**) which you then give to the barman, repeating your order. It is usual to stand at the bar with your drink. If you sit down, you get service at table and often have to pay extra, sometimes double. So think whether you want to sit and relax for some time, or whether in fact you just want a quick drink.*

*Maria first goes to the cash desk to pay*

---

1 What do Piera and Maria order to eat?
2 Do they have the same drink?

---

| | |
|---|---|
| CASSIERE: | Desidera? |
| MARIA: | Per me un cappuccino e una brioche. |
| PIERA: | E per me un caffè e una pasta. |
| CASSIERE: | 6.000 lire. |
| MARIA: | Ecco. |
| CASSIERE: | Ecco lo scontrino. |

*Maria and Piera go to the bar*

| | |
|---|---|
| MARIA: | Scusi! |
| BARISTA: | Sì, signorina. Mi dica. |
| MARIA: | Un cappuccino e una brioche, per favore. |
| BARISTA: | (*to her friend*) E lei? |
| PIERA: | Per me un caffè e una pasta. |
| BARISTA: | Un cappuccino e un caffè. Va bene. |

*Maria and Piera help themselves to the **brioche** and the **pasta** in the display case on the counter*

# Vocabulary notes

**prima colazione** breakfast
**desidera?** *lit.* 'you desire?' *The cashier is asking what Maria wants*
**ecco** here you are; *also* here is, here are; there is, there are
   (*pointing something out*)
**scusi** excuse me. *In a busy bar, use **scusi** or **mi scusi** to catch the
   barman's attention*
**mi dica** (*often just **dica***) *lit.* 'tell me'. *The barman is indicating
   that he is ready to listen to the order. The barman in the previous
   conversation said **Prego***
**lei** you (*formal*)
**una pasta** a pastry. ***Pasta** is also, of course, the generic word for
   all the various types of **spaghetti**, **macaroni**, etc.*

# Language points

## I numeri 'numbers'

| | | | |
|---|---|---|---|
| 1 | uno, una | 6 | sei |
| 2 | due | 7 | sette |
| 3 | tre | 8 | otto |
| 4 | quattro | 9 | nove |
| 5 | cinque | 10 | dieci |

*Examples:* **una birra, due caffè**
   The Italian unit of currency is the **lira**, plural **lire**. Decades of
inflation mean that **una lira** will not buy anything today. You will
be counting mostly in thousands, sometimes for very small items
in hundreds.

| | | | |
|---|---|---|---|
| 100 | **cento** | 200 | **duecento** |
| 1.000 | **mille** | 2.000 | **duemila** |

*Note:* **Mille** has a plural form **mila** but **cento** does not change
in the plural. When writing numbers in letters (e.g. on a cheque)
it is usual to join all the elements together in one, often long,
word, e.g. **cinquemilasettecento** (5.700). You will notice also that
the thousands are marked by a full stop (.) as in 10.000 and

not by a comma (,) which is used where English uses the decimal point.

## More about indefinite articles

Can you guess whether the word **scontrino** is masculine or feminine? Like most nouns ending in **-o** it is masculine. However, 'a till receipt' is **uno scontrino.** As you will perhaps know from listening to Italians speaking English, the Italian language avoids clusters of consonants and Italians find them difficult in English. The combination **n + s + c** is avoided by inserting an **o**: **uno scontrino**.

This applies to other words beginning with **s** + another consonant. For instance the English word 'sport' has been adopted into Italian. Like most foreign words used in Italian it is . . .? Yes, masculine. So you say **uno sport**.

The problem does not arise with feminine nouns because there is already the **-a** in **una**; **una spremuta**.

**Exercise 1** You are a waiter with a long list of drinks to get for a large group at a table on the terrace outside in the square. Here is the list, but the word for 'a' has been left out. Recite the list to the barman, filling that in.

_____ vino rosso, _____ gelato, _____ birra, _____ caffè,
_____ acqua minerale, _____ spremuta, _____ succo di frutta,
_____ tè, _____ vino bianco, _____ aranciata.

When you have checked your answers, say the words out loud to get used to the sound. It will also be helpful in memorizing them.

**Exercise 2** You are an Englishman who is on holiday in Italy with his family. They decide that since you have been learning Italian, you ought to do the ordering for them. So, be the interpreter to the barman in this bar. This means you have to put the words in italics into Italian in the spaces provided:

BARISTA: **Buongiorno. Prego.**
YOU: (to your wife) What would you like, darling?
YOUR WIFE: (1) *A white coffee.*
YOU: (to the barman) _____.
(to your daughter) And you, Jane?
JANE: (2) *An orangeade.*

YOU:   (to the barman) _____.
       (to your son) Mark?
MARK:   (3) *A fresh orange drink.*
YOU:   (to the barman) _____.
BARISTA: **E per Lei, signore?**
YOU:   (For yourself order (4) *a beer*. You deserve it after all that!) _____.

**Exercise 3** Read the following numbers out loud and then write them out as numerals:

1 sette
3 quattrocento
5 duemilacinquecento
7 diecimila

2 nove
4 ottocentotre
6 milletrecento
8 seimilacento

**Exercise 4** Here are some till receipts for various items of shopping. How much did the shopper spend in:

(Write the numbers in letters – and say them aloud to yourself)

"CAFFE VERSARI"
VERSARI VERA
P.ZA A.FERDINANDO 4
MONCALIERI (TO) T.641733
P.IVA 02484180019
65          12-07-1994
14:52          CASSA 1

REPARTO1          5.900
TOT          5.900
/FPA 42003098

---

CAFFE' DEL CENTRO SNC
C/O SHOPVILLE
"LE GRU"
VIA CREA 10
GRUGLIASCO (TO)
PART.IVA:06579670016
TEL.70.43.37  GRAZIE

VARIE          2'000
CAFFE'          1'700
VARIE          500
**TOTALE**          4'200
22/12/94          14-05
SC.FISC. N.          62
/FPD 12003164

---

FERRAMENTA
AMELOTTI ENRICO
VIA UMBERTO I 21/B
PECETTO (TO)
TEL. 011/8609979
P.IVA 02060930019

REPARTO1          2'200
**TOTALE**          2'200
02/09/95          18-15
SC.FISC. N.          45
/FPD 42005238

---

PANIFICIO
MEREU  SNC
STRADA GENOVA 174
M O N C A L I E R I
(TO)  TEL.647.17.92
PART.IVA:06773890014
GRAZIE

REPARTO1          1'300
**TOTALE**          1'300
04/09/95          18-13
SC.FISC. N.          253
/FPD 12000608

---

FARMACIA DR. MOSSO
V.BOCCARDO 2 TESTONA
MONCALIERI T.6471233
PART.IVA 00552520017

TICKET          6.000
TOTALE 1          6.000

CASS. 1 18:15 CASSA 1
25-03-95  SCONTR. N. 227
/F XT 13019304

---

GELATERIA
LA MELA STREGATA S.R.L.
PIAZZA CARDUCCI 122
TORINO ** TEL..677041
P.I. 02229270018

REPARTO1          5'000
REPARTO1          700
TOTALE          5'700

34          07-07-.994
14:12
/F16 11501985

1  il Caffè Versari
2  il Caffè del Centro
3  la ferramenta (*ironmonger's*)
4  il panificio (*baker's*)
5  la farmacia (*pharmacy/
   chemist's*)
6  la gelateria (*ice-cream bar*)
7  McDonald's

```
  * MCDONALD'S *
     S.I.R. SRL
  P.DUCA D'AOSTA,6



  P.I. 10807960157

                 0015
  17/03/95  CASS.6

  MISTA     5.800
  ACQUA G.  1.000
  ----------------
  TOTALE 6.800
  CONTAN    7.000
  RESTO     0.200

  0020A      12:58
        MILANO

  /\F25  11600067
```

Each receipt is a **ricevuta fiscale**. You are required by law to get a **ricevuta fiscale** for virtually everything you buy and the seller to provide it, as part of measures to reduce tax evasion introduced in recent years. Theoretically you could be fined if you failed to obtain the receipt.

## Greetings and courtesies

As in English, the greeting you use depends on the time of day and who you are talking to. **Buongiorno** is the equivalent of both 'good morning' and 'good afternoon'. It is used in any formal situation: going into a shop, in a hotel, in a bank, greeting someone you do not know well, greeting colleagues in the morning, etc.

# Dialogue 3 ▓▓

*Un appuntamento con il signor Rossi*

*Angela Smith has an appointment to see Signor Rossi. She goes into the outer office, where the secretary greets her*

1  What does the secretary invite Mrs Smith to do?
2  What words does Mr Rossi use to invite Mrs Smith to sit down?

SEGRETARIA: Buongiorno, signora. Mi dica.
SMITH: Buongiorno, signorina. Sono Angela Smith.
SEGRETARIA: Ah, signora Smith, buongiorno. Un attimo, prego. Si accomodi. (*She disappears into the inner office and a moment later Mr Rossi comes out with her*)
ROSSI: Buongiorno, signora Smith. Venga, venga. (*He motions to Mrs Smith to go into his office*)
SMITH: Buongiorno, signor Rossi.
ROSSI: S'accomodi, prego. (*He indicates a chair for Mrs Smith*) Come va?
SMITH: Bene, grazie. E lei?

## Vocabulary

| | |
|---|---|
| **sono** | I am |
| **un attimo** | just a moment |
| **s'accomodi, si accomodi** | sit down, make yourself comfortable |
| **prego** | *here* please, do (sit down) |
| **venga** | come this way (*lit.* 'come') |
| **come va?** | how are you? |
| **bene grazie, e lei?** | well thanks, and you? |
| **signor** (*abbr. to* **sig.**) | Mr |
| **signora** (*abbr. to* **sig.ra**) | Mrs |
| **signorina** (*abbr. to* **sig.na**) | Miss |

It is usual *not* to capitalize these titles. As yet, there is no Italian equivalent to 'Ms'. On the other hand, Italian women continue to use their maiden name after marriage, especially, but not only, in their professional capacity.

When you do not know a person's name, it is usual to refer to them as:

signore
signora
signorina

e.g. **Scusi, signora ...**

Note that the word **signore** has an **-e** on the end when it is used without the name, i.e. it becomes three syllables. In practice, too, the choice of **signora** or **signorina** depends partly on the age of the lady although **signorina** is not used a great deal. **Signora** is preferred.

# Dialogue 4

### Un incontro per la strada

*Mrs Martini meets her son's school teacher in the street. Her son, Marco, is at home with a cold*

> Why is the conversation a rather short one?

| | |
|---|---|
| INSEGNANTE: | Buongiorno, signora. Come va? |
| SIG.RA MARTINI: | Buongiorno, professore. Bene grazie, e lei? |
| INSEGNANTE: | Bene grazie. E Marco? |
| SIG.RA MARTINI: | Marco sta male. Ha un raffreddore. |
| INSEGNANTE: | Mi dispiace, signora. E suo marito? |
| SIG.RA MARTINI: | Sta bene, grazie. Lavora molto. |
| INSEGNANTE: | Mi scusi, devo andare. Arrivederla a presto. Auguri a Marco e saluti a suo marito. |
| SIG.RA MARTINI: | Arrivederla, professore. Buongiorno. |

## Vocabulary

| | |
|---|---|
| **insegnante** | teacher |
| **Marco sta male** | Marco is ill |
| **ha un raffreddore** | he has a cold |
| **mi dispiace** | I am sorry *lit.* 'it displeases me'. *You say it when expressing regret about something unpleasant or unfortunate. It is slightly different from* **mi scusi** *(see below)* |
| **e suo marito?** | and your husband? |
| **sta bene** | he's well |
| **grazie** | thank you |
| **mi scusi** | I am sorry, I apologize, excuse me (**mi** *is often omitted*) |
| **devo andare** | I have to go |
| **a presto** | see you soon |
| **auguri** | best wishes |
| **saluti** | greetings, say 'hello' to |

**Arrivederla** is a very formal way of saying 'goodbye'. It is often used by shopkeepers, bank clerks, etc. Less formal is **arrivederci**.

It is also very common, when saying goodbye in formal conversations, to add **buongiorno** too, as Mrs Martini does. After mid-afternoon, people often use **buonasera** (*lit.* 'good evening') both to open the conversation and to close it. **Buonanotte** means 'goodnight' and is used to say goodbye at night, really wishing someone a good night's sleep.

Mrs Martini's relationship with her son's teacher is formal so she calls him **professore** ('teacher'). It is usual to use titles like this when talking to professional people (e.g. **avvocato, dottore, ingegnere**).

Look at Dialogue 5 to find out what you say when you are greeting friends.

# Dialogue 5

### Ciao, Gianni

PAOLO: Ciao, Gianni. Come va?
GIANNI: Oh, ciao Paolo.
PAOLO: Tutto bene?
GIANNI: Sì, grazie, e tu?
PAOLO: Sì, tutto bene. Mi dispiace, devo scappare. Ciao. A presto.
GIANNI: Ciao.

# Vocabulary

| | |
|---|---|
| **tutto bene?** | *lit.* 'all well?' Is everything all right? |
| **scappare** | to run away. *Devo scappare is often used colloquially instead of devo andare* |

You say **ciao** both when you meet a friend and to say goodbye to him/her. You don't say **lei** to a friend, you use **tu**. You also use **tu** when talking to children, family, and colleagues. Italians, on the whole, these days, prefer to use **tu** once they get to know you or if they are working with you. It is similar to using first names.

# Language points

## Personal pronouns and verbs

You have now met the word **lei** several times. By convention it used to be written with a capital **L** although this convention is not nowadays observed except in formal letter-writing. You have also met **tu**. 'I' is **io**. You may have noticed that after **per** (a preposition) you have a different form.

| Pronoun subject with verb | | Pronoun after preposition | | |
|---|---|---|---|---|
| **io** | I | | **me** | me |
| **tu** | you (familiar) | **per** { | **te** for { | you |
| **lei** | you (formal) | | **lei** | you |

Personal pronouns as subjects of a verb ('I', 'you', 'he', 'we', etc) are usually not expressed in Italian as it is generally clear from the form of the verb who or what the subject of the verb is. Angela Smith said, for instance: **Sono Angela Smith.** She would only have said **Io sono Angela Smith** if she had been wanting to stress the 'I'.

The verb 'to be' (**essere**) is irregular in Italian. The following are the forms for the singular:

| | |
|---|---|
| **(io) sono** | I am |
| **(tu) sei** | you are (*familiar*) |
| **(lei) è** | you are (*formal*) |

The forms are different from each other and the subject pronoun is unnecessary.

The present singular of 'to have' – **avere**, is:

| | |
|---|---|
| **(io) ho** | I have |
| **(tu) hai** | you have (*familiar*) |
| **(lei) ha** | you have (*formal*) |

*Note:* The **h** is silent. This verb provides the only cases in Italian of an initial **h**.

**Exercise 5** Rewrite this short conversation between two friends as an exchange between two people whose relationship is formal, Sig. Rossi and Avv. Bruni.

*Buongiorno*

GIORGIO: Ciao, Marco, come va?
MARCO: Bene, grazie. E tu?
GIORGIO: Bene. Devo andare. Ciao.
MARCO: Ciao. *I have to go*

*Exercise 6* Look back over the dialogues and pick out the verbs used without subject pronouns. (*Note:* **Scusi** and **mi dica** are verbs in the command (imperative) form and would never have a pronoun with them. You are looking for other verbs.) Consult the Key to exercises to see if you found them.

# Reading 🔲

### Bar famosi

Read the passage and try to answer the questions. It is not necessary to understand every word.

---

1  When did Florian's open?
2  What are the ingredients of the aperitif which is the speciality of Harry's Bar?
3  If you were hungry would it be a good place to go?
4  What is the name of its owner?

---

(*Warning:* These bars are expensive!)

In Piazza San Marco a Venezia c'è un bar antico e famoso: il Florian. Esiste dal 1720. All'interno, c'è un senso di intimità nelle sale di stile '700. Fuori ci sono numerosi tavolini proprio in Piazza San Marco, con un'orchestrina che suona per i clienti. E' bello sedersi lì e guardare la piazza famosa e la gente che passa.

Un altro bar famoso a Venezia è l'Harry's Bar. E' un bar molto elegante. Offre naturalmente caffè, vino, whisky e così via, ma anche un aperitivo famoso, 'il Bellini', vino bianco frizzante con succo di pesca. Harry's è un bar ma è anche un ristorante molto buono. L'Harry's Bar era il locale preferito di Hemingway e ancora oggi è frequentato da molte persone famose, attori, scrittori e così via. Il proprietario, Arrigo Cipriani, è anche lui un personaggio famoso a Venezia.

## Vocabulary notes

**stile '700** eighteenth-century style (*the style of the years from 1700 to 1799*). *It is usual in Italian to refer to a century this way. The twentieth century is the '900 – Il novecento. It is an abbreviation for millenovecento*

**la gente** people. *La gente is singular, even though it refers to an idea which seems plural*

**frizzante** *of wine* sparkling

**pesca** peach

**Exercise 7** As a revision exercise, go over the chapter again and make a list of all the words used as greetings and courtesies in the various dialogues. Make sure you understand them and try to learn them.

It is wise to revise when learning. To do Exercise 7 you have to read this chapter again. This will help you remember it. It would be helpful to listen to the recording again. And, very importantly, do this again after each chapter. Gradually things which at first seemed difficult or strange, fall into place and become simple. **Auguri!**

# 2 Mi chiamo Harry, sono americano, e lei?

**My name's Harry, I'm American, and you?**

---

**In this lesson you will learn about:**

- Giving information about yourself
- Asking others for information about themselves
- More nouns
- Adjectives, singular
- More verbs in the present tense, singular
- Saying you like something/like doing something
- Saying you have to do something

---

## Dialogue 1 📼

*Sono americano, e lei?*

*An American businessman is finishing breakfast in a hotel in Bologna. As he eats he is reading the* International Herald Tribune. *An Italian, sitting at the next table, is watching him and eventually leans over*

---

1  Where is the American's home?
2  And the Italian's?
3  What explanation does the American give for his good Italian?
4  What seems to be the reason for the Italian's interest in the US?
5  Is the Italian pleased to be in Bologna?

| | |
|---|---|
| ITALIANO: | Mi scusi, signore. Buongiorno. Lei è americano? |
| AMERICANO: | Buongiorno. Sì, sono americano. Mi chiamo Harry McNamara. Abito a Boston. E lei? |
| ITALIANO: | Io sono italiano. Mi chiamo Pietro Mussi. Sono romano, di Roma. Lei parla molto bene l'italiano. |
| AMERICANO: | Grazie. Mia madre è italiana. E' siciliana. E' di Siracusa. |
| ITALIANO: | Ah, capisco. Mio fratello abita in America. Abita a Los Angeles. Mi piace molto l'America. E' un paese simpatico e interessante. Lei è in Italia in vacanza o per lavoro? |
| AMERICANO: | Sono qui per lavoro. E lei? E' a Bologna per lavoro? |
| ITALIANO: | Sì, sono qui per lavoro. Vengo spesso a Bologna. Mi piace. E' una città simpatica e interessante. Ora devo andare. Arrivederci a stasera, forse? |
| AMERICANO: | Sì, sono qui per una settimana. A stasera. |
| ITALIANO: | Arrivederci. Buona giornata. |

## *Vocabulary*

| | |
|---|---|
| **mi chiamo** | my name is (*lit.* 'I call myself') |
| **abito** | I live |
| **lei parla molto bene l'italiano** | you speak Italian very well |
| **mia madre** | my mother |
| **capisco** | I understand |
| **mio fratello** | my brother |
| **mi piace** | I like |
| **in vacanza** | on holiday |
| **per lavoro** | for work |
| **vengo spesso** | I often come |
| **simpatico** | nice, friendly. *There is no exact translation. When you say a person or a place is* **simpatico** *it means you like them* |
| **a stasera** | see you this evening |
| **forse** | perhaps |
| **buona giornata** | have a nice day |

# Language points

## Adjectives

In Italian adjectives 'agree with the noun they qualify', that is: if the noun is masculine, the adjective must be in the masculine form. If the noun is feminine, the adjective must be in the feminine form. Look back over Dialogue 1. Underline or highlight all the adjectives you can find or write them on a piece of paper.

You probably picked out: **americano, italiano, romano, italiana, siciliana, simpatico, interessante**.

Look to see which nouns they qualify. You have two men talking who say: **Io sono americano; io sono italiano**. But Harry says his mother is **italiana, siciliana**.

You also had adjectives used to qualify the words

|  | **paese** (*m.*) | **simpatico, interessante** |
| and | **città** (*f.*) | **simpatica, interessante** |

Adjectives are of two types:

* *italiano/italiana, americano/americana*

A man is **americano**; a woman is **americana**, i.e. the -**o** is the masculine ending and -**a** is the feminine ending. Many adjectives for nationality are of this sort. *Note:* They are written with a small letter.

| Country | Adjective |
| Australia | australiano/a |
| Brasile | brasiliano/a |
| Gran Bretagna | britannico/a |
| Messico | messicano/a |
| Spagna | spagnolo/a |
| Svizzera | svizzero/a |
| Sud Africa | sudafricano/a |

This applies not to only adjectives of nationality: **un paese è simpatico, una città è simpatica**.

* *interessante, ends not in -o or -a, but in -e*

The second group of adjectives in Italian ends in -**e**. Many adjectives of nationality, for instance, end in -**e**:

| Inghilterra | inglese |
| Irlanda | irlandese |

| | |
|---|---|
| Galles | gallese |
| Scozia | scozzese |
| Canada | canadese |
| Nuova Zelanda | neozelandese |
| Francia | francese |
| Giappone | giapponese |
| Olanda | olandese (**Paesi Bassi** = 'the Netherlands') |

British citizens note: many Italians don't understand the difference between British and English. Scots, Welsh and Northern Irish should try not to feel too offended when Italians assume they are English. Americans (and others) should note that America can be **America**, but also **Stati Uniti** 'United States' – see Lesson 5. The adjective **statunitense**, derived from **Stati Uniti**, is sometimes heard. The usual everyday word is **americano**.

Now, here's some good news: adjectives which end in an -**e** do not have separate masculine and feminine forms. A man and a woman both say:

sono 〔 inglese
francese
canadese

And you say:

è 〔 un paese 〕 interessante
una città

(talking of the USA) **è un paese** (*m.*) **simpatico e interessante**
(talking of Bologna) **è una città** (*f.*) **simpatica e interessante**

*Note:* Adjectives usually follow the noun in Italian

**Exercise 1** Say, in Italian, what nationality you think the following people might be. *Example:* **Luciano Pavarotti**. *Answer:* **Luciano Pavarotti è italiano**.

| | |
|---|---|
| 1 Gérard Depardieu | 4 Brigitte Bardot |
| 2 Placido Domingo | 5 Robert de Niro |
| 3 Sofia Loren | 6 Meryl Streep |

And these cities. *Example:* **Los Angeles**. *Answer:* **Los Angeles è una città americana**.

| | |
|---|---|
| 7 Roma | 10 Toronto |
| 8 New York | 11 Sydney |
| 9 Rio de Janeiro | 12 Tokyo |

# Language points

## More about nouns – nouns ending in -e

Nouns ending in **-e**, like **paese, madre**, form the third big group of nouns in Italian. The first two are those which end in **-o** (masculine) and those which end in **-a** (feminine). Some nouns in the third group are masculine and some are feminine. Where they relate to people it is easy to guess which gender: **madre** 'mother' is feminine; **padre** 'father' is masculine.

But in most cases you have to learn the gender. **Paese** is masculine. It helps to learn the noun with an adjective of the **-o/-a** type which shows gender, e.g. **un paese simpatico**.

## More about verbs

In the text you met the following verbs in the first person singular:

io sono   mi chiamo   abito   vengo   devo

**Io** was used when the Italian said **io sono italiano** because the Italian man was contrasting his nationality with the American's. In English we would stress the '*I*' using our voice. After the first verb it is no longer necessary for him to use **io** because the ending of the verb tells us who the subject is. Can you tell which verb ending indicates **io**? It is **-o**.

When you look up a verb in the dictionary, you will find the *infinitive form*. For very many Italian verbs this will end in the letters: **-are**. In the text you met some verbs of this type in the first person, that is to say in the 'I' form:

abitare      parlare
abito        parlo

Here are some more:

lavorare   studiare   telefonare   fumare   ballare   cantare
lavoro     studio     telefono     fumo     ballo     canto

You can possibly guess at the meaning of them. You can check this in the glossary at the back of the book.

The **tu** form of verbs ends in **-i**:

lavori     studi     telefoni     fumi     balli     canti

This is the case with *all* verbs.

For **-are** verbs *only*, the **lei** form ends in **-a**. So you get:

*parlare*

| | |
|---|---|
| **(io) parlo** | I speak, I am speaking |
| **(tu) parli** | you speak, you are speaking (*familiar*) |
| **(lei) parla** | you speak, you are speaking (*formal*) |

*Note:* The present tense in Italian can translate both the English simple present ('I speak') and the English present continuous ('I am speaking'). So, if the forms seem difficult, console yourself with the knowledge that the one tense will do two jobs for you.

You also met some verbs which are irregular: **sono**, **vengo**, **devo**, and one of a different pattern from the **-are** type: **capisco**. These verbs too have **-o** to indicate 'I', the first person singular, even though they do not, in other ways, fit the pattern of the **-are** verbs. Their infinitives are:

| | | |
|---|---|---|
| **sono** | **essere** | to be |
| **vengo** | **venire** | to come |
| **devo** | **dovere** | to have to, must |
| **capisco** | **capire** | to understand |

In Lesson 1, you met the forms of **essere**. Even with this very irregular verb, the **tu** form ends in **-i**.

There was another verb in the passage: **mi chiamo**, *lit.* 'I call myself'. It is used when in English we would say 'my name is ...' or 'I'm called ...' **Chiamare** is also an **-are** verb. For the time being, however, don't worry about **mi chiamo**. **Chiamo** by itself means 'I call', 'I am calling'. We will come back to this later.

***Exercise 2*** Look at the drawings below and match each with one of these verbs:

canta    fuma    lavora    telefona    balla    studia

**Chiara**        **Lucia**        **Paolo**

| Luigi | Anna | Marco |

Imagine you are doing all these things. How would you say it?
*Example:* (**io**) **canto**

**Exercise 3** Look back at Dialogue 1 and work out how you would say in Italian:

> My name is Charlie Hardcastle. I am South African. I live in Johannesburg. I speak English and French. My mother is French, from Bordeaux. Bordeaux is a nice, friendly city.

## Mi piace

*Lit.* 'it is pleasing to me'; it is the everyday way of saying 'I like':

| **Mi piace** | la pizza<br>Roma<br>la musica | or **Mi piace** | parlare italiano<br>ballare<br>studiare |
|---|---|---|---|

**Mi piace** can be followed by (1) a noun ('I like pizza') or (2) the infinitive of a verb ('I like speaking Italian/to speak Italian'). We shall return to **mi piace**. You have also met **mi dispiace**, which literally means 'it is displeasing to me', but we would normally say 'I am sorry'. It is not the opposite of **mi piace**. See Lesson 3.

## Dovere

This verb, like **mi piace**, is followed by an infinitive: **devo andare**, **devo scappare**.

*Exercise 4* How would you say you like the following:

1 working (to work)
2 New York
3 singing
4 Rome
5 speaking Italian
6 Luciano Pavarotti

*Exercise 5* How would you say you have to do the following:

1 to telephone
2 to work
3 to come
4 to study

# Reading 1

### Mi chiamo Paolo Bianchi

*An Italian doctor is talking about himself*

1 What is the doctor's name?
2 Where does he come from?
3 Where does he live?
4 Where does he work?
5 Can you say something about what he looks like?
6 Is he married?
7 What does he like doing in his leisure time?

Mi chiamo Paolo Bianchi. Sono italiano. Sono di Milano. Sono alto e biondo. Sono medico e lavoro in un ospedale a Milano. Naturalmente abito a Milano. Sono sposato e ho due figli. Mia moglie si chiama Luisa. E' insegnante. Mi piace giocare a tennis, mi piace anche la musica classica.

# *Vocabulary*

| | |
|---|---|
| **alto** | tall, high |
| **biondo** | fair-haired |
| **sposato** | married |
| **figlio** | son; *figli* (*pl.*) *can mean 'sons' or 'sons and daughters'* |
| **moglie** | wife |

> You probably found you could get quite a lot of the information you were asked for. The answers are printed in the Key.

# Language point

## Saying what you do for a living

Paolo says **Sono medico**. When you say what your job is, the word for the occupation can function as an adjective and so 'a' can be omitted. You will also hear: **Sono un medico**. Here are some other jobs:

| | | | |
|---|---|---|---|
| **albergatore/trice** | hotelier | **avvocato/tessa** | lawyer |
| **casalinga** | housewife/ home-maker | **commesso/a** | shop assistant |
| **dentista** | dentist | **cuoco/a** | cook |
| **ingegnere** | engineer | **infermiere/a** | nurse |
| **segretario/a** | secretary | **insegnante** | teacher |
| **uomo d'affari** | businessman | **studente/tessa** | student |

*Note:* Some of these words have a masculine and feminine form as indicated. Nouns ending in **-ista** are masculine or feminine according to the sex of the person described. There are many women lawyers and doctors in Italy but it is not usual to make a feminine form for the words **avvocato** and **medico**. Indeed this is a field in which some women have strong views and feel the feminine form belittles them. As for the feminine for **uomo d'affari**, a businesswoman would call herself ... well, it depends on the precise nature of her work. She might be **una donna-manager**, or simply **manager** (yes, using the English word). If she actually owns companies she could perhaps be **donna d'affari**, but to some people it sounds odd.

**Exercise 6** Here is another person's description of himself. The verbs have been left out. Fill in the gaps using the verbs listed. You may use a verb more than once.

**abito, sono, lavoro**

Mi chiamo Silvio, Silvio Mancini. (1) ____ italiano. (2) ____ di Roma. Ma (3) ____ a Firenze. (4) ____ in una banca a Firenze. (5) ____ cassiere. Mi piace il mio lavoro.

**Exercise 7** You have just met Giorgio at a reception and he gives you a short portrait of himself. Complete what Giorgio says using the words below. Use each word once only.

**scusi, madre, devo, sportivo, lavoro, chiamo, mi, abito, ospedale, giocare**

Mi ____ Giorgio. Sono italiano. ____ a Napoli. Mia ____ abita a Roma con mio fratello. Sono medico in un ____ a Napoli. Mi piace il mio ____. Sono ____ e mi piace ____ a golf e a tennis. Mi ____; ____ scappare. ____ dispiace. Arrivederci.

In these passages you met some more adjectives: **sposato**, **alto**, **biondo**. You will notice these adjectives all end in **-o**. Keep an eye open to see what happens when Paolo's wife, Luisa, talks about herself. Don't forget to listen to the recordings as you read.

# Reading 2  

## *Mi chiamo Luisa Lucchini*

*Paolo's wife is talking about herself*

> 1 What does Luisa teach?
> 2 Does she like sports?
> 3 Why does she like Milan?

Mi chiamo Luisa, Luisa Lucchini. Sono italiana. Sono bionda, e sono alta. Sono di Bologna ma abito e lavoro a Milano. Sono insegnante. Lavoro in un liceo e insegno storia e geografia. Sono sposata e ho due figli. Mio marito si chiama Paolo. E' medico e lavora in un ospedale qui a Milano. Io sono sportiva. Mi piace giocare a tennis e a golf. Amo la musica lirica e quando ho tempo mi piace andare alla Scala. Mi piace Milano. E' una città grande, vivace, interessante e stimolante.

## Vocabulary

| | |
|---|---|
| **un liceo** | a high school, upper secondary school |
| **amo** | I love |
| **la musica lirica** | opera |

Did you notice that Luisa says:

$$\text{sono} \left\{ \begin{array}{l} \textbf{italiana} \\ \textbf{bionda} \\ \textbf{alta} \end{array} \right. \text{?}$$

**Exercise 8** Match the nouns on the left with the adjectives on the right. Take into account sense and gender. Some adjectives can go with more than one word. How many reasonable and grammatically correct combinations can you make?

| | |
|---|---|
| una birra | vivace |
| un signore | australiana |
| un vino | romana |
| una signora | alto |
| un lavoro | americano |
| un paese | sportivo |
| una madre | interessante |
| un marito | simpatico |
| una città | bionda |
| una signorina | americano |
| un professore | sposato |
| un fratello | bianco |

You have now learned to give other people some simple, basic information about yourself. It is also useful to be able to do the same about other people.

# Dialogue 2 🔲

## *Suo marito, come si chiama?*

*Luisa Lucchini, the Milanese teacher, is talking to a Canadian tourist
in the hotel where they are both spending their holiday. They have
talked about themselves. Now they are talking about their husbands*

---

1  What new piece of information do you learn about Paolo's leisure
   activities?
2  Is the Canadian woman's husband Canadian too?
3  What is his job?
4  Does he enjoy sports?
5  Where do the couple live?

---

CANADESE:  E suo marito, come si chiama?
LUISA:     Si chiama Paolo.
CANADESE:  Che lavoro fa?
LUISA:     E' medico. Lavora in un ospedale a Milano.
CANADESE:  E come passa il suo tempo libero?
LUISA:     E' molto sportivo. Gioca a tennis e ama anche il golf.
           Gli piace anche la musica classica. Suona il pianoforte.
           E' molto bravo. Spesso la sera ascolta musica. E suo
           marito, come si chiama?
CANADESE:  Si chiama Bill. Non è canadese, è scozzese.
LUISA:     Che lavoro fa?
CANADESE:  Lavora in una banca a Toronto. E' commercialista. La
           banca è una banca inglese.
LUISA:     E' sportivo, ama lo sport?
CANADESE:  No, non è sportivo. Invece è appassionato per il fai-
           da-te.
LUISA:     Oh, che bello!
CANADESE:  Dipende!

## *Vocabulary*

| | |
|---|---|
| **che lavoro fa?** | what's his job? |
| **commercialista** | accountant, financial adviser (*has a degree in economics and business studies*) |
| **ascolta** | he listens to |

| | |
|---|---|
| **il fai-da-te** | do-it-yourself |
| **oh, che bello!** | oh, how lovely! |
| **dipende** | it depends |

# Language point

## Talking about other people – third person singular of -are verbs

Pick out the verbs used by Luisa and the Canadian woman to talk about their husbands. You should have found:

**si chiama; fa; lavora; passa; è; gioca; ama; suona; ascolta**

These forms are, as you will realise, the same as those for **lei**, the formal 'you'. In fact, **lei** is also the word for 'she'. 'He' is **lui**. And, as usual, neither was used by the two speakers because it was quite clear who they were talking about.

You may perhaps be puzzled by the fact that **lei** is the formal 'you' and **lei** is 'she', and the form of the verb used is the same. The origin is reputed to lie in the human tendency to flatter people. The Italian for 'your lordship' was **la Signoria Vostra** and it was usual to address his lordship using the third person: 'Will your Lordship have his coffee here or on the terrace?' Gradually this form of address was extended to everyone. **Signoria Vostra** is not now used in daily conversation but it does still appear on formal invitations, usually abbreviated to **S.V. Lei**, on the other hand, is very much part of everyday language and you should use it in preference to **tu** when in doubt. It is better to be too formal than too familiar. The use of **lei** often seems odd at first to learners of Italian but it soon becomes second nature. The confusion with 'she' which learners fear is not the problem it at first seems.

Now we can see the full singular pattern of an **-are** verb:

> (io) parlo
> (tu) parli
> (lei) parla
> (lui) parla
> (lei) parla

**Il signor Smith parla molto bene l'italiano.**

And of **essere:**

```
(io) sono
(tu) sei
(lei) è
(lui) è
(lei) è
```

***Exercise 9*** Pretend to be the following people and talk about yourself.

1 A woman with the following attributes: you are Australian; tall and blonde; married; and you work in Sydney.
2 You are a Canadian man and you are married. Your wife is English. You live in Milan.
3 You are an Italian man, you are Sicilian, from Palermo. Your name is Salvatore. You live in Bologna. You work in a bank. You are married and your wife is Scottish. She is a teacher.

How would you say the same things about someone else?

4 She is Australian, tall and blonde, married and she works in Sydney.
5 He is Canadian. He is married. His wife (**sua moglie**) is English. He lives in Milan.
6 He is Italian, Sicilian, from Palermo. His name is Salvatore. He lives in Bologna and works in a bank. He is married and his wife is Scottish. She is a teacher.

***Exercise 10*** Try to describe yourself using the words you have met in this chapter. This exercise of course has no set answer – it depends on you. Try also to describe someone else – a friend or member of your family.

# 3 In città

## In town

In this lesson you will learn about:

- Finding your way around the sights
- Asking for and understanding directions to specific places
- Definite articles (i.e. 'the')
- Asking questions
- Negative sentences
- Ordinal numbers

## Dialogue 1

### A Perugia

*Jack is visiting Perugia, a lively modern city but with roots going back to the Etruscans, whose civilization preceded that of the Romans in Italy. Maria is showing Jack a brochure containing a plan of the city and pictures of some of the sights*

1  Can you guess what the Palazzo Comunale is used for?
2  Where do people like to stroll in the evening?
3  Why might you want to go to the garden at the end of Corso Vannucci?

JACK:    Che cos'è questo?
MARIA:   Questo è il Palazzo Comunale, il municipio. Si chiama anche il Palazzo dei Priori.
JACK:    E' magnifico. E questo?
MARIA:   E' la cattedrale.
JACK:    (*Pointing to another photo*) Questa è una fontana?

MARIA: Sì. E' la Fontana Maggiore. E' l'opera di Nicola e Giovanni Pisano.

JACK: E' molto bella. E la via, come si chiama?

MARIA: E' Corso Vannucci. E' molto importante per la città. La sera la gente viene qui a fare la passeggiata. In fondo c'è un giardino con un panorama molto bello sulla valle e verso Assisi.

JACK: E questo?

MARIA: Questo è l'arco etrusco.

JACK: E il museo famoso, dov'è?

MARIA: La Galleria Nazionale? L'entrata è qui, in Corso Vannucci.

## Vocabulary notes

**questo/a** this
**il municipio** the town hall
**il Palazzo dei Priori** the Palace of the Priors (*in the Middle Ages Perugia was a city state; the Priori were the elected officers who governed it*)
**opera** work (*produced by a creative artist*)
**la via** the street
**la sera** the evening. *Here:* in the evenings
**fare la passeggiata** to go for a walk. *In much of Italy **la passeggiata** is not just exercise: it is a social event. You walk up and down the main street, stopping to chat to friends, looking at everyone else and generally seeing what is going on*
**c'è (ci è)** there is
**un panorama** a view. *A number of nouns ending with -**ma** are masculine. Hint: learn it with an adjective which shows gender, e.g. **un panorama magnifico***
**in fondo** at the far end, at the bottom
**verso** towards

## Language points

### The definite article

| |
|---|
| **il** for masculine nouns<br>**la** for feminine nouns |

| | | | |
|---|---|---|---|
| **un palazzo** | a palace | **il palazzo** | the palace |
| **un giardino** | a garden | **il giardino** | the garden |
| **una fontana** | a fountain | **la fontana** | the fountain |
| **una via** | a street | **la via** | the street |

*Note:* For *both* masculine and feminine nouns beginning with a vowel the word for 'the' is **l'**.

| | | | |
|---|---|---|---|
| **un arco** | an arch | **l'arco** | the arch |
| **un'acqua minerale** | a water[1] | **l'acqua** | the water |

1 You say this when ordering a glass of water; it is usual to order spring/mineral water rather than ask for it from the tap.

*Note also:*

| | | | |
|---|---|---|---|
| **uno scontrino** | a till receipt | **lo scontrino** | the till receipt |
| **uno studente** | a student | **lo studente** | the student |

Words which have **uno** for 'a', have **lo** for 'the' (see Lesson 1). This also applies to nouns beginning with **z**, pronounced 'ts' or 'ds' (see 'The sounds of Italian'), e.g. **lo zucchero** ('sugar').

## Questo

This can be a pronoun or an adjective. When it replaces (as a pronoun) or describes (as an adjective) a feminine noun it becomes **questa**.

## Asking questions

*Yes–no questions* are made simply by using a rising intonation for the last word:

| | |
|---|---|
| **Questa è una fontana.** | This is a fountain. |
| **Questa è una fontana?** | Is this a fountain? |
| **Harry è americano.** | Harry is American. |
| **Harry è americano?** | Is Harry American? |
| **Paolo lavora in un ospedale.** | Paolo works in a hospital? |
| **Paolo lavora in un ospedale?** | Does Paolo work in a hospital? |
| **Giorgio abita a Firenze.** | Giorgio lives in Florence. |
| **Giorgio abita a Firenze?** | Does Giorgio live in Florence? |

You do not need 'do' or 'does' as in English, nor the word order change which English requires with the verb 'to be'. Word order is, however, more flexible in Italian than in English, so you will often hear in everyday speech:

> **E' una fontana, questa?**
> **E' americano, Harry?**
> **Lavora in un ospedale, Paolo?**
> **Abita a Firenze, Giorgio?**

The first form (i.e. statement with voice raised at the end: **Questa è una fontana?**) should be your model.

The answer will normally be either **sì** or **no**, 'yes' or 'no'.

When asking a question in a way that seems to be expecting confirmation that the information in the question is correct, e.g.

> You do work in a hospital, don't you?

simply tag on to the statement: **vero?** or (sometimes) **non è vero?**

> **Lavori in un ospedale, vero?**
> **Questa fontana si chiama la Fontana Maggiore, vero?**

*Information questions* require a question word. The subject, if expressed, follows the verb:

> **Come si chiama il medico?** What's the doctor's name? (*lit.* 'How does the doctor call himself?')
> **Che cos'è questo?** What's this?
> **Come va suo marito?** How is your husband?

Question words met so far:

> **Come?** How?
> **Come va?** How are you?
> **Che ...?** *Che + noun means 'which', 'what?'*
> **Che lavoro fa?** What is your job? (What work do you do?)
> **Che cosa?** What? (*often just **cosa?***)

*Note:* **Una cosa** means 'a thing'; so **che cosa** is *lit.* 'which, what thing'.

**Exercise 1** Look back at the dialogues in Lesson 2. Make a list of the questions you find in them.

**Exercise 2** Opposite are pictures of some famous places in Italy. For each there is a question and the answer. Complete the answer with the correct word for 'the'. If you do not know what the word means, it does not really matter because you can find the correct

**1** The Doges' Palace in Venice.

**3** The Basilica of San Pietro in Rome.

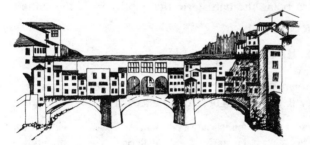

**2** The Ponte Vecchio in Florence.

**4** The Leaning Tower of Pisa.

**5** The Campanile by Giotto in Florence.

gender from the **un, una** in the question. Try guessing and then check from the glossary.

1 Questo è un palazzo?
Sì, è _____ Palazzo Ducale a Venezia.
2 Questo è un ponte?
Sì, è _____ Ponte Vecchio a Firenze.
3 Questa è una basilica?
Sì, è _____ Basilica di San Pietro a Roma.
4 Questa è una torre?
Sì, è _____ Torre Pendente di Pisa.
5 Questo è un campanile?
Sì, è _____ Campanile di Giotto a Firenze.

Technically the Leaning Tower of Pisa is also a **campanile**, being the bell tower for the cathedral of Pisa, **il duomo di Pisa**. Cathedrals are sometimes called **cattedrale**, more often **duomo**. The famous Leaning Tower is part of a particularly lovely group of buildings, the third being the **battistero**, the baptistery of the cathedral.

## Vocabulary

More town vocabulary: the first group is very guessable. Use the glossary if you can't guess or to check if you are unsure.

| | | | |
|---|---|---|---|
| **aeroporto** | **ambasciata** | **banca** | **cinema** (*m.*) |
| **consolato** | **farmacia** | **galleria** | **pizzeria** |
| **ristorante** (*m.*) | **stazione** (*f.*) | **supermercato** | **teatro** |
| **ufficio postale** | | | |

The following are more difficult to guess:

| | | | |
|---|---|---|---|
| **albergo** | hotel | **cambio** | foreign currency exchange |
| **chiesa** | church | **fermata dell'autobus** | bus stop |
| **mercato** | market | | |

## Dialogue 2

### C'è una banca qui vicino?

*A tourist needs to change some money. He stops a passerby*

---

1 What does the tourist ask for first?
2 The passerby suggests he goes to a foreign exchange bureau. Why?

---

TURISTA: Scusi, c'è una banca qui vicino?
PASSANTE: Una banca, sì. E' in Piazza Garibaldi.
TURISTA: Dov'è Piazza Garibaldi? E' lontano?
PASSANTE: No, è qui vicino. Vede l'albergo Bristol? (*pointing down the road*)
TURISTA: Sì.
PASSANTE: Piazza Garibaldi è subito dopo, sulla sinistra.
TURISTA: Grazie. E' aperta la banca a quest'ora?
PASSANTE: Penso di no. Lei deve cambiare valuta o travellers cheques?
TURISTA: Sì, travellers cheques.
PASSANTE: C'è un ufficio cambio lì, sulla destra, subito dopo la farmacia.
TURISTA: Oh, grazie. Buongiorno.
PASSANTE: Prego. Buongiorno.

## *Vocabulary*

| | | | |
|---|---|---|---|
| **vicino** | near | **penso di no** | I think not, I don't think so |
| **lontano** | far | | |
| **qui** | here | **valuta** | currency |
| **qui vicino** | near here | **subito** | immediately, suddenly |
| **vede l'albergo?** | do you see the hotel? | | |
| | | **dopo** | after |
| **lì** | there | **sulla sinistra** | on the left |
| **aperto** | open | **sulla destra** | on the right |

**Exercise 3** Make the question you need in the following circumstances, using a sentence on the pattern of: **C'è una banca qui vicino?**

1 You are hungry and want something to eat.
2 You have a headache and want to buy something for it.
3 It's getting late and you realize you are going to have to spend the night in this town.
4 You're tired of walking and want to get a bus to your destination.
5 You need to do some food shopping.

# Language point

## Dove and dov'è

You may need to look for a specific place, not *a* bank but *the* bank you want to use. You will need to ask 'where is' – **dov'è**. *Note:*

**dove** (*stress the first syllable*)          where
**dov'è** (**dove è**) (*stress on the* **è**)          where is

# Dialogue 3

### Scusi, dov'è il consolato americano?

*Our tourist has lost his passport and needs the consulate. He stops another passerby*

| Where *is* the American Consulate? |
| --- |

TURISTA:     Mi scusi, lei sa dov'è il consolato americano?
PASSANTE:   Mi dispiace, non lo so. Ma c'è l'Azienda per il Turismo in Via Mazzini. Provi a chiedere lì.
TURISTA:     E dov'è Via Mazzini?
PASSANTE:   E' la seconda via a destra. L'Azienda per il Turismo è sulla sinistra.
TURISTA:     Grazie. Buongiorno.
PASSANTE:   Prego. Buongiorno.

## Vocabulary

| | |
| --- | --- |
| **lei sa** | do you know? |
| **non lo so** | I don't know (*lit.* 'I don't know it') |
| **provi a chiedere** | try asking |

# Language points

## Negative sentences

To make a sentence negative, put **non** before the verb:

| | |
|---|---|
| **Jane è americana.** | Jane is American. |
| **Jane non è americana.** | Jane isn't American. |
| **Piero abita a Milano.** | Piero lives in Milan. |
| **Piero non abita a Milano.** | Piero doesn't live in Milan. |
| **Mi piace New York.** | I like New York. |
| **Non mi piace New York.** | I don't like New York. |
| **Capisco.** | I understand. |
| **Non capisco.** | I don't understand. |

In the last dialogue you met: **non lo so**. You can say **non so** but Italians usually say:

| | | | |
|---|---|---|---|
| **lo so** | I know (it) | **non lo so** | I don't know (it) |

**So** is from **sapere**, an irregular verb.

*Note:* Do not confuse **no** ('no') and **non** which is used with a verb to make a negative sentence.

***Exercise 4* Vero o falso?** Read the following statements and say whether they are true or false.

1 New York non è in Irlanda.
2 Luciano Pavarotti non è biondo.
3 Roma non è una città interessante e bella.
4 Il Teatro alla Scala non è a Milano.
5 Assisi non è lontano da Perugia.

Which of these are true for you?

6 Non sono americano/a.
7 Non abito in Italia.
8 Non sono sposato/a.
9 Non parlo francese.
10 Non lavoro in una banca.
11 Non mi piace il fai-da-te.
12 Per me, questo esercizio è molto difficile.

*Exercise 5* Someone is pestering you with questions. The answer
to them all is 'no'. You feel a bit irritated by the onslaught so
answer them, stressing the 'no' answer by giving the full sentence
in the negative. You may find it helpful to look back to Lesson 2
and check the 'you' and 'I' verb endings. *Example:* **Lei fuma?**
*Answer:* **No, non fumo.**

1  Lei lavora qui?
2  Abita in questa città?
3  E' qui in vacanza?
4  E' americano/a?
5  Parla francese?

## Ordinal numbers

You know the numbers 1–10 (Lesson 1). Here are the corresponding ordinal numbers. The abbreviated way of writing each is
given in brackets.

| first | **primo** | (1°) | sixth | **sesto** | (6°) |
|---|---|---|---|---|---|
| second | **secondo** | (2°) | seventh | **settimo** | (7°) |
| third | **terzo** | (3°) | eighth | **ottavo** | (8°) |
| fourth | **quarto** | (4°) | ninth | **nono** | (9°) |
| fifth | **quinto** | (5°) | tenth | **decimo** | (10°) |

After **decimo**, take off the final vowel from a given number and
add: **-esimo**.

Ordinal numbers agree with the noun they refer to:

**Il primo giorno**      the first day
**La prima sera**        the first evening

## Directions for finding places

The general word for 'street' is **strada**. In naming them, they are
usually called **via**, e.g. **via Cavour**. **Strada Rosero** would be a name
used in a rural area and would indicate where the road leads to.
Streets are often named after important historical figures, events
or even dates. **Corso** means a particularly important street, **viale**
(*m.*) a wide, tree-lined street. **Una piazza** is a square, **un piazzale**
a large square.

*Question:* **Dov'è la Banca Popolare?**

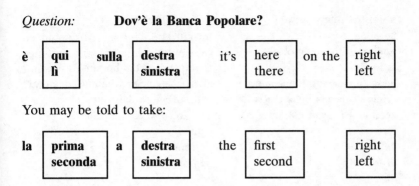

You may be told to take:

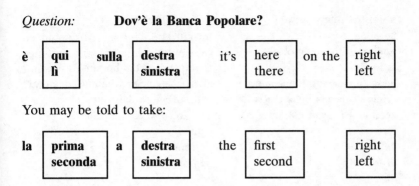

Often you will be told what you *have to* do (see Lesson 1):

**Lei deve prendere la seconda sulla sinistra.**
You have to take the second on the left.

**Lei deve girare a destra.**
You have to turn right.

You may hear:

**Prenda la quarta a sinistra.**
Take the fourth left.

**Giri a destra qui e poi è sempre diritto.**
Turn right here and then it's straight on.

These last two forms are 'commands', imperatives, like **dica**, **scusi**, **provi**. More about them soon.

Another way of posing the question is: **Per la stazione, per favore?**

If you want *a* supermarket, *a* bank etc., that is any one rather than a specific one, you say:

**C'è    un supermercato        qui vicino?**
**        una banca**

## *Vocabulary*

Here is a summary of vocabulary for giving directions:

| | |
|---|---|
| **dov'è** ... | where is ... |
| **per** ... | *roughly* what is the way to ... |
| **a destra/sulla destra** | to the right, on the right |

| | |
|---|---|
| **a sinistra/sulla sinistra** | to the left, on the left |
| **poi** | then, next |
| **sempre dritto** (*or* **diritto**) | straight on |
| **in fondo** | at the end, at the bottom |
| **dopo (il cinema, il museo ecc.)** | after (the cinema, the museum, etc.) |
| **prima di (prima della chiesa)** | before (before the church) |
| **accanto a (accanto al palazzo)** | next to (next to the palace) |
| **dietro** | behind |
| **davanti a** | in front of |
| **di fronte a** | opposite |
| **oltre** | beyond |
| **è lontano?** | is it far? |
| **vicino** | near |
| **è a 100 metri** | it's 100 metres (*100 yards approx.*) away |
| **è a 5 minuti** | it's 5 minutes away |
| **a piedi** | on foot |
| **in macchina** | by car |
| **fino a** | as far as |
| **il semaforo** | the traffic lights |

*Hint:* When you are given directions, it is a good idea to repeat the main points to the person who gave them, e.g. **seconda a sinistra, poi sulla destra.** In this way you check you have understood and it helps you memorize what was said.

## More verbs, present tense singular: verbs with an infinitive ending in -ere

You have already met the verbs ending in **-are**. A second group have an infinitive ending in **-ere**:

| *vedere* (*to see*) | *prendere* (*to take*) | *chiedere* (*to ask*) |
|---|---|---|
| (io) vedo | prendo | chiedo |
| (tu) vedi | prendi | chiedi |
| (lui) vede | prende | chiede |
| (lei) | | |

They differ very little from the **-are** verbs. The third person singular has **-e** where the first group has **-a**. Other verbs you have met which belong to this group are commonly used only in the third person singular:

| piacere | dipendere |
|---------|-----------|
| piace   | dipende   |

**Piacere** 'to be pleasing' is not a regular verb, but few parts of it are used frequently. **Dovere** 'to have to' is also an irregular verb but follows the **-ere** pattern for the present tense singular endings, although with the stem changing:

devo
devi
deve

One further point about **-ere** verbs. Some have the stress on the first **e** of the infinitive, some on the previous syllable: **ved_ere** but **pr_endere**. This has no bearing on any other part of the verb. Where stress is on the antepenultimate syllable, this is given in the glossary. When in doubt, check in a dictionary where the stress should fall.

***Exercise 6*** Here is a map of the centre of Torino. You are standing at the spot marked x. Overleaf are some instructions. Follow them and work out where you get to.

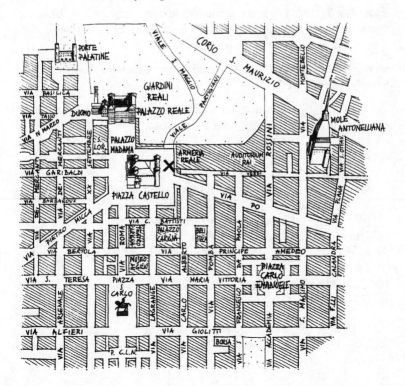

1 Prenda Via Po, qui, sulla nostra sinistra. Vada sempre dritto sotto i portici, sul lato sinistro, fino alla quarta via sulla sinistra: Via Montebello. Ed è lì in Via Montebello, sulla destra, dopo il cinema Massimo.

2 Allora, lei deve girare la piazza verso sinistra e prendere Via Roma. Vede, è lì, sulla sinistra. Prosegua per Via Roma, sotto i portici, e arriva in _____.

3 Lei deve fare il giro della piazza verso destra poi sulla destra trova il cortile di Palazzo Reale. Attraversi il cortile diagonalmente, verso sinistra. Passi sotto l'arco; arriva in una via stretta ed è lì sulla destra.

**Exercise 7** Work out how to explain to an Italian how to get to your home/place of work from the bus stop/railway station/motorway exit (**uscita**).

*Example:* **L'uscita è 'corso Marconi'. Sempre dritto per 200 metri; al secondo semaforo, a sinistra, e poi la prima sulla destra. La casa è sulla sinistra, il numero 23.**

**Exercise 8** Here are some sentences and, separately in a list, some verbs. Can you pick the correct verb in the correct form to complete the sentence? Use each verb once only.

**abito**, **abita**, **chiama**, **chiedo**, **chiedere**, **dipende**, **lavora**, **piace**, **prenda**, **prendi**, **vedi**, **vedo**

1 Io non _____ la banca. Dov'è?
2 Non so se vengo. _____ dal mio lavoro.
3 Devo _____ la strada. Non _____ in questa città e non so dov'è il duomo.
4 _____ la terza sulla sinistra e il museo è lì.
5 Un attimo. _____ a questo signore se la banca è qui vicino.
6 Il mio amico _____ a Milano, proprio in centro.
7 Mi _____ molto la fontana. E' bella.
8 Questo Palazzo si _____ il Palazzo Pubblico. E' molto antico.
9 Carlo _____ al museo di arte moderna. E' un lavoro molto interessante.
10 Ecco il bar Roma. Tu _____ Enzo? Deve essere qui. Ah sì. Ciao, Enzo. Cosa _____?

# Reading

## A Roma

1 What is the origin of the name of Palazzo Venezia?
2 Why do you think the Museum of Italian Unification is in the Vittoriano?
3 Why was the Campidoglio important in Ancient Rome?
4 Why do you think the Via dei Fori Imperiali is so called?
5 Between which two Piazze does Via del Corso run?

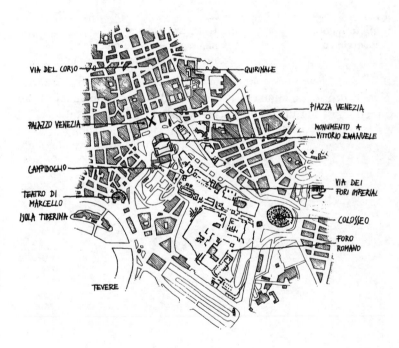

Siamo a Roma, in Piazza Venezia. Dietro di noi c'è Palazzo Venezia, in passato residenza degli ambasciatori di Venezia, oggi un museo. Davanti a noi, a destra, c'è il Vittoriano, il monumento al re Vittorio Emanuele II, il primo re d'Italia dopo l'unificazione nel 1861. Qui si trova anche l'Altare della Patria e la tomba del Milite Ignoto. All'interno del Vittoriano c'è il Museo del Risorgimento. Oltre questo monumento si trova il Campidoglio, il centro religioso della Roma antica e ancora oggi il cuore della città.

Alla sinistra del Vittoriano c'è Via dei Fori Imperiali e in fondo il Colosseo. A destra e a sinistra di questa via ci sono i ruderi del Foro Romano.

Sulla nostra sinistra c'è la famosa Via del Corso, la strada principale della città. Lunga più di un chilometro, finisce in Piazza del Popolo.

## Vocabulary

| | |
|---|---|
| **il re** | the king |
| **il Milite Ignoto** | the Unknown Soldier |
| **il Risorgimento** | the name given to the nineteenth century movement for Italian unity |
| **i ruderi** | ruins |

*Note:* Vittorio Emanuele was the second Victor Emmanuel of the Kingdom of Sardinia, but the first king of the united Italy.

# 4 In viaggio

**Travelling**

---

**In this lesson you will learn about:**

- Travelling – by train, bus, air
- Numbers 11–99
- Telling the time
- Verbs with infinitives in **-ire** (singular)
- Relative pronouns (the man who . . ., the book which . . .)
- Impersonal **si**

---

## Dialogue 1 ▄▄

### *Devo andare a Torino*

*While in Milan, Angela Smith needs to go to Turin for a day. She enquires at the Milan Central Station (**Milano–Stazione Centrale**) about the journey*

---

1  How frequent are the trains on the Milan–Turin line?
2  How many towns does the **rapido** stop at?
3  How much, in total, does Angela's ticket cost?

---

IMPIEGATO:   Buongiorno, dica.

SMITH:       Buongiorno. Devo andare a Torino. Posso fare l'andata e il ritorno in una giornata?

IMPIEGATO:   Certo, signora. C'è un treno quasi ogni ora e ci mette meno di due ore. A che ora vuole partire?

SMITH:       Verso le otto.

IMPIEGATO:   Allora, c'è un treno che parte alle 8.20. Arriva a Torino alle 10.13.

| SMITH: | E' un rapido? |
|---|---|
| IMPIEGATO: | No. C'è un rapido alle 9.10. Ferma solo a Novara e a Vercelli e arriva a Torino alle 10.55. |
| SMITH: | Benissimo. Prendo quello. E' necessario prenotare per domani? |
| IMPIEGATO: | No, se arriva alla stazione un po' prima della partenza. |
| SMITH: | E per tornare? Vorrei essere a Milano prima delle venti. |
| IMPIEGATO: | C'è un treno quasi ogni ora, alle 15.50, alle 16.50, alle 17.50. Alle 17.08 c'è l'Intercity; arriva alle 19.30. |
| SMITH: | Perfetto. Mi dia un'andata e ritorno per domani per il rapido. |
| IMPIEGATO: | Prima o seconda classe? |
| SMITH: | Preferisco prima classe. Quanto costa? |
| IMPIEGATO: | 35.000 lire. Più il supplemento rapido, 10.000. |
| SMITH: | Va bene. Prima classe con supplemento rapido. |

## Vocabulary

| | |
|---|---|
| andare | to go |
| posso ...? | can I ...? |
| in giornata | in the day |
| quasi | almost |
| meno di | less than |
| a che ora vuole partire? | at what time do you want to leave? |
| verso | at about |
| ferma solo a Novara ... | it stops only at Novara ... |
| quello | that one |
| tornare | to come back |
| domani | tomorrow |
| vorrei ... | I'd like, I should like ... |

## Language points

### Ogni

| | |
|---|---|
| ogni ora | every hour |
| giorno | day |
| dieci minuti | ten minutes |

**Ogni quanto c'è un treno per Torino?**
How often do the trains for Turin run? (*lit.* 'every how much?')

## *Vocabulary*

### Il treno

| | |
|---|---|
| **Ferrovie dello Stato – FS** | Italian State Railways |
| **l'orario (dei treni)** | the (train) timetable |
| **biglietto (di andata e ritorno)** | a (return) ticket |
| **biglietteria** | ticket office |
| **fare il biglietto** | to buy a ticket |
| **dove devo cambiare?** | where do I have to change? |
| **arrivo** | arrival |
| **partenza** | departure |
| **rapido** | express |
| **supplemento rapido** | a supplement payable for travelling on an express train |
| **prenotare, prenotazione** | to book a seat, booking (*sometimes obligatory on fast trains*) |
| **binario** | track (*the platform trains leave from is given as* **binario** ...) |
| **da che binario parte il treno per Verona?** | which platform does the train for Verona leave from? |
| **un viaggiatore** | a traveller |
| **viaggiare** | to travel |
| **il treno è in orario** | the train is on time |
| **anticipo** | early |
| **ritardo** | late |
| **partenza** | leaving |
| **arrivo** | arriving |

### Numbers 11–99

We can't put it off any longer! You need to learn the remaining numbers, 11–99. If necessary, remind yourself of the numbers in Lesson 1. The numbers 11–19 are perhaps the most difficult for the learner. They divide into two groups according to the way they are formed:

| | |
|---|---|
| 11 undici | |
| 12 dodici | |
| 13 tredici | 17 diciassette |
| 14 quattordici | 18 diciotto |
| 15 quindici | 19 diciannove |
| 16 sedici | |

You will recognize part of each as being similar to **dieci** (10) but in the first group that comes at the end and in the second at the beginning of the word. Notice too that the stress of the first group is irregular, falling on the third syllable from the end.

From 20 to 99 the numbers are plain sailing:

| | |
|---|---|
| 20 venti | 30 trenta |
| 21 ventuno | 31 trentuno |
| 22 ventidue | 32 trentadue |
| 23 ventitrè | 33 trentatrè |
| 24 ventiquattro | 34 trentaquattro |
| 25 venticinque | 35 trentacinque |
| 26 ventisei | 36 trentasei |
| 27 ventisette | 37 trentasette |
| 28 ventotto | 38 trentotto |
| 29 ventinove | 39 trentanove |

| | |
|---|---|
| 40 quaranta | 70 settanta |
| 50 cinquanta | 80 ottanta |
| 60 sessanta | 90 novanta |

Note that the final vowel is **i** for **venti** and **a** for all the others. Also that it is dropped when the word is combined with **uno** and **otto**, e.g. **settantuno**.

Reminder: this applies only to the numbers 21–98. It does not apply to **cento**: **centouno**.

The accent on **ventitrè** etc. is to indicate the stress.

**Exercise 1** Here are some addresses. How would you say the house numbers? *Example:* **Via Tiziano 25.** *Answer:* **Venticinque.**

1 Corso Vittorio Emanuele 18
2 Via Mazzini 77

3 Via San Francesco 52
4 Piazza della Repubblica 39
5 Corso Cavallotti 61

**Exercise 2** Work out how to say these famous dates in history in Italian. *Note*: In Italian you always say: **millenovecento** ... – i.e. 'one thousand nine hundred ...' and not 'nineteen hundred ...'

| | | |
|---|---|---|
| 1 1066 | 2 1215 | 3 1492 |
| 4 1789 | 5 1848 | 6 1918 |

## Che ora è? Che ore sono?

To ask someone 'what's the time?' you can say either **che ora è?** or **che ore sono? Ora** means 'hour', plural **ore**.

| | |
|---|---|
| **E' l'una** | It's one o'clock |
| **Sono le due** | It's two o'clock |
| **Sono le tre ... e così via** | It's three o'clock ... and so on |

But at 12 noon and 12 midnight respectively:

**E' mezzogiorno**
**E' mezzanotte**

For minutes past, you simply use **e**:

| **Sono le cinque e cinque** | It's five past five |
|---|---|
| **dieci** | ten |
| **venti** | twenty |
| **venticinque** | twenty-five |

and for minutes to, **meno**:

| **Sono le sei meno venticinque** | It's twenty-five to six |
|---|---|
| **venti** | twenty |
| **dieci** | ten |
| **cinque** | five |

For quarters and halves:

| **Sono le cinque e un quarto** | It's a quarter past five |
|---|---|
| **le cinque e mezzo** | half past five |
| **le sei meno un quarto** | a quarter to six |
| **E' mezzogiorno e un quarto** | It's a quarter past twelve |
| **e mezzo** | half past twelve |
| **meno un quarto** | a quarter to twelve |

When giving the times of trains, flights, etc. Italians use the 24-hour clock which avoids the possibility of misunderstanding:

**Il treno parte alle sedici e cinquanta.**
The train leaves at 16.50.

Note also that when you are saying 'at 16.50' the **a** ('at') combines with **le** or **l'**:

| | |
|---|---|
| **Parto all'una** | I'm leaving at one |
| **alle due** | at two |

More about this later.

***Exercise 3*** What times are the clocks showing? Use the conversational way of telling the time.

*Example:* **Sono le dieci e venticinque.**

1          2          3

4          5

***Exercise 4*** Say at what time you:

1 get up
2 leave for work
3 have lunch
4 finish work
5 arrive home

## Verbs – group 3, ending in -ire

Angela used **preferisco**. You have already met **capisco**. The third group of verbs in Italian has an infinitive ending in **-ire**. In the present tense, but not in most other tenses, this group of verbs divides into two sub-groups.

(1)

|            | *capire*  | *preferire*  | *finire*  |
|------------|-----------|--------------|-----------|
| (io)       | capisco   | preferisco   | finisco   |
| (tu)       | capisci   | preferisci   | finisci   |
| (lui/lei)  | capisce   | preferisce   | finisce   |

(2)

|            | *partire* | *dormire* | *sentire* |
|------------|-----------|-----------|-----------|
| (io)       | parto     | dormo     | sento     |
| (tu)       | parti     | dormi     | senti     |
| (lui/lei)  | parte     | dorme     | sente     |

The second sub-group has the same endings as **-ere** verbs, while the first have an extra syllable: **-isc-**. Try to learn, as you go along, which group each type of **-ire** verb belongs to.

You have now seen the forms for the singular of all regular verbs in Italian. Verb tables often look daunting but study the summary table below carefully and you will see that the differences between the groups are small:

| *-are* | *-ere* | *-ire (1)* | *-ire (2)* |
|--------|--------|------------|------------|
| -o     | -o     | -isco      | -o         |
| -i     | -i     | -isci      | -i         |
| -a     | -e     | -isce      | -e         |

Don't forget, the Italian present can express the meaning of both the English simple present ('I speak') and also the English present continuous ('I am speaking').

**Exercise 5** Here are pictures of Carla doing various things. Match each drawing with one of the sentences in the list opposite.

a

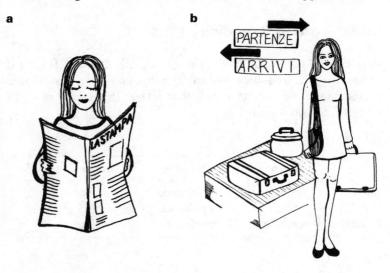

b

c

d

**e** **f**

**g** **h**

1 Carla balla in discoteca
2       visita un museo
3       prende un caffè
4       guarda la TV
5       legge il giornale
6       scrive una lettera
7       parte per le vacanze
8       dorme

How would you say *you* were doing each of these actions? You
need to change the endings of the verbs to the **io** form. *Example:*
**Ballo in discoteca.**

*Exercise 6* Giorgio has been telling you about himself. Tell someone else what he said, i.e. rewrite his words so that you are talking about him, changing the endings of the verbs from the 'I' form to the 'he' form. *Example:* **Giorgio è pilota.**

*Sono* (1) pilota. *Abito* (2) a Verona e *lavoro* (3) per una compagnia privata. Spesso *devo* (4) portare gente a Roma o a Bruxelles. Generalmente *parto* (5) da Verona presto e *arrivo* (6) a Roma per le 9. La sera *torno* (7) a Verona e *finisco* (8) di lavorare alle 18 o alle 19. Se non è possible tornare *dormo* (9) all'albergo, ma *preferisco* (10) tornare a Verona. Ma non *decido* (11) *io*, decide il cliente.

## Ci mette . . .

**Ci mette** is used to say how long it takes:

**Il treno ci mette due ore.**        The train takes two hours.

**Per fare questo, ci metto mezz'ora.** To do this, I take half an hour.

**Mettere** in other contexts means 'to put' and works like **prendere** in the present tense.

# Dialogue 2

### Vorrei andare in Piazza Castello

*In Torino Angela wants to go to Piazza Castello. It is raining as she gets off the train so she thinks she'll take the bus. She finds a bus information office in the station*

---

1 If Angela takes the number 63, does it take her right to Piazza Castello?
2 Where does she have to get off?
3 What is the bus which will take her right into Piazza Castello?

---

ANGELA:       Buongiorno. Vorrei andare in Piazza Castello. Che autobus devo prendere?
IMPIEGATO:    Può prendere il 4, il 12 o il 63. Scende in Via XX Settembre dietro il duomo. Trova una piccola via che la porta in Piazza Castello.

ANGELA: Dov'è la fermata?

IMPIEGATO: E' in Via Sacchi, accanto alla stazione.

ANGELA: Non c'è un autobus che mi porti proprio in Piazza Castello?

IMPIEGATO: C'è il 15, che deve prendere in Via XX Settembre. La lascia proprio in Piazza Castello.

ANGELA: Sembra un po' difficile. E piove. Dove posso trovare un taxi?

## Vocabulary

| | | | |
|---|---|---|---|
| **può** | you can | **sembra un po' difficile** | it seems a bit difficult |
| **scende** | you get off | **piove** | it's raining |
| **la lascia** | it leaves you | **trovare** | find |

## Language points

### Che

The word **che** has a number of uses. Among them are: to make a question (*interrogative adjective or pronoun*):

**Che autobus devo prendere?**  Which bus must I take?
**Che ora è?**  What time is it?
**Che cosa devo fare?**  What must I do?

or to show the relationship between a noun followed by a phrase and the main part of the sentence (*relative pronoun*):

**Trova una piccola via che la porta in Piazza Castello.**
You'll find a little street which takes you into Piazza Castello.

As a relative pronoun (as in the last example), **che** can refer to people or things, and be subject or object of the clause it introduces. In this it differs from – and is easier than – both English and French.

#### People, subject

**L'amica che viene stasera abita proprio in Piazza Castello.**
The friend who is coming this evening lives right in Piazza Castello.

### People, object

**Giorgio è una persona che conosco bene.**
Giorgio is a person (who) I know well.

### Things, subject

**Tu vedi il taxi che arriva?**
Do you see (can you see) the taxi that is arriving?

**L'Albergo Londra che è in Via Londra è molto famoso.**
The Hotel Londra which is in Via Londra is very famous.

### Things, object

**Il libro che cerco è di un amico.**
The book (that) I am looking for belongs to a friend.

## Proprio

This is an adverb meaning: 'exactly', 'really', 'indeed', 'right', 'just'.

**Arrivi proprio al momento giusto.**
You are arriving (have come) exactly at the right moment.

**Abita proprio in centro.**
He lives right in the centre.

**Sei proprio gentile.**
You really are kind.

## Un po'

A very commonly used abbreviation for **un poco**, 'a little'.

| | |
|---|---|
| **Vuole un po' di vino?** | Would you like a little wine? |
| **Parla italiano?** | Do you/does he/she speak Italian? |
| **Un po'.** | A little. |

**Poco** without **un** can also be an *adverb*:

| | |
|---|---|
| **Legge poco.** | He reads little (i.e. he doesn't read very much). |
| **Dorme poco.** | He doesn't sleep very much. |
| **E' poco simpatico.** | He's not very nice. |

and an *adjective*:

**poca gente**    few people, not very many people

# Reading 1

*Come si fa a prendere l'autobus?*

1  Where do you usually buy bus tickets?
2  Is the cost related to the distance travelled?
3  Why might the foreigner find travelling by bus more pleasant than driving?

Quando si prende l'autobus in Italia, occorre generalmente acquistare il biglietto prima di salire. Di solito questo si fa dal tabaccaio, dal giornalaio, al bar o in qualsiasi posto dove si vede un cartello che annuncia la vendita dei biglietti. Salendo sull'autobus, occorre obliterare il biglietto con la macchinetta. Nelle città generalmente si paga lo stesso prezzo per qualsiasi percorso, senza badare alla distanza. Però è meglio informarsi sul posto del sistema in vigore. Viaggiare in autobus è un modo simpatico e qualche volta anche divertente per conoscere una città, a contatto con la gente e senza il problema di trovare un parcheggio una volta arrivati a destinazione. E costa relativamente poco. Di solito è più economico acquistare un blocchetto di dieci biglietti che un biglietto solo. Chi sale senza biglietto paga una multa.

## *Vocabulary*

| | |
|---|---|
| **occorre** | it is necessary to, you need to |
| **acquistare** | to purchase, buy |
| **prima di salire** | before getting on |
| **di solito** | usually |
| **dal tabaccaio** | at the tobacconist's |
| **dal giornalaio** | at the newsagent's |
| **in qualsiasi posto** | in any place |
| **un cartello** | a sign, a notice |
| **la vendita** | the sale |
| **salendo** | as you get on |
| **macchinetta** | little machine |

| | |
|---|---|
| **si paga lo stesso prezzo** | you pay the same price |
| **senza badare a** | regardless of |
| **è meglio informarsi** | it's better to find out (inform oneself) |
| **sul posto** | on the spot, in the place |
| **un modo** | a way |
| **qualche volta** | sometimes |
| **un parcheggio** | a parking place, a car park |
| **una multa** | a fine |

# Language points

## Salire/scendere

'To get on' (a bus) is **salire** and 'to get off' is **scendere**. These verbs are also used to refer to getting into and out of other vehicles. The literal meanings are 'to go up' and 'to go down', respectively. **Scendere** is a regular verb, **-ere** type. **Salire** is irregular.

> **Scusi, per il duomo, dove devo scendere?**
> Excuse me, for the cathedral, where should I get off?

## Chi

**Chi**, like **che**, has more than one use. It can mean 'who?' when asking questions:

> **Chi vuole venire con me?** Who wants to come with me?
> **Chi è?** Who is it?

It can also be used, as in this passage, to mean 'the person who', 'those who', 'anyone who':

> **chi sale senza biglietto** anyone who gets on without a ticket

This is much used in proverbs; in English we would say 'he who'.

> **Chi va piano, va sano e va lontano.**
> (*Lit.* 'He who goes slowly, goes safely and a long way'.)
> *In other words:* More haste, less speed.

It can also mean 'some ... others':

> **Per andare a Roma c'è chi preferisce l'aereo, chi la propria macchina, chi il treno.**

For going to Rome, some prefer to travel by air, others to use
their own car and others the train.

## Come si fa? **Impersonal** si

There were a number of examples of this in the last passage. **Si**
has more than one meaning and a very common and useful one is
'one' in the sense of 'one does such and such', i.e. in generalisations.
In English we often, instead, say 'you', 'they', or use the passive:
e.g. 'How do you/they do it?' 'How is it done?'

**Come si fa a prendere l'autobus?**
How does one go about taking the bus?

*Note:* You can also say:

**Come si fa *per* ... andare alla stazione?**

Can you pick out the other cases of **si** in the text?
Here are some common and useful phrases with **si**:

**Come si dice in italiano *useful*?**
What is the Italian for *useful*? (*lit.* 'how does one say ...')

| **Come si** | **scrive** | **questa parola?** |
| | **pronuncia** | |

| How is this word | written? |
| | pronounced? |

**Qui si parla inglese.**
English is spoken here.

**Si può parcheggiare qui?**
Can one/you park here?

**Si mangia bene e si paga poco.**
(*of a restaurant*) The food is good and it's not expensive (*lit.*
'One eats well and one pays little').

## Qualsiasi

**Qualsiasi** means 'any' in the sense of 'it doesn't matter which',
'whichever'.

| **qualsiasi percorso** | any journey |
| **qualsiasi paese** | any country |
| **qualsiasi cosa** | anything (*in positive sentences*) |

# Reading 2

*L'aeroporto*

> 1 Why is travelling by air so easy for English-speaking travellers?
> 2 In what case are announcements made in English as well as Italian?

Viaggiare in aereo, per una persona di madre-lingua inglese, è facile. Perchè? Perchè l'aeroporto è un posto dove si usa molto la lingua inglese. Questo è vero anche per l'aereo. E il personale capisce sempre l'inglese. In genere tutto viene annunciato in inglese e in italiano, soprattutto per i voli diretti verso un paese in cui la lingua principale è l'inglese. Il vocabolario poi non è difficile. Il viaggiatore prende un *volo*; c'è anche un verbo, *volare*. Il volo *parte* da un aeroporto e *arriva* in un altro. Per la *partenza* il viaggiatore deve prima fare il 'check-in', poi deve passare per l'esame elettronico del bagaglio e il *controllo dei passaporti*. Poi va a una precisa *porta* o *uscita*, da dove sale sull'aereo. Esattamente come in tutti gli aeroporti del mondo.

## *Vocabulary*

| | | | |
|---|---|---|---|
| **perchè?** | why? | **un volo** | a flight |
| **perchè** | because | **mondo** | world |
| **soprattutto** | especially, above all | | |

# 5 Vorrei comprare ... Quanto costa?

## I'd like to buy ... How much does it cost?

In this lesson you will learn about:

- Comparing one thing with another
- 'False friends'
- Asking if you may do something, saying you want to or have to do something
- Saying what you would like, could or ought to do
- The plural of nouns, adjectives and definite articles
- This and that – **questo e quello**
- The plural subject and strong pronouns ('we', 'they')
- The plural of regular verbs and some irregular ones
- Asking how much something costs

## Dialogue 1 ▯▯

*Vorrei una guida*

*Joe has just arrived in Florence and he wants to start exploring, but first he needs a guidebook and a good map. He goes into a likely-looking bookshop*

1 What type of guidebook does Joe choose?
2 Is he offered a choice of maps?

COMMESSA: Buongiorno, signore. Desidera?
JOE: Vorrei una guida della città.
COMMESSA: In italiano o in inglese?

| Joe: | Preferisco l'inglese, se è possibile. |
|---|---|
| Commessa: | Ecco. C'è questa, illustrata. E' molto bella. E c'è anche questa, tascabile. E' più pratica, forse. |
| Joe: | Posso vedere? Infatti, ha ragione. La guida piccola è più pratica. Quanto costa? |
| Commessa: | 19.000 lire, signore. |
| Joe: | Va bene. Prendo questa. |
| Commessa: | Altro, signore? |
| Joe: | Sì. Vorrei anche una pianta della città. |
| Commessa: | Per il momento abbiamo solo questa. Guardi pure. Secondo me, è la migliore. |
| Joe: | E' molto chiara. La prendo. Quant'è? |
| Commessa: | 28.000 lire in tutto. La pianta costa 9.000. |
| Joe: | Ecco 50.000. |
| Commessa: | 29, 30, 40, 50.000. Grazie, Signore. Arrivederla. Buongiorno. |
| Joe: | Buongiorno. |

## Vocabulary notes

**vorrei** I'd like (*polite way of asking for something in a shop – see below*)

**tascabile** *lit.* 'pocketable' (*una tasca means 'a pocket'*)

**più** more

**posso vedere?** may I see? (*see below*)

**ha ragione** you're right

**abbiamo** we have

**guardi pure** please have a look/please do have a look

**altro?** anything else?

**la prendo** I'll take it, *lit.* 'I take it' (*present tense*)

**quanto costa?** how much does it cost, how much is it? *referring to a specific item* (**costare** *means 'to cost'*)

**quant'è?** (**quanto è**) how much does it come to in total, how much is it? *usually referring to all the items bought*

## Language points

### The comparative

To compare two people or objects, you use **più**:

| | |
|---|---|
| **questa guida è più pratica** | this guidebook is more practical |
| **piccola** | smaller |
| **interessante** | more interesting |

In Italian few words actually change in the comparative form; most are simply preceded by **più**. Exceptions are:

| | | | |
|---|---|---|---|
| **migliore** | better | **maggiore** | bigger |
| **peggiore** | worse | **minore** | smaller |

But you can also say: **più buono**, **più cattivo**, **più grande** and **più piccolo**. Purists prefer the first forms, but the second are frequently heard.

To say things from the other point of view, you use **meno**, 'less':

**Questo libro è meno importante.**
This book is not so important (less important).

**Vorrei una guida meno grande.**
I'd like a smaller guidebook.

To compare one thing with another, in phrases such as 'smaller than', 'more interesting than', use **di**:

Questo libro è più interessante di quello.
Firenze è più piccola di Roma.
Firenze è meno grande di Roma.

**Il più grande, la più grande** means 'the biggest':

Di tutte le città italiane, Roma è la più grande.
Questo ristorante è caro, ma secondo me è il migliore della città.
Questa cartolina è la più bella di tutte.

*Note:* **la più bella** } **di** the most beautiful } in
**il migliore** } the best }

However, **più** can also mean 'plus' and **meno** can mean 'minus':

| | |
|---|---|
| **Due più due fa quattro.** | $2 + 2 = 4$ |
| **Quattro meno due fa due.** | $4 - 2 = 2$ |

**Exercise 1** **Vero o falso?** Say if the following statements are true or false.

1 L'Italia è più grande del Canada.
2 Un albergo è più caro di un campeggio.

3  L'Everest è più alto dell'Etna.
4  L'elefante è più feroce del leone.
5  Napoli è più tranquilla di Venezia.

## False friends

**Infatti** is frequently used by Italians when agreeing with something someone has said. It means 'indeed' rather than 'in fact' which is **in effetti**, **in realtà**. You have seen that Italian is highly guessable. Many Italian words resemble English words. Language professionals refer to such words as *cognates*. Cognates make the learner's task easier. However, there are some cases where the similarity is misleading. These words are sometimes called *false friends*. One *false friend* you have already met is **simpatico** which does not mean quite the same as 'sympathetic' in English. If a person is **simpatico**, you find him congenial, likeable but he does not necessarily feel sympathy for you.

In the cases of both of these words, it is not disastrous if you get the word wrong. Indeed it is often more a laughing matter and everyone will probably enjoy it. For instance Italians use **suggestivo** to mean 'beautiful' and it has no hint of the meaning given to 'suggestive' in English, hence Italian tourist brochures which refer to 'suggestive views'. But it makes all the difference to your Italian if you pay attention to the points where the two languages differ and try to get things right.

## *Vocabulary*

### *Common false friends*

| | | | |
|---|---|---|---|
| **accidenti!** | good heavens! | **un incidente** | an accident |
| **attualmente** | at present | **veramente** | actually |
| **bravo** | good, clever | **coraggioso** | brave |
| | (*at something*) | **congresso** | conference |
| **conferenza** | lecture | **lettura** | reading |
| **educato** | polite | **colto, istruito** | educated |
| **fattoria** | farm | **fabbrica** | factory |
| **ginnasio** | high school | **palestra** | gymnasium |
| **largo** | wide | **grande** | large |
| **libreria** | bookshop | **biblioteca** | library |
| **morbido** | soft | **malsano, morboso** | morbid |

| occorrere | be necessary | **succedere** | happen, occur |
|---|---|---|---|
| **sensibile** | sensitive | **sensato** | sensible |

*Exercise 2* What does the following short paragraph mean? Mind the *false friends*!

Alberto è un ragazzo molto educato. Attualmente frequenta il ginnasio. E' uno studente molto bravo. Gli piace la lettura e va spesso nelle librerie a guardare e comprare libri.

## Asking if you may do something, saying you want to or have to do something

The word **posso ...?** means literally 'can I, may I ...?' You first met it in Lesson 4. **Posso**, like **devo**, is part of an irregular verb and one which is just as useful. Indeed, there is a trio, **dovere**, 'to have to', **potere**, 'to be able to' and **volere**, 'to want', which, combined with an infinitive, enable you to say a lot of useful things. You have met the present of **dovere** (singular). Here are the other two:

| *potere* | *volere* |
|---|---|
| posso | voglio |
| puoi | vuoi |
| può | vuole |

You can now make combinations. Here are a few:

| posso | parlare |
|---|---|
| | finire |
| voglio | partire |
| | andare |
| devo | lavorare |
| | giocare |
| e così via ... | (*and so on*) |

You can now also, of course, ask people if they are able, willing or have to do something.

| *Formal* | **Può portare questo per me?** |
|---|---|
| | Can you carry this for me? |
| | **Vuole andare a Firenze domani?** |
| | Do you want to go to Florence tomorrow? |
| | **Deve veramente partire? Mi dispiace.** |
| | Do you really have to leave? I'm sorry. |

| *Informal* | **Puoi finire questo per me?** |
|---|---|
| | **Vuoi giocare a tennis?** |
| | **Devi andare a Roma?** |

(The meanings of the verbs are exactly as above.)

## Saying what you'd like, and what you could or ought to do

When you are requesting something, in a shop for instance, it is more polite to say **vorrei**, 'I'd like' than **voglio**, 'I want'. **Vorrei** is the first person singular of a different part of the verb called the *conditional*. We shall look at the conditional in detail in Lesson 15. Also useful are two other first person singular conditionals:

| **potrei** | I could |
|---|---|
| **dovrei** | I ought to |

**Dovrei andare a Roma domani, potrei partire con il treno delle 7.00, ma vorrei aspettare la telefonata di Giorgio prima di decidere.**

I ought to go to Rome tomorrow, I could leave on the 7 a.m. train but I should like to wait for Giorgio's phone call before deciding.

## Si può?

You saw in Lesson 3 you can use this to ask if something is possible. And of course you can use it to say it is impossible:

**Si può prenotare un posto al cinema per questo film?**
**No, signore, mi dispiace, non si può.**

Can one book a seat in the cinema for this film?
I'm sorry, Sir, it is not possible.

**Exercise 3** Below are pairs of sentences. Pair the sentences in the first group below with logical follow-ups from those in the second group.

1 Vado a Parigi, ma non parlo francese.
2 Non mi piace la pizza.
3 Potrei prenotare due posti per il film stasera?
4 Andiamo in questa libreria.
5 Sono stanco.

a Mi dispiace, signore, ma non si può.
b Dovrei studiare la lingua.
c Vorrei andare a dormire.
d Potrei prendere gli spaghetti alla bolognese?
e Vorrei comprare una guida della città.

**Exercise 4** How would you say the following in Italian?

1 I want to go to Rome.
2 I'm sorry, I can't go to Rome.
3 May I see the book?
4 Can you play tennis tomorrow?
   Sorry, I can't. I have to go to Milan.
5 I don't want to leave tomorrow.
6 Is it possible to leave for Rome tonight?
   I'm sorry, it's not possible.
7 I'd like a beer.
8 Is it possible to pay by credit card? (**pagare con la carta di credito**)
9 Can you (*people generally*) see Etna from here?

## Secondo me

This means 'according to me' but is a very useful way of expressing the idea 'in my opinion', 'I think that . . .' It can be adapted:

| secondo | me |
|---------|------|
|         | te |
|         | lei |
|         | lui |
|         | Paolo |

# Dialogue 2

### Cinque cartoline per favore

*Joe intends to send postcards to friends back home. He goes into a Tabaccheria which has some attractive displays of cards*

> 1 How many postcards does Joe buy?
> 2 Which country does he plan to send them to?

TABACCAIO: Dica.
JOE: Posso vedere le cartoline?
TABACCAIO: Certo, faccia pure.
JOE: Quanto costano?
TABACCAIO: Queste qui, normali, costano 400 lire l'una. Le grandi costano 1000 l'una.
JOE: Allora, prendo cinque di quelle normali e cinque grandi. Sono molto belle, le grandi, ma un po' care.
TABACCAIO: Sì, sono bellissime, ma se deve scrivere a molte persone . . . Allora, sono settemila lire in tutto. Vuole anche i francobolli?
JOE: Sì, mi dia dieci francobolli per gli Stati Uniti.
TABACCAIO: Via aerea?
JOE: Sì, grazie.
TABACCAIO: Metto i francobolli qui nella busta con le cartoline. Le do anche dieci etichette 'via aerea'. Desidera altro?
JOE: No, grazie. Quant'è?

# Language points

## Plurals of nouns

| Singular ending | Plural ending |
|---|---|
| **-o** (*m.*) | **-i** |
| **-a** (*f.*) | **-e** |
| **-e** (*m.* and *f.*) | **-i** |

*Examples:*

| un francobollo | dieci francobolli | un palazzo | due palazzi |
|---|---|---|---|
| una cartolina | cinque cartoline | una fontana | tre fontane |
| uno studente | cento studenti | una torre | due torri |

*Exception:* Monosyllabic nouns, and nouns ending in a consonant or a stressed vowel, do not change in the plural:

| due bar | tre computer | dieci caffè |
|---|---|---|

## Plural of adjectives

Adjectives form their plurals in the same way:

| Singular | Plural |
|----------|--------|
| americano | americani |
| bello | belli |
| | |
| americana | americane |
| bella | belle |
| | |
| inglese | inglesi |
| interessante | interessanti |

So we have:

| | |
|---|---|
| un signore americano | due signori americani |
| un libro interessante | due libri interessanti |

**Exercise 5** The bar is very busy and the barman is working fast. But either he is flustered or he is not hearing properly. He repeats the orders to the customers, but in each case he gets it wrong. Be the customers and correct him as indicated.

*Example:* **Un vino rosso, vero?** No, two _____.
*You say:* **No, due vini rossi.**

1 **Un caffè, vero?** No, three _____.
2 **Un'aranciata, vero?** No, four _____.
3 **Una birra, vero?** No, five _____.
4 **Un'acqua minerale, vero?** No, six _____.
5 **Una spremuta di arancia, vero?** No, seven _____.
6 **Un cappuccino, vero?** No, eight _____. (*to customer number five, as the barman turns away*) **Oh, questo barista è decisamente strano.**

## Plural of definite articles

| | Singular | Plural |
|---|----------|--------|
| *Feminine* | la | le |
| | l' | le |
| *Masculine* | il | i |
| | l' | gli |
| | lo | gli |

*Examples:*

| | |
|---|---|
| la strada | le strade |
| l'acqua | le acque |
| il francobollo | i francobolli |
| l'americano | gli americani |
| lo studente | gli studenti |

*Note:*

(1) **lo stato** –means 'the state' and so: **gli Stati Uniti d'America**.
(2) **le**, the feminine plural article, is not shortened when the next word starts with a vowel.

**Exercise 6** Here are some nouns, sometimes with adjectives describing them. What would be the correct word for 'the' to use with each one?

*Example:* \_\_\_\_\_ **pianta tascabile** *Answer:* **la pianta tascabile**

| | | | |
|---|---|---|---|
| 1 | \_\_\_\_\_ albergo caro | 6 | \_\_\_\_\_ studente americano |
| 2 | \_\_\_\_\_ città tranquilla | 7 | \_\_\_\_\_ uffici pubblici |
| 3 | \_\_\_\_\_ ragazzi educati | 8 | \_\_\_\_\_ monumento importante |
| 4 | \_\_\_\_\_ cartoline grandi | 9 | \_\_\_\_\_ scontrini |
| 5 | \_\_\_\_\_ francobolli italiani | 10 | \_\_\_\_\_ città italiane |

## Questo/quello

These may be used as an adjective, with a noun, or as a pronoun, standing for a noun.

**Prendo questo.** (*pr.*)  I'll have this one (referring to a masculine noun).
**Mi piace quella fontana.** (*adj.*)  I like that fountain.

– **Vuoi comprare questa cartolina?** (*adj.*) – **No, preferisco quella.** (*pr.*)
– Do you want to buy this postcard? – No, I prefer that one.

**Questo** (*pr.*) **è più grande; quello** (*pr.*) **è più interessante.**
This one is bigger; that one is more interesting.

**Quello**, when used in front of a noun, has forms like those of the definite article:

| | | | |
|---|---|---|---|
| il palazzo | quel palazzo | i palazzi | quei palazzi |
| l'albergo | quell'albergo | gli alberghi | quegli alberghi |
| lo stato | quello stato | gli stati | quegli stati |

la fontana    quella fontana    le fontane    quelle fontane
l'acqua       quell'acqua       le acque      quelle acque

The changes are to do with sound and the smooth flow of speech from the tongue; the forms are those that flow for Italian. Say them to yourself.

*Exercise 7* Look back at Exercise 6. Instead of 'the' in each case, what would you put for 'that'/'those'?

## Plural subject pronouns

| | |
|---|---|
| **noi** | we |
| **voi** | you (*more than one person*) |
| **loro** | they |

Don't forget that more often than not Italians omit the subject pronoun. However, these pronouns, unlike the singular ones (see Lesson 1), can also be used after a preposition ('with', 'in', 'from'); and with **secondo**:

| | |
|---|---|
| **Noi siamo con loro.** | We are with them. |
| **Parte con voi?** | Is he leaving with you? |
| **Vuole venire con noi.** | He wants to come with us. |
| **secondo loro** | in their opinion |

In other words, they are also the *strong pronouns*.

## Plural of regular verbs

| -*are* | -*ere* | -*ire* |
|---|---|---|
| -iamo | -iamo | -iamo |
| -ate | -ete | -ite |
| -ano | -ono | -ono/iscono |

| *parlare* | *vedere* | *partire* | *finire* |
|---|---|---|---|
| parliamo | vediamo | partiamo | finiamo |
| parlate | vedete | partite | finite |
| parlano | vedono | partono | finiscono |

Look closely: the differences are small. For all verbs, the **noi** form is -**iamo**. For **voi**, the distinguishing or characteristic vowel of the infinitive appears: **-ate**, **-ete**, **-ite**. For the **loro** form, the **-are** verbs have **-ano**, the others **-ono**. Also for the **loro** form, the stress moves from the penultimate syllable to the antepenultimate. The stressed vowel is indicated above by the underlining. Note also, that verbs like **finire** have the extra **-isc-** only in the third person in the plural.

**Exercise 8** How would you complete these sentences in Italian? We give you the verb to use. Don't forget to leave out the pronoun ('we', 'you', etc.).

1 (We prefer) Roma a New York. (**preferire** – it works like **finire**)
2 (We arrive) a casa alle sei e mezzo. (**arrivare**)
3 (They are buying) una guida di Roma. (**comprare**)
4. Gianni e Carlo, (do you understand) inglese? (**capire**)
5 Anna e Giorgio (are leaving) alle otto. (**partire**)
6 Gli studenti (are having) un caffè. (**prendere**)

## Quanto costa?

Now do you understand why the question is sometimes **quanto costa?** sometimes **quanto costano? Costare** is an **-are** verb so:

**Quanto costa?**      How much does it cost?
**Quanto costano?**    How much do they cost?

**Quant'è?** or **quanto fa?** are usually used to enquire about the total cost: how much does it come to?

## Plural of irregular verbs:

| essere | avere | potere | dovere | volere |
| --- | --- | --- | --- | --- |
| siamo | abbiamo | possiamo | dobbiamo | vogliamo |
| siete | avete | potete | dovete | volete |
| sono | hanno | possono | devono | vogliono |

As you study these you will realize that, for the most part, the irregularities are sound changes in the 'root' of the verb, not in the endings.

**Exercise 9** Here are two short paragraphs. Most of the verbs have been left in the infinitive. Can you write down the correct form in each case?

A Mio marito ed io (1 andare) in discoteca questa sera. Generalmente la sera (2 guardare) la TV, (3 leggere) o (4 invitare) amici. Ma questa sera (5 volere) cambiare.

B Gli italiani (1 lavorare) molto. Generalmente (2 cominciare) a lavorare alle 7.30, alle 8.00 o alle 8.30. A mezzogiorno molti (3 tornare) a casa per mangiare, altri (4 mangiare) in città. (5 Finire) di lavorare alle 6 o alle 7 di sera. Se (6 volere) andare al cinema o a teatro (7 dovere) mangiare rapidamente. Il teatro comincia alle 9.

| | |
|---|---|
| **molti** | many people |
| **altri** | others, other people |
| **se** | if |

# Reading

## *Il mercato in Italia*

> 1 Why is it easy to visit a market in Italy?
> 2 Why are the restaurants and bars full on market day?

Per lo straniero in Italia, un divertimento e un piacere è la visita al mercato locale. Ogni paese ha un mercato almeno una volta alla settimana e questo è vero anche nelle grandi città dove ci sono mercati di quartiere. Il turista ammira la frutta e la verdura: tutto è sempre fresco e disposto con arte per attirare il cliente. Spesso ci sono contadini che vengono dalla campagna con i loro prodotti: uova, frutta e verdura, noci, funghi, dipende dalla stagione. Generalmente c'è anche un venditore di formaggi, una bancarella di pesce e spesso un macellaio che vende la carne. In più ci sono vestiti, articoli da cucina, scarpe e sandali, borse, biancheria da casa, un po' di tutto, insomma. Il mercato è anche un luogo di incontro per la gente del paese e della campagna circostante. I bar, i ristoranti e le strade sono pieni di persone che chiacchierano con animazione.

## *Vocabulary*

| | | | |
|---|---|---|---|
| **lo straniero** | the foreigner | **piacere** | pleasure |
| **un divertimento** | entertainment | **almeno** | at least |

| | | | |
|---|---|---|---|
| **la verdura** | vegetables | **macellaio** | butcher |
| **attirare** | to attract | **vestiti** | clothes |
| **contadini** | peasants, farmers, country people | **cucina** | kitchen, cooking |
| | | **scarpe** | shoes |
| **uova** | eggs | **borse** | bags, handbags |
| **noci** | walnuts | **biancheria da** | household linen |
| **stagione** | season | **casa** | |
| **formaggi** | cheeses | **chiacchierare** | to chat, chatter |
| **pesce** | fish | | |

*Exercise 10* Review the first five lessons. You should find that things which seemed difficult or strange at first are becoming more understandable.

# 6 Appuntamenti

## Engagements

## Dialogue 1 ▭

### Vorrei parlare con il signor Rossi

*Angela Smith calls Signor Rossi to arrange a meeting next week to
discuss their new project*

1 When would Mrs Smith like to have a meeting with Mr Rossi?
2 After agreeing to the meeting, what suggestion does Mr Rossi
  make to Mrs Smith?

| | |
|---|---|
| SMITH: | Pronto, ditta Rossi? |
| SEGRETARIA: | Sì, buongiorno. Desidera? |
| SMITH: | Vorrei parlare con il signor Rossi. |
| SEGRETARIA: | Chi parla? |
| SMITH: | Sono Angela Smith. |
| SEGRETARIA: | Ah, buongiorno signora Smith. Un attimo, per favore. Le passo subito il signor Rossi. |

| | |
|---|---|
| ROSSI: | Pronto. Buongiorno, signora, come va? |
| SMITH: | Bene grazie, e lei? Senta, vengo in Italia la settimana prossima. Possiamo vederci per parlare del nuovo progetto? |
| ROSSI: | Buona idea. Quando le va bene? |
| SMITH: | Martedì devo andare a Torino. Suggerisco mercoledì alle nove. Va bene? |
| ROSSI: | Sì, anche per me va bene. Mercoledì, 17 giugno. |
| SMITH: | Giusto. |
| ROSSI: | E mercoledì sera, se lei è libera, venga a cena con me e mia moglie. |
| SMITH: | Grazie, è molto gentile. Accetto con piacere. Arrivederci alla settimana prossima. |

| | |
|---|---|
| **ditta** | company, firm |
| **cena** | supper, evening meal |

# Language points

## Hours, days, weeks, months, years

You should be able to work out what these mean:

| | |
|---|---|
| un secondo | 60 secondi = un minuto |
| un minuto | 60 minuti = un'ora |
| un'ora | 24 ore = un giorno |
| un giorno | 7 giorni = una settimana |
| una settimana | 4 settimane = un mese |
| un mese | 12 mesi = un anno |
| un anno | |

Do you remember how to say 'wait a moment' (Lesson 1)?

| **un attimo** *or often:* | **attenda** } | **un attimo** |
|---|---|---|
| | **aspetti** } | |

# *Vocabulary*

Here are some more words related to days, months and years.

| **oggi** | today |
|---|---|

| | |
|---|---|
| **ieri** | yesterday |
| **l'altro ieri** | the day before yesterday |
| **domani** | tomorrow |
| **dopodomani** | the day after tomorrow |
| **la settimana prossima** | next week |
| **la settimana scorsa** | last week |
| **mattina** }<br>**mattino** } | morning (*both masculine and feminine forms exist – use either*) |
| **pomeriggio** | afternoon |
| **ogni giorno** | daily (*adverb*) |
| **quotidiano** | daily (*adjective*); *also* (*as noun*) daily newspaper |
| **ogni settimana** | weekly |
| **ogni mese** | monthly |
| **il giorno dopo** | the day after |
| **il giorno prima** | the day before |
| **l'indomani** | the next day (*the day after the one being talked about, usually in the past*) |
| **quindici giorni** }<br>**due settimane** } | a fortnight |

Do you remember the words for 'evening' and 'night'?

**Exercise 1** Using the words given above, how do you think you might say the following? Don't forget, **mese** and **anno** are masculine.

1 next month
2 last month
3 next year
4 last year
5 annually

Can you guess how you might say:

6 tomorrow morning
7 yesterday afternoon

*Note:* 'This morning', 'this evening' and 'tonight' are usually: **stamattina, stasera** and **stanotte**, i.e. **questa** is abbreviated to **sta**. 'This afternoon' is **questo pomeriggio** or **oggi pomeriggio**.

## *I giorni della settimana*

Here are the days of the week:

| | |
|---|---|
| lunedì | venerdì |
| martedì | sabato |
| mercoledì | domenica |
| giovedì | |

*Note:* All have irregular stress and are written without capital letters. All are masculine, except **la domenica**.

| | |
|---|---|
| **arrivo lunedì** | I arrive/am arriving on Monday |
| **arrivo il lunedì** | I arrive on Mondays (*regularly*) |
| **a sabato** | see you on Saturday |
| **a domani** | see you tomorrow |
| **a stasera** | see you this evening |
| **alla settimana prossima** | see you next week |

## *I mesi dell'anno*

Here are the months of the year:

| | | |
|---|---|---|
| gennaio | maggio | settembre |
| febbraio | giugno | ottobre |
| marzo | luglio | novembre |
| aprile | agosto | dicembre |

Again, no capital letters are used and all are masculine.
When giving the date you say:

| | |
|---|---|
| il primo dicembre | il due dicembre |
| l'otto dicembre | il trentun dicembre |

i.e. you use the ordinal for 'the first' only. Note also that **trentun** works like **un**, as do other numbers ending in **un**.

There is more than one way of asking what the date is:

| | |
|---|---|
| **Qual è la data (di) oggi?** | What's the date today? |
| **Oggi è il venti aprile.** | Today is the twentieth of April. |

**Di** is optional. Or, when you know the month but are not sure of the day:

| | |
|---|---|
| **Quanti ne abbiamo oggi?** | What's the date today? |
| **Oggi ne abbiamo 20.** | It's the 20th. |
| **Che giorno è oggi?** | What day is it today? |

'On' with a date is omitted:

**Arrivo il diciassette giugno.**   I'm arriving on seventeenth of June.

That is the usual word order; the number is *not* put after the month. And when abbreviating the order is the European one:

3.11.95 = il tre novembre 1995

To say simply 'in July' you can use either **a** or **in**:

**Mark, il mio amico inglese, viene in Italia a luglio.**
Mark, my English friend, is coming to Italy in July.

**Exercise 2** Say these dates aloud in Italian and then write them down:

| | | | |
|---|---|---|---|
| 1 | 1 May | 4 | 11 June |
| 2 | 25 December | 5 | 25 April |
| 3 | 14 July | 6 | 20 September |

The last two dates are often used for street names. They mark respectively the liberation of Italy at the end of the Second World War; and the date in 1870 when the Papal States fell to the troops of the then recently unified Italian state, thus completing it.

7 Work out the date of your own birthday, **compleanno**.

### Le quattro stagioni

Here are the four seasons:

| | | | |
|---|---|---|---|
| l'inverno | la primavera | l'estate (*f.*) | l'autunno. |

You say: **in inverno, in primavera, in estate, in autunno**. With **inverno** and **estate**, **di** can also be used.

## *Vocabulary*

## Al telefono

| | |
|---|---|
| **telefonare** *a* **una persona** | to telephone someone |
| **chiamare una persona** | to call someone |
| **un gettone** | telephone token – *in the past public telephones required this* |
| **moneta**, *pl.* **monete** | coins |
| **carta telefonica** | telephone card |
| **una cabina telefonica** | telephone box |
| **pronto** | hello (***pronto*** *also means 'ready'*) |
| **chi parla?** | who is calling/speaking? |
| **con chi parlo?** | who am I talking to? who's speaking? |
| **sono Giorgio** | (this is) Giorgio speaking |
| **c'è Carla?** | is Carla there/available? |
| **sì, c'è/no, non c'è** | yes, she's here/no, she's not here |
| **teleselezione** | direct dialling |
| **prefisso** | area (or country) code |
| **centralino** | operator |
| **interno** | extension |
| **attenda (resti) in linea** | hold the line |
| **le passo ...** | I'm putting you through to ... |
| **mi sente?** | can you hear me? |
| **è caduta la linea** | I (we)'ve been/were cut off |
| **scusi, ho sbagliato numero** | I'm sorry, I've dialled the wrong number |
| **telefonino, telefono cellulare** | cellular telephone |
| **numero verde** | freephone number (*starts with 167*) |
| **segreteria telefonica** | telephone answering machine |
| **un abbonato** | subscriber |
| **un elenco telefonico** | telephone directory |

Italians vary in how they say telephone numbers. It is usual to say:

nove tre sei sette uno cinque sei     9367156

but some people group the numbers:

novantatrè, sessantassette, quindici, sei

We advise the first system.

The dialling tone in Italy is a short tone followed by a longer tone. When the number is ringing you hear a long tone, repeated. If the number is engaged you get a repeated short tone.

**Exercise 3** Look at the information below from an Italian telephone directory and say which number you would call if:

1 you saw a building on fire
2 you saw someone collapse in the street
3 you saw a bridge collapse
4 you needed the telephone number of someone whose number was not yet in the directory
5 you wanted to find out the exact time

| NUMERI DI EMERGENZA | |
| --- | --- |
| Soccorso pubblico di emergenza | 113 |
| Carabinieri – pronto intervento | 112 |
| Vigili del fuoco – pronto intervento | 115 |
| Soccorso stradale – Automobile Club d'Italia | 116 |
| Emergenza sanitaria | 118 |
| Pronto soccorso autoambulanze | 118 |
| Telefono azzurro – Linea gratuita per i bambini | 19696 |
| Sveglia automatica | 114 |
| Ora esatta | 161 |
| Informazioni elenco abbonati | 12 |

# Dialogue 2

## *Andiamo al cinema*

*Alberto telephones Marisa to ask her to go to the cinema with him*

1 Which days can Alberto not manage?
2 Where do they decide to meet?

ALBERTO: Pronto. Casa Rossini? C'è Marisa?
MARISA: Sì, sono io. Chi parla?
ALBERTO: Ciao, Marisa. Sono Alberto. Senti, danno quel nuovo film al Lux la settimana prossima. Sai, il film che ha avuto il Leone d'oro al Festival di Venezia. Che dici? Andiamo a vederlo?
MARISA: Sì, volentieri. Quando?
ALBERTO: Lunedì non posso perchè ho una riunione. Va bene martedì?

MARISA:   Mi dispiace, faccio sempre aerobica il martedì.

ALBERTO:   E io il mercoledì gioco sempre a tennis con Raffaele. Giovedì ti va bene?

MARISA:   Giovedì, vediamo un attimo. Il 10, vero?

ALBERTO:   Sì, il 10 ottobre.

MARISA:   *consulting her diary* Sì, sono libera. Per me va benissimo giovedì. Dove ci troviamo?

ALBERTO:   Andiamo a mangiare la pizza prima? Ti vengo a prendere alle 7.00.

MARISA:   Perfetto. A giovedì allora. Ciao.

ALBERTO:   Ciao, a giovedì.

# Language points

## A + the definite article – articulated prepositions

You have now met a number of examples and it is time to give you the whole picture. The spelling reflects the way **a** combines with the definite article in speech:

| | | | |
|---|---|---|---|
| a + il | → | al | al supermercato |
| a + l' (*m.*) | → | all' | all'aeroporto |
| a + lo | → | allo | allo stadio |
| a + la | → | alla | alla stazione |
| a + l' (*f.*) | → | all' | all'entrata |
| a + i | → | ai | ai negozi |
| a + gli | → | agli | agli scavi |
| a + le | → | alle | alle casse |

**gli scavi**   excavations (archaeological)      **la cassa**   till, cash desk

Look back to **quel** in Lesson 5. It works the same way.

The same thing happens with four other common, short prepositions: **da, su, in** and **di**. The examples are from earlier lessons:

| | |
|---|---|
| un panorama *sulla* valle | *sulla* destra, *sulla* sinistra |
| salire *sull* 'autobus | informarsi *sul* posto |
| *dal* tabaccaio | *dal* giornalaio |

**In** and **di** change when they combine with the article:

> in + il → nel
> di + il → del

metto i francobolli *nella* busta
i mesi *dell'*anno,                    i giorni *della* settimana
prima *della* partenza         una guida *della* città

These forms are called *articulated prepositions*. The full table can be found in the Grammar section at the end of the book.
  *Warning!* These very common prepositions (**a**, **di**, **da**, **in**, **su**) should be handled with care! They are arguably the trickiest thing to learn to use correctly in Italian. On the other hand, you should not be too inhibited by this warning as a mistake in a preposition does not usually obscure your meaning. However, note for instance:

| | |
|---|---|
| **Abito a Roma** | I live in Rome |
| **in Italia** | in Italy |
| **Devo andare a Roma** | I have to go to Rome |
| **in Italia** | to Italy |

Italian uses **a** to mean 'to' or 'in' when talking about towns and cities and **in** when talking about countries, regions, etc. *Note also:* You use the article as well as **in** with countries which are plural:

**Devo andare negli Stati Uniti**
**nei Paesi Bassi** (Netherlands)
**nelle Antille** (West Indies)

It makes sense to learn usages as you go along. For instance **a** can mean 'to', 'in', 'at', or even 'on' in some cases:

| | |
|---|---|
| **Andiamo al cinema** | Let's go to the cinema |
| **Siamo al cinema** | We are at the cinema |
| **Abita a Roma** | He lives in Rome |
| **Marco è al telefono** | Marco's on the phone |

Another tricky preposition is **da**. Da can mean 'at the house/establishment of', as in the examples given above: **dal tabaccaio** means 'at the tobacconist's', cf. French 'chez'.
  **Fra** and **tra** are interchangeable and mean 'among', 'between', 'through', and with an expression of time, 'in . . .'s time'.

**fra Milano e Genova**          between Milan and Genoa

| | | | |
|---|---|---|---|
| **fra un'ora** | | in an hour's time | |

Other common prepositions are listed below. There are fewer idiomatic uses with these.

| | | | |
|---|---|---|---|
| **con** | with | **senza (di)** | without |
| **per** | for, through, by | **attraverso** | across, through |
| **contro (di)** | against | **dietro (di)** | behind |
| **davanti a** | in front of | **accanto a** | beside, next to |
| **di fronte a** | opposite | **in fondo a** | at the bottom of |
| **sopra (di)** | above | **oltre** | beyond |
| **in mezzo a** | in the middle of | **dopo (di)** | after |
| **prima di** | before | **entro\*** | by (+ point in time) |

\* **Finiamo entro giovedì**    We'll finish by Thursday

Where (**di**) is indicated, **di** is used before a pronoun:

**senza di lui**   without him     **contro di me**   against me

*Exercise 4* The following information comes from the brochure of a gymnasium. Complete it by putting articulated prepositions in the blanks. We indicate which preposition you should use (e.g. **su**) but leave you to work out how it combines with the definite article. *Note:* **Salute** is feminine. You should be able to work out the gender of the other nouns.

```
                          Servizi offerti
            Biblioteca (su) _____ salute e (su) _____ sport
                        Ampio parcheggio
       La possibilità (in) _____ bella stagione di allenarsi
                 (a) _____ aperto tra il verde

                             Orario:
   (da) _____ lunedì (a) _____ venerdì (da) _____ ore 9.00 (a) _____
                          ore 21.15
        il sabato (da) _____ ore 10.00 (a) _____ ore 12.30
```

| | | | |
|---|---|---|---|
| **salute** | health | **ampio parcheggio** | large car park |
| **allenarsi** | to train, to work out | | |

And this is from an advertising brochure for a self-service restaurant:

---

Per il pranzo (in) \_\_\_\_ corso (di) \_\_\_\_ intervallo di lavoro, per la cena che segue (a) \_\_\_\_ shopping, per ritrovarsi con gli amici prima (di) \_\_\_\_ spettacolo in una sala (di) \_\_\_\_ centro, per una sosta ristoratrice fra una scoperta e l'altra (in) \_\_\_\_ la città in cui si fa turismo . . . la soluzione è Brek.

---

| | | | |
|---|---|---|---|
| **pranzo** | lunch | **cena** | supper |
| **spettacolo** | show | **sala** | hall (theatre, cinema, etc.) |
| **sosta** | pause, stop | **scoperta** | discovery |

*Note:* **Shopping** is considered as beginning with **s** + consonant, as in **lo sci**.

## Reflexive/reciprocal verbs

Mi chiamo Harry.
Come si chiama?

We explained in Lesson 2 that **chiamare** means 'to call' and **mi chiamo** means 'I call myself', i.e. 'my name is'. The infinitive is **chiamarsi**. A verb which works this way is called a *reflexive verb*, i.e. one that 'turns back on itself'. The present tense of **chiamarsi** is:

| | |
|---|---|
| mi chiamo | ci chiamiamo |
| ti chiami | vi chiamate |
| si chiama | si chiamano |

**Mi, ti,** etc. are called *reflexive pronouns*. In the infinitive form the reflexive pronoun follows the verb and is written joined to it. Sometimes there is a direct equivalence between an Italian verb and an English verb:

| *divertirsi* | *to enjoy onself* |
|---|---|
| **mi diverto** | I enjoy/am enjoying myself |
| **ti diverti** | you enjoy/are enjoying yourself |
| **si diverte** | he/she enjoys/is enjoying himself/herself |
| **ci divertiamo** | we are enjoying ourselves |
| **vi divertite** | you are enjoying yourselves |
| **si divertono** | they are enjoying themselves |

But often this is not the case. Common reflexive verbs are:

| | | | |
|---|---|---|---|
| **alzarsi** | to get up | **coricarsi** | to lie down |
| **addormentarsi** | to fall asleep | **svegliarsi** | to wake up |
| **riposarsi** | to rest | **lavarsi** | to wash (oneself) |
| **pettinarsi** | to comb/do one's hair | **vestirsi** | to dress, get dressed |
| **accorgersi** | to notice | **sposarsi** | to get married |
| **rendersi conto** | to realize | | |

**Accomodarsi**, 'to make onself comfortable', is used particularly in the formal invitation: **s'accomodi**, 'take a seat', 'sit down'.

In the plural some verbs are used with the reflexive pronoun to indicate the action is *reciprocal*:

| | |
|---|---|
| **Dove ci troviamo?** | *lit.* 'Where shall we find each other?' *i.e.* where shall we meet? |
| **Non si parlano.** | They don't talk/are not speaking to each other. |
| **Si vedono ogni sabato.** | They see each other each Saturday. |

Grammatically sophisticated readers may rest assured, the reflexive pronouns, **mi**, **ti**, etc. can mean both 'myself' and 'to myself', 'yourself' and 'to yourself', i.e. they can be *direct* and *indirect* objects of the verb.

*Note:* Common ways of saying 'goodbye' between friends are: **ci vediamo** or **ci sentiamo**, meaning: 'see you soon' and 'we'll telephone each other' respectively.

***Exercise 5*** The printer has got the following sentences muddled up. They describe what I do every morning. Put them into a more logical order.

1 Mi pettino.
2 Non mi alzo subito.
3 Mi vesto.
4 Vado in bagno.
5 Mi sveglio alle sette.
6 Mi lavo.

***Exercise 6*** Lucio has done a series of drawings of his morning routine. What does he do? Here are the verbs you need: **pettinarsi, fare la doccia, vestirsi, svegliarsi, fare colazione, alzarsi, prepararsi**.

**1**

**2**

**3**

**4**

**5**

**6**                    **7**

## More irregular verbs

| andare | venire | fare | sapere | dire |
|--------|--------|------|--------|------|
| vado | vengo | faccio | so | dico |
| vai | vieni | fai | sai | dici |
| va | viene | fa | sa | dice |
| andiamo | veniamo | facciamo | sappiamo | diciamo |
| andate | venite | fate | sapete | dite |
| vanno | vengono | fanno | sanno | dicono |

You need to find your own way of learning these verbs. You will need them a lot – but also hear them a lot which will help you.

– **Dove vai?**
– **Vado a fare la spesa. Perchè non vieni con me?**
– **Buona idea, così faccio la spesa anch'io.**

– Where are you going?
– I'm going shopping. Why don't you come with me?
– Good idea, that way I'll do my shopping too.

**Anna dice che non sa dove abita Luisa. Come facciamo a trovare la sua casa?**
Anna says she doesn't know where Luisa lives? How shall we find her house?

**Exercise 7** Here are two lists. The first contains questions and the second answers but again they have become muddled. Can you sort them out?

| | | | |
|---|---|---|---|
| 1 | Vuoi venire con me? | a | Si, vogliamo un po' di frutta e di verdura. |
| 2 | Da dove vengono? | b | Sì. Viene a trovarlo stasera. |
| 3 | Che cosa dicono del progetto? | c | Al cinema. |
| 4 | Che cosa fai? | d | Non posso oggi. |
| 5 | Andate al mercato? | e | Scrivo una lettera. |
| 6 | Dove vanno Giorgio e Maria? | f | Vengo io. |
| 7 | Lucia sa che Giorgio arriva oggi? | g | Non sanno che esiste. |
| 8 | Chi viene con noi? | h | Da Roma. |

## Telling people to do something – the imperative

You have met a number of examples of this. For instance:

**Giri a destra.**     **Prenda la terza sulla sinistra.**
Turn right.           Take the third on the left.

**Scusi.**           **Senta.**
Excuse me.           Listen.

All these are examples of the *imperative*, the form of the verb used to give orders or instructions. They were all used in the formal form, addressed to people when using **lei**. How can we make sense of this?

| *-are* verbs | | all other verbs | |
|---|---|---|---|
| scusare | scusi | prendere | prenda |
| girare | giri | sentire | senta |
| parlare | parli | dire | dica |
| accomodarsi | s'accomodi | venire | venga |

The rule is that for verbs other than **-are** ones, the ending is **-a**, even if you are not quite sure what to attach it to! In fact, it is usually the first person singular of the verb, without **-o**. (**veng(o)**, **dic(o)**).

But what about friends? Alberto said to Marisa: **senti**. But you have not met other forms as you have mostly met formal conversations. The rule is:

| *-are* verbs: *-a* | all other verbs:  *-i* |
|---|---|
| scus*a* | sent*i* |
| gir*a* | |
| parl*a* | |

You may have observed that it is exactly the opposite of the formal form and wonder how to get it right. We suggest: choose two imperatives you hear frequently in Italy and make them your models. For instance, **scusare** and **sentire**. Your friends will say to you: **Oh scusa, Joe/Mary/Mike/Ann** (substitute your own name). In the street people you don't know will say: **Scusi, signore/signora/ signorina**, as appropriate. Similarly friends will attract your attention by saying: **Senti, Joe,** etc., and people you do not know well will say: **Senta, signore,** etc. These two make excellent models. Other verbs you commonly hear are:

*-are* verbs

| **tu** | | **lei** | |
|---|---|---|---|
| guarda<br>aspetta | Joe | guardi<br>aspetti | signore |

*Other verbs*

| **tu** | **lei** | **tu** | **lei** |
|---|---|---|---|
| prendi<br>abbi pazienza<br>vieni<br>di' | prendi<br>abbia pazienza[1]<br>venga<br>dica | fa'<br>va'<br>da' | faccia<br>vada<br>dia |

1 *Lit.* 'have patience', *i.e.* be patient.

In fact for regular **-ere** and **-ire** verbs, the **tu** form of the present is also the imperative form. This is also true for some irregular verbs (**vieni**). In the case of **dire, fare, andare** and **dare**, the full form is usually abbreviated, as (') shows.

## Andiamo! 'Let's go!'

To include yourself in a suggestion, you use the **noi** form of the verb, but *never* use the **noi**. This is also an imperative.

| | |
|---|---|
| **Telefoniamo a Gianni!** | Let's call/phone Gianni! |
| **Mangiamo alle otto!** | Let's eat at 8 o'clock! |
| **Facciamo gli spaghetti!** | Let's make spaghetti! |

To tell several people to do something, you use the **voi** form of the verb, again without **voi**.

| | |
|---|---|
| **Andate presto!** | Go quickly! |

## Telling someone *not* to do something

You simply use **non** and the verb:

Non dica questo.
Non giri a sinistra, vada dritto.

Except when you are using **tu**. Then you use **non** + infinitive:

Non dire questo.
Non girare, va' dritto.

*Exercise 8* You and your friend Mario are on your way, by car, to Giorgio's house. You know the way and Mario doesn't. So you have to give him directions. The verbs have been left out. Choose the correct ones from the list which follows to make sense of your instructions. You may use two of them twice. As Mario is a friend, you use **tu** when talking to him.

**rallenta, prendi, girare, va', gira, sta', facciamo, cerca, andare**

1 _____ la seconda sulla destra.
2 Qui, _____ a destra.
3 E poi _____ sempre dritto un po'.
4 Non _____ troppo veloce.
5 Ora al semaforo _____ a sinistra.
6 _____ sempre sulla sinistra perchè devi girare di nuovo.
7 No, non _____ qui.
8 Ecco _____ un po' e.
9 _____ questa via.
10 _____ un parcheggio in questa piazza.
11 _____ l'ultimo pezzo a piedi perchè non si può parcheggiare.

*Exercise 9* There's an air traffic controllers' strike – again. You are an airline employee and a passenger wants information about his flight.

You: (1)  (Yes,) **signore.** (*Say 'tell me', using dire, indicating you are ready to listen*)

PASSENGER: **Quando parte il mio volo?**

You:  (2) (Give me) **il biglietto per favore. Mi dispiace, signore, il volo per Amsterdam ha due ore di ritardo.**

PASSENGER: **Ma non è possibile! Devo essere a Amsterdam a mezzogiorno.**

You:  (3) (Be patient), **signore.** (4) (Forgive me). **Non posso fare niente.** (5) (Make yourself comfortable) **al bar o nel ristorante.** (6) (Wait) **con calma ...**

# Reading

*La domenica in Italia*

---

1  Why is it difficult for families to be together on Saturdays?
2  Can you list five activities which an Italian family might be engaged in during a winter Sunday?
3  Where do many people enjoy going on summer Sundays?

---

La domenica è un giorno molto importante per gli Italiani. Il sabato molti adulti non lavorano ma i bambini sono a scuola la mattina. La domenica è dunque il giorno in cui tutti i membri della la famiglia sono a casa. Spesso il venerdì o il sabato, si sente l'augurio 'Buona domenica!' La domenica è il giorno in cui si invitano i familiari a pranzo a mezzogiorno. Il pomeriggio si va a fare una passeggiata in campagna o nei parchi o semplicemente si passeggia lungo la via principale della città, che è spesso zona pedonale. Certe persone, invece, d'inverno preferiscono passare il pomeriggio al cinema. Durante la stagione calcistica, i tifosi vanno allo stadio a vedere la partita. Se però devono accompagnare la famiglia a spasso, seguono la partita alla radio. E' divertente vedere questi signori camminare con la radiolina all'orecchio per seguire, anche da lontano, la loro squadra. In inverno dalle città del nord c'è l'esodo verso la montagna per sciare; invece d'estate è il mare o la campagna che attirano i gitanti. La sera, sulle strade che vanno in città, qualsiasi città, si formano code di automobilisti che tornano per prepararsi a una nuova settimana di lavoro. Il lunedì arriva sempre troppo presto.

## *Vocabulary*

| | | | |
|---|---|---|---|
| **dunque** | so, therefore | **augurio** | wish, greeting |
| **spesso** | often | **(auguri!** | best wishes!) |
| **i familiari** | relatives | **il calcio** | soccer |
| **pedonale** | traffic-free, reserved for pedestrians | **calcistico** | to do with soccer |
| **pedoni** | pedestrians | **un tifoso** | a fan |
| **spasso** | walk or outing for pleasure | **camminare** | to walk |
| **esodo** | exodus | **orecchio** | ear |
| **una gita** | a trip, an excursion | **un gitante** | tripper |
| **casa** | house, home | **una coda** | a queue |

# 7 Giriamo

## Let's get out and about

## Dialogue 1 🔲

*All'albergo (1)*

*Frances is touring Italy with her husband and some friends, husband and wife. They haven't booked accommodation, it's low season. Frances has been delegated to go into the Albergo della Fontana in a little Tuscan town to see whether they have rooms for tonight*

1 How many rooms does Frances want?
2 What are the important points about the rooms for her and her party?
3 Before deciding to take the rooms what does she ask to do?

| | |
|---|---|
| DIRETTORE: | Buona sera, signora, desidera? |
| FRANCES: | Avete una camera? |
| DIRETTORE: | Sì, signora. Una camera singola o doppia? |
| FRANCES: | In realtà, vorrei due camere, due camere doppie. Una per me e mio marito, una per i nostri amici. |
| DIRETTORE: | Preferite un letto matrimoniale o due letti? |
| FRANCES: | Veramente non importa. |
| DIRETTORE: | Con bagno o senza? |
| FRANCES: | Oh, con bagno, per favore. E preferiamo camere tranquille. |
| DIRETTORE: | Certo, signora. Per una notte? |
| FRANCES: | No, per due notti. |
| DIRETTORE: | Abbiamo due camere tranquille. Danno sul cortile dietro l'albergo. Ma qui in ogni modo c'è poco traffico. |
| FRANCES: | Potrei vedere le camere? |
| DIRETTORE: | Senz'altro. Prendo le chiavi. Venga pure. |

## Vocabulary

| | |
|---|---|
| **i nostri amici** | our friends |
| **veramente** | really (**vero** means 'true'; lit. 'truly') |
| **danno sul cortile** | they overlook the courtyard (implied: 'at the back of the hotel') |
| **in ogni modo** | in any case |
| **c'è poco traffico** | there's not much traffic |
| **senz'altro** | of course |
| **le chiavi** (sing. **la chiave**) | the keys |

### More vocabulary for hotels

| | |
|---|---|
| **una camera singola** | a single room |
| **doppia** | double |
| **una camera a un letto** | a single room (room with one bed) |
| **due letti** | double (room with two beds) |
| **una camera matrimoniale** | a room with a double bed. Italian double beds are generous |
| **con bagno** | with bath |
| **doccia** | shower |
| **aria condizionata** | air conditioning |

# Language points

## Non importa

**Non importa** means 'it doesn't matter', 'it's not important'. **Importa** is a verb (**importare**), and the subject is 'it' which is not stated. A verb used in this way is called an *impersonal* verb: the subject is not a person. Look out for others.

## The plural of nouns and adjectives ending in -co and -go

Most nouns and adjectives ending in **-go** keep the hard **g** sound in the plural and therefore insert an **h** to indicate this:

un albergo                    due alberghi

Nouns ending in **-co** are less predictable. Generally speaking those in which the *penultimate* syllable bears the main stress keep the hard **c** and therefore insert an **h**:

un arco etrusco               due archi etruschi
un vino bianco                due vini bianchi

When the stress is on the *antepenultimate* syllable however there is usually a sound change:

un medico simpatico           due medici simpatici

*Exception:*

un amico                      due amici

*Note:* Feminine nouns and adjectives in the feminine ending in **-ca** and **-ga** all keep the hard sound and insert the **h**, including:

un'amica                      due amiche

These are points which fall into place the more Italian you hear. Lists of exceptions are confusing for the beginner, so we are not giving them. But **amico** is such a common word, you should learn it. If in doubt, consult a dictionary. But, as ever, don't worry too much as mistakes do not usually impair communication. As your Italian becomes more sophisticated you can gradually aim to get these details correct.

*Exercise 1* In the hotel conversation singulars and plurals were used:

**una camera   due camere       un letto   due letti**

Here are some more words, sometimes with adjectives, to put into the plural – remind yourself of the forms first (Lesson 5). In numbers 1–8, change to two of everything. *Example:* **un letto** *Answer:* **due letti**

1  un giorno                    5  una banca
2  una settimana                6  un giornale
3  un mese interessante         7  un cappuccino
4  un nuovo progetto            8  una birra

In the next group you have definite articles ('the'). Make the whole word group plural. *Example:* **il francobollo francese** *Answer:* **i francobolli francesi**

 9  il nuovo film               13  la nuova galleria
10  lo spettacolo               14  la strada che va in città
11  il giornale interessante    15  l'adulto responsabile
12  il supermercato francese    16  il vino rosso

# Dialogue 2  ▭

*All'albergo (2)*

*Having satisfied herself the rooms are pleasant, Frances continues the conversation*

---
1  What is and what is not included in the price?
2  Where is the garage?
---

FRANCES:    Qual è il prezzo di una camera per una notte?
DIRETTORE:  120,000 lire, signora.
FRANCES:    E' inclusa la colazione?
DIRETTORE:  No, signora. Sono inclusi le tasse e il servizio, ma la colazione non è compresa nel prezzo.
FRANCES:    Va bene. Vado a chiamare mio marito e i nostri amici. Oh, c'è un garage?
DIRETTORE:  Sì, signora. Quando esce, giri a sinistra. Poi deve passare sotto l'arco, a sinistra. Il garage è dietro

l'albergo, in fondo al cortile. Posso avere un documento, per cortesia?

FRANCES: Ecco il mio passaporto.

## Vocabulary

| | |
|---|---|
| **il prezzo** | the price |
| **la colazione** | breakfast |
| **compreso, incluso** | (*very similar in meaning*) included |
| (*from* **comprendere, includere**) | |
| **quando esce** | when you go out |
| **in fondo a** | at the bottom of, at the end of |
| **per cortesia** | *another way of saying* please. *Yet another is:* **per piacere** |
| **un documento** | an identification document, *usually a passport or an identity card* |

## Language points

### Uscire 'to go out'

| | |
|---|---|
| esco | usciamo |
| esci | uscite |
| esce | escono |

### Vado a chiamare mio marito

When you say you are going to do something, you need to use **a**
after **andare**, before the second verb.

| | |
|---|---|
| **Vado a mangiare.** | I am going to eat. |
| **Andate a vedere il nuovo film?** | Are you going to see the new film? |
| **Va a lavorare.** | He/she is going to work. |

***Exercise 2*** Joe McDonald needs to book into a hotel for the night.
Here is his conversation with the receptionist. Unfortunately the
printer has got the order all wrong and forgotten to indicate
whether Joe or the receptionist is talking. Can you sort it out so
that it makes sense?

1  Per quante notti?
2  Singola o doppia?
3  Sessantamila lire.
4  Abbiamo una singola con doccia. Va bene?
5  E' compresa la colazione?
6  Ecco la chiave. E' il numero 32.
7  Va bene.
8  Buona sera. Avete una camera?
9  No, non è compresa.
10 Una notte.
11 Grazie.
12 Posso avere un documento?
13 Singola.
14 Qual è il prezzo?
15 Certo, ecco la mia carta d'identità.

## Dialogue 3

### *Vorrei un po' di frutta*

*Mrs Rossi is shopping at her local market. She stops at a fruit and vegetable stall*

> 1  The fruitseller says the small oranges have certain qualities. What are they?
> 2  Which other fruit does she want?
> 3  How much will her apples cost her?

FRUTTIVENDOLO:     Buongiorno, signora. Desidera?
SIG.RA ROSSI:      Buongiorno. Vorrei un po' di frutta. Quanto costano le arance?
FRUTTIVENDOLO:     2000 al chilo le grandi, 1800 le piccole. Sono molto dolci, quelle piccole, ottime per la spremuta.
SIG.RA ROSSI:      Allora, un chilo. E ho bisogno anche di banane.
FRUTTIVENDOLO:     Quante?
SIG.RA ROSSI:      Cinque o sei. Ecco, così va bene. E due pompelmi.
FRUTTIVENDOLO:     Benissimo, signora. Altro?
SIG.RA ROSSI:      Ci sono delle mele buone?
FRUTTIVENDOLO:     Queste a 2000 al chilo, del Trentino, sono molto buone.
SIG.RA ROSSI:      Mezzo chilo, per favore.
FRUTTIVENDOLO:     Ecco. E poi?
SIG.RA ROSSI:      Basta così per oggi. Quant'è?
FRUTTIVENDOLO:     Settemila, signora.

| Sig.ra rossi: | Ecco (*giving him a 10.000 lire note*). |
| Fruttivendolo: | Otto, nove, diecimila. Grazie, signora, arrivederla, buongiorno. |

## Vocabulary

| dolce | sweet | del Trentino | from the Trentino, |
| ottimo | very good | | *in northern Italy* |
| ho bisogno di | I need (*see below*) | basta così | *lit.* 'it's enough like |
| una mela | an apple | | that'. That'll be all |

## Language points

### Ho bisogno di . . .

**Avere bisogno di**, *lit.* 'to have need of', corresponds to the English 'to need'.

| Ho bisogno di francobolli. | I need some (postage) stamps. |
| Ho bisogno di sapere la risposta. | I need to know the answer. |
| Hai bisogno di me? | Do you need me? |

### Altro?

When asking a customer if she (he) needs anything else a shop-keeper may say: **altro?** In the context this means 'anything else?' **Altro** is the word for 'other':

| un altro caffè | another coffee |
| l'altro giorno | the other day |

*Note* the way you say 'two, three, etc. more/other':

| Altri due caffè | Two more coffees |
| Altre tre persone | Three other people |

Other ways of encouraging the customer to buy more are:

| E poi? | And then? Next? |
| Dopo? | After (that)? |
| E' tutto? | Is that all? |

And ways of saying 'no' are:

| | |
|---|---|
| **No, grazie.** | No, thank you. |
| **Basta, grazie.** | That's all, thanks. |
| **No, basta così.** | *lit.* 'No, it's sufficient like that' |
| **No, va bene così.** | No, *lit.* 'it's all right like that' |

(**Così** means 'in this way', 'in that way', 'thus'.)

## Basta

**Bastare** is a verb but normally used only in the third person singular and plural. It can have a specific subject:

| | |
|---|---|
| **Bastano queste banane?** | Are these enough bananas? |
| **Bastano diecimila lire?** | Are 10.000 lire enough? |

or be used impersonally followed by an infinitive or a noun:

| | |
|---|---|
| **Basta chiedere.** | It's sufficient to ask, *i.e.* All you need do is ask. |
| **E' lontano. Si può arrivare in una giornata?** | It's a long way. Can one get there in one day? |
| **Basta partire presto.** | So long as one starts early (All you need do is start early). |
| **Basta telefonare.** | All you need to do is telephone. |

Or, from a leaflet about cancer prevention:

**Basta una telefonata per prenotare una visita preventiva gratuita per te e per i tuoi cari ...**
All it needs is a telephone call to book a free check-up for you and your loved ones ...

## Weights and measures

The system used in Italy, as elsewhere in Europe, is the metric system. For weight, the basic measures are the gram (**grammo**) and the kilogram (**chilogrammo**) – 1,000 grams. Lightweight items such as ham, sweets/candies, are sold by the **etto**. **Un etto** = 100 grams, which is about ½ oz. less than ¼ lb. So you have:

| | |
|---|---|
| un etto | = 100 grammi |
| mezzo chilo | = 5 etti = 500 grammi |
| un chilo | = 1.000 grammi |

The liquid measure is the litre:

```
un litro
mezzo litro
un quarto (di litro)
```

## La frutta

The word is similar to the English collective noun 'fruit', i.e. you do not usually use it in the plural. The most commonly found, in season, include (the singular is given for clarity):

| | | | |
|---|---|---|---|
| **l'albicocca** | apricot | **l'arancia** | orange |
| **la ciliegia** | cherry | **la fragola** | strawberry |
| **il limone** | lemon | **la mela** | apple |
| **il melone** | melon | **la pera** | pear |
| **la pesca** | peach | **il pompelmo** | grapefruit |
| **la prugna** | plum | **la susina** | (*also*) plum |
| **l'uva** | grapes | | |

*Note:* **Uva** is a singular noun meaning 'grapes':

| | |
|---|---|
| **L'uva è molto buona.** | The grapes are very good. |
| **Un chilo di uva bianca, per piacere.** | A kilo of white grapes, please. |

## Plurals of nouns ending in -cia, -gia

A stressed **-i** remains in the plural:

    la farmacia    le farmacie    un'allergia    molte allergie

If the **-i-** is there only to show that the **-c-** or **-g-** is soft, then:

(a) **-cia**, **-gia**, preceded by a vowel becomes **-cie**, **-gie**:

    una ciliegia        un chilo di ciliegie

(b) **-cia**, **-gia**, preceded by a consonant becomes **-ce**, **-ge**:

    un'arancia        un chilo di arance

Difficult? Yes, but we needed to tell you for the next exercise! When you are *speaking* Italian, in the case of (a) and (b) it makes no difference to the sound, so don't worry. But, in the next exercise, try to get it right, since it is fresh in your mind. You can always look it up when you have to write.

*Exercise 3* You are at a fruit stall in a market. Ask how much the fruits listed above cost. There is one 'trick question' – watch out for it.

# Dialogue 4 ▣

*Ho bisogno di formaggio*

*Mrs Rossi is in a grocer's shop*

> 1 How much **pecorino** does Mrs Rossi buy?
> 2 What else does she buy besides cheese?

| | |
|---|---|
| COMMESSO: | Buongiorno, signora, desidera? |
| SIG.RA ROSSI: | Ho bisogno di formaggio oggi. C'è del pecorino? |
| COMMESSO: | Dolce o piccante? |
| SIG.RA ROSSI: | Piccante. Tre etti. |
| COMMESSO: | Ecco. Altro? |
| SIG.RA ROSSI: | Sì. Del prosciutto crudo. |
| COMMESSO: | Prosciutto di Parma o nostrano? |
| SIG.RA ROSSI: | Quanto costano? |
| COMMESSO: | Il nostrano 32.000 lire al chilo, quello di Parma 39.000. E' molto buono quello nostrano. |
| SIG.RA ROSSI: | Allora lo prendo. Basta un etto. |
| COMMESSO: | (*slices some and then weighs it*) 120 grammi. Va bene così? |
| SIG.RA ROSSI: | Sì, va bene. Quant'è? |
| COMMESSO: | 6.500 il pecorino. E poi, 3.800 il prosciutto. 10.300 in tutto. Grazie, arrivederla. Buongiorno. |

## *Vocabulary notes*

**formaggio** cheese

**pecorino** a cheese made with ewes' milk. *According to how long it has been matured it is **dolce** 'mild' or **piccante** 'strong flavoured'*

**prosciutto crudo** cured ham. *Usually known in English as* 'Parma ham' *although ham is cured in a similar way in other parts of Italy;* **prosciutto** *can also be* **cotto** *'cooked'*

**nostrano** local. *Used particularly of wine, cheese, ham, fruit. etc. The word is, of course, linked with **nostro** which you met earlier in the lesson, meaning 'our'*

*Exercise 4* Say out loud and then write down in words the prices in this last conversation.

## Language points

### Some ham, some cheese – the partitive

To express the idea 'some' of something, not all, you use the articulated preposition **del**, i.e. **di** + the definite article:

| | | | |
|---|---|---|---|
| **del formaggio** | some cheese | **delle mele** | some apples |
| **del prosciutto** | some ham | | |

### 20.000 lire al chilo

When giving the price 'per kilo', 'per litre', etc. Italian uses: **al chilo, al litro.**

*Exercise 5* Sig.ra Rossi has made a shopping list. How would she tell the shop assistant she wants *some* of the following? *Example:* **banane.** *Answer:* **Vorrei delle banane.**

| | | |
|---|---|---|
| 1  limoni | 4  formaggio | 7  arance |
| 2  francobolli | 5  uva | 8  pesche |
| 3  caffè | 6  acqua minerale | 9  pane (bread) |

### Un etto di prosciutto

When you specify a quantity, however, you just use **di**:

un chilo di mele     un litro di vino     un po' di formaggio

## Dialogue 5

### Ci sono altri colori?

*Joe, in Florence, wants to buy presents to take home. He, like many other tourists, goes to the very large street market near the church*

*of San Lorenzo. He is looking at sweaters, with his young sister in mind. There is one he likes displayed on a stall ('a sweater' is **una maglia**)*

---

1  Who does the salesgirl assume he is buying for?
2  What colour sweater catches his eye?
3  Why does he take an L?

---

| | |
|---|---|
| JOE: | *(trying to attract the salesperson's attention)*<br>Senta! Posso vedere quella maglia? |
| VENDITRICE: | Sì, signore. E' molto bella, questa maglia. Fatta a mano. |
| JOE: | Quanto costa? |
| VENDITRICE: | Solo 70,000. E' per sua moglie? |
| JOE: | No, per mia sorella. Ha 16 anni. Ci sono altri colori? |
| VENDITRICE: | *(pointing to a pile of sweaters)* Sì signore. Guardi. C'è verde, rosa, blu, beige ... |
| JOE: | Mi piace quella verde. |
| VENDITRICE: | Sua sorella, com'è? Di che misura ha bisogno? |
| JOE: | Le piace portare le maglie grandi. |
| VENDITRICE: | Allora deve prendere una L. |
| JOE: | Va bene. Prendo quella verde. |

**fatto/a a mano**   hand made (made by hand)
**misura**   size (*for clothes, shoes etc.*)

## Language point

### I colori

(Singular: **il colore**)

| | |
|---|---|
| **azzurro** | blue (darker than **celeste**) |
| **bianco** | white |
| **giallo** | yellow |
| **grigio** | grey |
| **nero** | black |
| **rosso** | red |

| | |
|---|---|
| **arancione** | orange |
| **celeste** | blue (sky blue, paler than **azzurro**) |
| **marrone** | brown |
| **verde** | green |

| | |
|---|---|
| **blu** | dark or navy blue |
| **rosa** | pink |
| **viola** | violet |

The colours have been grouped above according to the way the adjectives work. The first group have four forms: **rosso**, **rossa**, **rossi**, **rosse**:

**buoni vini rossi**          good red wines

The second group have two forms: **verde**, **verdi**:

**una mela verde**          one (a) green apple
**due mele verdi**          two green apples

The remainder have one form only:

**una maglia blu**          a dark blue sweater
**due maglie blu**          two dark blue sweaters

*Note also:*

| | | | |
|---|---|---|---|
| **chiaro** | light (*when used with a colour*), *also means* clear | **scuro** | dark |
| **verde chiaro** | light green | **verde scuro** | dark green |

**Exercise 6** It takes a while to absorb verb forms. Here is some more practice. The verb is given in the infinitive. Write the correct form for the various subjects suggested. Where it might be more usual to leave the subject pronoun out, it is put in brackets. *Example: lavorare*

**Carlo. Carlo lavora. Anna e Paola. Anna e Paola lavorano.**

1  *comprare*
   Anna, che cosa (a) _____ (tu)?
   Io (b) _____ un libro.
   Gianna, tu e Piero, che cosa (c) _____?
   (Noi) (d) _____ una maglia per Piero.

2 *leggere*
   Io (a) _____ poco. Non ho tempo.
   Paolo invece (b) _____ molto.
   Si dice che gli Italiani (c) _____ poco. Non so se è vero.

3 *preferire*
   Io (a) _____ la maglia rossa.
   Giorgio invece (b) _____ quella celeste.

4 *parlare*
   Questi studenti (a) _____ russo, francese e italiano.
   Io invece (b) _____ solo italiano.
   Mario (c) _____ inglese e francese?
   E tu? (d) _____ un'altra lingua?

5 *vivere*
   Giorgio e Anna (a) _____ in città.
   Noi (b) _____ in campagna.

# Reading 🔘🔘

**Che cosa pensano gli Italiani?**

> 1  What do Italians say about Ornella Muti?
> 2  What percentage of Italians say they are Catholics?
> 3  Do these self-professed Catholics go to confession regularly?
> 4  When asked to say what they considered the pleasures of life, what did Italians put in first place?
> 5  And what came second and third?

Un libro recente* rivela delle risposte forse sorprendenti a varie domande fatte agli Italiani. Ad esempio, secondo un sondaggio recente, gli Italiani considerano Ornella Muti la donna più bella del mondo. Impariamo che il 70% degli Italiani si considera cattolico praticante ma fra di loro il 46% si confessa una volta all'anno, il 12% meno di una volta all'anno e il 9% non si confessa mai. E quando si chiede agli Italiani quali sono i piaceri della vita, che cosa scopriamo? Al primo posto mettono il fatto di essere Italiani. Il sesso è soltanto in settima posizione, dopo il cibo, la musica, i viaggi, le risate e la lettura.

* *L'opinione degli Italiani*, Istituto CIRM a cura di Nicola Piepoli. (Sperling & Kupfer Editori) 1994

(Passage freely adapted from an article in *Anna*, 4 February 1995.)

## *Vocabulary*

| | | | |
|---|---|---|---|
| **rivelare** | to reveal | **i piaceri della vita** | the pleasures of life |
| **una risposta** | an answer | **scopriamo** | we discover |
| **una domanda** | a question | **il sesso** | sex |
| **ad esempio** | for example | **il cibo** | food |
| **sondaggio** | opinion poll | **viaggi** | journeys, travelling |
| **donna** | woman | **le risate** | (good) laughs |
| **impariamo** | we learn | | |
| **una volta all'anno** | once a year | | |
| **non si confessa mai** | never goes to confession | | |

# 8 Un po' di geografia

## A little geography

In this lesson you will learn about:

- The basics of the geography of Italy
- Vocabulary for talking about parts of the country
- Distances and area
- Forming the past participle e.g. cultivated, grown
- The passive
- **Bellissimo** – saying 'it's very beautiful'
- Adverbs
- Expressing your likes – **mi piacciono, mi piacerebbe**
- Personal pronouns, indirect object form ('to me', 'to him')

# Reading 1 📼

*Un po' di geografia*

Are the following statements true or false?

1 The summit of Mont Blanc is in Italy.
2 The highest mountains in Europe are to be found in the Appennines.
3 Three quarters of Italy's land area is flat.
4 Water for crops is not a problem for agriculture in the Po Plain.
5 Milan and Turin have recently developed manufacturing industry.
6 The Alps are volcanic mountains.
7 Etna is an extinct volcano.
8 Sicily is the southernmost island of Italy.
9 Tourism is very important to the Italian economy.

L'Italia è una penisola a forma di stivale. Montagne e colline occupano una superficie pari a oltre tre quarti del territorio italiano. L'Italia è povera di pianure.

Al nord un arco di montagne, le Alpi, la separa dai paesi confinanti. Nell'arco alpino si trovano le montagne più alte d'Europa: il Monte Bianco, m. 4810, il Monte Rosa, m. 4634, e il Cervino, m. 4478, chiamato 'Matterhorn' in inglese. Di questi tre, solo il Monte Rosa ha la cima interamente in territorio italiano.

Ai piedi delle montagne si estende da ovest ad est la Pianura Padana, cioè del fiume Po. Il Po, il più grande fiume italiano, è lungo 652 km. La pianura, di gran lunga la più grande d'Italia, (46 000 km²) è irrigata dalle abbondanti acque che scendono dalle montagne. Perciò è da secoli intensamente coltivata. Sulla ricchezza di questa agricoltura fiorente è basato lo sviluppo dell'industria che è oggi l'attività economica dominante della pianura. Città come Milano e Torino hanno una lunga storia industriale; più recente è lo sviluppo eccezionale in città medie di industrie varie che vanno dall'abbigliamento e gli alimenti, ai prodotti 'high-tec'.

La pianura è chiusa a sud da un'altra catena di montagne: gli Appennini, che si allungano per 1190 km. fino a Reggio Calabria e anche in Sicilia. Gli Appennini sono montagne vulcaniche. Tutti conoscono il nome di due vulcani italiani: il Vesuvio, attualmente inattivo, e l'Etna, ancora in attività.

La Sicilia e la Sardegna sono due grandi isole italiane. Ci sono poi numerose isole piccole, tra cui Lampedusa, a sud-ovest dell'isola di Malta, che è più vicina alle coste della Tunisia che a quelle siciliane. Il mare e le isole, con le montagne e la campagna, costituiscono mete turistiche piacevolissime. Va ricordato che il turismo è un settore importantissimo dell'economia italiana.

## *Vocabulary*

| | | | |
|---|---|---|---|
| **stivale** (*m.*) | boot | **fiorente** | flourishing |
| **pari a** | equal to | **sviluppo** | development |
| **povero/a** | poor | **alimenti** | foods |
| **cioè (ciò è)** | that is, i.e. | **chiuso/a** | closed |
| **di gran lunga** | by far, by a long | **catena** | chain |
| | chalk | **meta** | destination |
| **è da secoli** | it has been | **piacevole** | pleasant |
| **coltivata** | cultivated for | | |
| | centuries | | |

### *Landscape and places*

| | |
|---|---|
| **paese** | (1) country (*e.g France, New Zealand*); (2) village |
| **confine** | border, boundary |
| **frontiera** | frontier |
| **luogo** | place |
| **posto** | place; *also:* seat; job |
| **regione** | *Italy is divided into twenty administrative* regions |

| | | | |
|---|---|---|---|
| **provincia** | | *each region is divided into* provinces | |
| **comune** | | *the* **comune** *is the base administrative level. Each* **comune** *has a mayor* (**sindaco**) | |
| **città** | | city, town, *not necessarily very large* | |
| **centro** | | centre, *often '***centro storico***', the old, central part of a city* | |
| **periferia** | | outskirts, suburbs | |
| **villaggio** | | village (*as well as* **paese**) | |
| **frazione** | | outlying village of a **comune** | |

| | | | |
|---|---|---|---|
| **bosco** | wood | **isola** | island |
| **cima** | summit | **pianura** | plain |
| **collina** | hill | **spiaggia** | beach |
| **costa** | coast | **superficie** | surface |
| **fiume** | river | | |

# Language points

## The points of the compass

The words for the points of the compass each have corresponding adjectives:

| | |
|---|---|
| nord – settentrionale | sud – meridionale |
| est – orientale | ovest – occidentale |

The compass points can be combined as in English: **sud-ovest**, **nord-est**. Given the shape of Italy, it is more frequent to talk of the north and south than east and west; the north and south are in fact very different. It is common to refer to the south as **il mezzo-giorno**; the word also means 'south'.

## Measuring distances and area

**chilometro** (*abbr.* km.)
**metro** (m.)                  **un chilometro = mille metri**
**centimetro** (cm.)          **un metro = cento centimetri**
**millimetro** (mm.)          **un centimetro = dieci millimetri**
**un chilometro quadrato (1 km²)** one square kilometre
**un ettaro = 100 m²** = 2.471 acres

## Past participles

These correspond to the English form ending in '-ed', 'cultivated', 'irrigated', 'walked', 'talked', etc. The passage contained a number:

Questa pianura è *irrigata* ...
E' intensivamente *coltivata*.
Sulla ricchezza ... è *basato* lo sviluppo ... (= lo sviluppo è basato)

The past participle is formed according to the type of verb:

| | | | |
|---|---|---|---|
| **-are** verbs: | drop **-are**, add **-ato**: | **parlare** | **parlato** |
| **-ere** verbs: | drop **-ere**, add **-uto**: | **cadere** | **caduto** |
| **-ire** verbs: | drop **-ire**, add **-ito**: | **finire** | **finito** |

In English there are irregular forms ('thought', 'seen', 'gone'), and so there are in Italian, particularly in the second group. There is a list of common ones in the Grammar summary at the end of the book.

Some past participles are often used as adjectives: **una porta aperta/chiusa** 'an open/shut door'.

Past participles are much used in newspaper headlines:

**Città inondata, ospedale evacuato.**
City flooded, hospital evacuated.

**Sulla riforma, governo battuto due volte.**
Government beaten twice on the reform.

Some people find reading newspapers, especially the section called **cronaca**, which contains news items of a non-political sort (crime, road accidents etc.), a good way of getting language practice.

## The passive

The passive is formed with **essere** and a past participle, just as in English it is formed with 'to be' and the past participle:

**La pianura è *coltivata***
The plain is cultivated

**Lo sviluppo è *basato* sulla ricchezza dell'agricoltura.**
Development is based on the wealth of the agriculture.

**Il servizio è *incluso***
Service is included.

*Note:* The past participle agrees with the subject, behaving like an adjective.

To say who or what things were done by, i.e. to express the agent, use **da**:

**L'albergo è gestito dal proprietario.**
The hotel is managed by the owner.

**La pianura è circondata da montagne.**
The plain is surrounded by mountains.

A common use is after **deve essere, può essere**:

**Il lavoro deve essere finito domani.**
The work must be finished tomorrow

**Exercise 1** *Y*ou are a busy executive and are getting your secretary organized. How will you tell him/her:

1 The fax must be sent this morning. (**spedire un fax**)
2 The meeting can be organized for Monday. (**organizzare una riunione**)
3 The hotel can be booked by telephone. (**prenotare un albergo**)
4 The booking can be confirmed by fax. (**confermare una prenotazione**)
5 The tickets must be collected at midday. (**ritirare i biglietti**)
6 Rome can be informed by fax. (**informare Roma via fax**)
7 The taxi can be called in (**fra**) 10 minutes. (**chiamare un taxi**)

You need not worry too much about the passive as it works the same way as the passive in English. It tends to belong to formal language. We shall meet it and the past participle again. However, don't forget *impersonal si*. We met it in Lesson 4 and it often conveys ideas which in English would be in the passive:

**Qui si parla italiano.** Italian is spoken here.
**Come si scrive questa parola?** How is this word written/spelt?

# Dialogue

*Fare il ponte nel Bel Paese*

*Several times in the year a public holiday falls close to a weekend and Italians – and others working in Italy – like to make a long*

*weekend of it, taking a holiday on the days between the weekend
and the public holiday. This is called: **fare il ponte**, making a bridge.
Here, George, an American working temporarily in Milan, asks a
colleague for advice about how he and Jane, his wife, might spend
the long weekend*

1 Why does George ask Andrea for advice?
2 What does George want to avoid?
3 What conflict is there between George and Jane's interests?
4 In which town is there a Roman arena?
5 What is the name of the really restful place Andrea suggests?

GEORGE: Senti, Andrea, mi puoi dare un consiglio? Vorrei
suggerimenti per il fine settimana del 25 aprile. Jane ed
io abbiamo pensato di fare il ponte e partire per quattro
o cinque giorni. Tu che conosci bene l'Italia, che cosa
mi suggerisci? Vogliamo a tutti i costi andare via e
cambiare aria.

ANDREA: Cosa preferite, città o campagna? Un lago forse? O il
mare? C'è anche la montagna.

GEORGE: A Jane piace visitare le città. S'interessa molto di
architettura, di cose antiche. Io vorrei riposarmi, non
vorrei passare troppo tempo in macchina. E mi piacciono di più i posti tranquilli, i paesi piccoli, i panorami
belli.

ANDREA: Perchè non andate nel Veneto?

GEORGE: Conosciamo già Venezia e ci piacerebbe evitare posti
troppo affollati.

ANDREA: Appunto. Nel Veneto puoi trovare città per Jane e posti
più tranquilli per te. Ad esempio, Verona è una città
vivacissima, ricca di monumenti.

GEORGE: Davvero? Che cosa c'è da vedere a Verona?

ANDREA: C'è l'Arena, un anfiteatro romano, c'è la chiesa di S.
Zeno, romanica, bellissima; ci sono anche altri monumenti e tanti angoli pittoreschi. Poi potreste continuare
verso Vicenza e vedere qualche opera del Palladio.[1] Per
te c'è Marostica, una cittadina medievale; c'è Asolo, un
posto veramente riposante, in una bellissima posizione
in collina. E poi c'è l'altopiano di Asiago ...

GEORGE: Vedo che non mancano le possibilità; grazie.

1 Palladio was a Renaissance architect.

# Language points

## Bellissimo

Often, instead of using the word **molto** to convey the idea: 'very', Italians use **-issimo**. Just remove the final vowel of the adjective and add **-issimo**.

***Exercise 2*** Jane and George are telling someone about their weekend. George echoes everything Jane says. *Example:*

J: **Verona è una città molto interessante.**
G: **Interessantissima.**

J: Il Veneto è molto bello.
G: (1) _____

J: Marostica è una cittadina molto simpatica.
G: (2) _____

J: Asolo è un posto molto tranquillo.
G: (3) _____

J: Le ville del Palladio sono molto eleganti.
G: (4) _____

J: E' stato un weekend molto piacevole.
G: (5) _____

## Adverbs

To form an adverb, add **-mente** to the feminine of the adjective:

lento/a                        lentamente

Adjectives ending in **-e**:

semplice                    semplicemente

Adjectives ending in **-ale** and **-are** lose the **-e**:

finale                         finalmente
attuale                       attualmente
regolare                     regolarmente

Common adverbs *not* formed from adjectives are:

**bene**          well          **male**          badly

| | | | |
|---|---|---|---|
| **presto** | quickly | **sempre** | always |
| **spesso** | often | **subito** | at once |

**-issimo** can be added to four of these adverbs:

| | | | |
|---|---|---|---|
| bene | sto benissimo | spesso | viene spessissimo |
| male | canta malissimo | presto | partiamo prestissimo |

*Note:* **Molto** can be an adverb and an adjective. As an adverb it is invariable.

**I libri sono molto interessanti.** (*adverb*)
The books are very interesting.

**Ho molti libri sulla geografia italiana.** (*adjective*)
I have lots of books on Italian geography.

*Exercise 3* Complete these statements inserting an adverb formed from the adjective given:

1 La porta si chiude _____ (automatico).
2 Anna è contenta e canta _____ mentre lavora (allegro).
3 Non hanno molto tempo e così mangiano _____ (veloce).
4 Il treno viaggia _____ (lento).
5 Il dottor Rossi fa molto _____ (buono) il suo lavoro.
6 Anna mi telefona _____ (regolare).

## Mi piacciono

You will remember **mi piace** (Lesson 2) means 'it is pleasing to me'. Therefore when it is a *plural* thing you like – for instance, quiet places, as George does – then you have to say 'quiet places are pleasing to me', **mi piacciono i posti tranquilli**.

*Exercise 4* How would you say you like:

1 Roma
2 le montagne
3 visitare monumenti storici
4 le isole piccolissime
5 questi spaghetti (**spaghetti** *are, as you can see from the form and the adjective* **questi**, *plural*)

But what about talking about other people's likes? You need to be able to say 'it is/they are pleasing to you, to him' etc. Here's how:

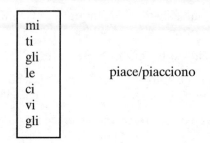

| mi | |
| ti | |
| gli | |
| le | piace/piacciono |
| ci | |
| vi | |
| gli | |

These pronouns are called *indirect object pronouns*. Pronouns because they stand instead of nouns, indirect object because they contain the idea '*to* me', not simply 'me'. To express this particular idea in English, we have a direct object: 'I like *it*'. But remember that in Italian what you are saying is: 'it is pleasing *to me*'.

*Exercise 5* How would you ask: (a) a friend, i.e. using **tu** (b) an acquaintance, i.e. using **lei** (c) two people, using **voi**

1 Do you like Italian wines? 2 Do you like Venice? 3 Do you like studying Italian?

## Mi piacerebbe

This means: 'it would be pleasing to me'. In other words, 'I should like'. It is the same part of the verb you met in **vorrei**, 'I should like'. They are very similar in meaning, but you tend to use **vorrei** when choosing/asking for things (e.g. when making purchases, ordering drinks, food, etc.). **Mi piacerebbe** has a plural form for use when what you would like is plural: **mi piacerebbero**.

You can talk about what other people would like in the same way as with **piace**:

| mi | |
| ti | |
| gli | |
| le | piacerebbe/piacerebbero |
| ci | |
| vi | |
| gli | |

**Mi piacerebbe** is much used followed by verbs:

Mi piacerebbe visitare le isole Tremiti.
Ci piacerebbe vedere il Vesuvio.

**Exercise 6** Here are some things you might like to do when you are in Italy:

Mi piacerebbe vedere la Torre Pendente di Pisa.
Mi piacerebbe andare in gondola a Venezia.
Mi piacerebbe gettare una moneta nella fontana di Trevi.
Mi piacerebbe assistere ad una gara di Formula 1 a Imola.
Mi piacerebbe sciare sulle pendici dell'Etna.
Mi piacerebbe visitare Pompei ed Ercolano.
Mi piacerebbe vedere lo Stromboli, il vulcano nelle isole Eolie.

*Now add some of your own ...*

## Qualche opera del Palladio

This means 'some works by Palladio'.
    **Qualche** means *some* but it is always followed by a singular noun:

| | |
|---|---|
| **qualche volta** | sometimes |
| **qualche libro** | some books |
| **qualche cosa** | something (*often abbreviated to:* **qualcosa**) |

## Che cosa c'è da vedere a Verona?

Note this use of the preposition **da** (see Lesson 6). Similarly:

| | |
|---|---|
| **Cosa c'è da fare?** | What is there to do? |
| **C'è qualcosa da mangiare?** | Is there something to eat? |
| **Cosa prende da bere?** | What will you have to drink? |

## C'è, ci sono

These mean 'there is', 'there are'. **C'è** is the same as **ci è**.

A Verona c'è un teatro romano.
A Venezia ci sono tanti canali.

**Exercise 7** Here is a list of some of the interesting places and artefacts to be seen in the little Tuscan town of Cortona. Answer the question, **A Cortona, che cosa c'è da vedere?**, deciding whether you should say: **c'è** or **ci sono**.

1 Il lampadario etrusco nel Museo dell'Accademia Etrusca.
2 La via Crucis a mosaico di Gino Severini.
3 Le strade pittoresche del quartiere alto della città.
4 Il panorama sulla Val di Chiana.
5 Le opere del pittore Luca Signorelli.
6 La fortezza Medicea.
7 I dipinti del Beato Angelico nel Museo Diocesano.

**Il Beato Angelico**, Dominican monk and painter, ?1400–1455, in English usually **Fra Angelico**.

**Luca Signorelli**, 1445–1523, was born in Cortona.

**Gino Severini**, 1883–1966, was also born in Cortona although he lived and worked mostly in Paris.

# Reading 2 ▣

## *Nord–Sud*

1 What is the essence of the problem of the south?
2 Are there more or fewer unemployed, per 1000 population, in the south?
3 What six differences between north and south are quoted as part of the reason for the economic differences?
4 What might attract a tourist to the south?

Il 'problema del mezzogiorno' è da anni un' importante questione della politica italiana. In che cosa consiste il problema? Nel fatto che il sud è in genere più povero del nord. Si può prendere qualsiasi indicatore di ricchezza: il reddito pro capite, il tasso di disoccupazione, il numero di macchine o di telefoni per 100 persone e si trova che il nord è più ricco del sud. Ci sono perfino più squadre di calcio di serie A nel nord che nel sud.

Perchè? Ci sono tanti motivi, molto complessi: una storia diversa, costumi diversi, un clima diverso, terreno diverso, una più lunga e più diffusa industrializzazione nel nord ... perfino il fatto che íl sud è più lontano dal centro economico dell'Europa. Purtroppo il problema sembra difficile da risolvere.

Per il turista però le differenze sono altre. Il sud è ricco di resti dell'antica civiltà greca, ad esempio. L'assenza di industria e una minore densità di popolazione vogliono dire meno inquinamento,

campagne e coste bellissime e anche tra la gente un calore umano
che forse si perde in una società più prospera.

## Vocabulary

| | |
|---|---|
| **reddito pro capite** | per capita income |
| **inquinamento** | pollution |
| **calore umano** | human warmth |

# 9 Buon appetito

**Enjoy your meal**

---

### In this lesson you will learn about:

- Italian food
- Ordering a meal
- Object pronouns, direct and indirect, e.g. 'me', 'her', 'them', 'to me', 'to her', 'to them'.
- Making your point clear – those little words
- **Viene fatto**, **va fatto** – 'it's done', 'it should be done' – another form of the passive

---

## Dialogue 1 🔘

*Al ristorante*

*Mr and Mrs Rossi have taken Angela to one of their favourite restaurants. They are just finishing their* **antipasto**

---

1 Why does Signora Rossi say ham and melon is good in the summer?
2 How does the waiter describe the fish?
3 In spite of its name, '**manzo alla California**' is a speciality of an Italian region according to the waiter. Which one?

---

| | |
|---|---|
| ANGELA: | E' molto saporito questo prosciutto. Mi piace moltissimo prosciutto e melone. |
| SIG.RA ROSSI: | Sì, d'estate è buono, è leggero. |
| CAMERIERE: | *(taking plates away)* E come primo, cosa prendete, signori? |
| SIG. ROSSI: | *(consulting the menu)* Cosa prende per primo, |

|  | signora? Ci sono i tortellini, il risotto, gli gnocchi, le tagliatelle al pomodoro e basilico, al pesto ... |
|---|---|
| ANGELA: | (*looking at her copy*) Per me il passato di verdura. |
| SIG.RA ROSSI: | Buona scelta. Lo prendo anch'io. E tu, Massimo? |
| SIG. ROSSI: | Per me, il risotto. |
| CAMERIERE: | E come secondo? Abbiamo dell'ottimo pesce stasera. Oppure c'è un arrosto di vitello speciale ... |
| ANGELA: | Che cosa è il 'manzo alla California'? |
| CAMERIERE: | E' una specialità lombarda, signora. E' uno stufato di manzo cotto molto lentamente con aceto di vino e panna. (*They make their selection.*) |

## Vocabulary

| | |
|---|---|
| **saporito** | tasty |
| **prosciutto e melone** | Parma ham and melon; *considered a dish, hence the singular verb* |
| **leggero** | light |
| **scelta** | choice |
| **passato di verdura** | sieved or liquidized vegetable soup |
| **uno stufato di manzo** | a beef stew |
| **cotto** | cooked |

It is assumed readers have eaten pasta and know dishes such as **tortellini**, **gnocchi**; they are virtually untranslatable but a book on Italian food would explain them.

## Vocabulary notes

I pasti del giorno *'the meals of the day'*

**pasto** a meal
**prima colazione** breakfast
**pranzo** lunch, dinner. *Pranzo is the main meal of the day, sometimes eaten in the evening. In that case the midday meal is often called **colazione**. There are regional variations*
**cena** supper
**spuntino** snack (*Note: **uno spuntino***)
**merenda** a snack between lunch and supper, *usually for children*
**antipasto** hors d'oeuvre, starter

**primo (piatto)** first course (*see below*)
**secondo** main course (*meat or fish*)
**contorno** vegetable (*served with the main course*)
**verdure** vegetables
**dolce** pudding, dessert
**formaggio** cheese
**ristorante** restaurant (*usually fairly big*)
**trattoria** restaurant (*small, usually family run*)
**pizzeria** *specializes in* **pizza** *but often offers other dishes, particularly* **pasta**
**tavola calda** *serves 'fast food', Italian style, to take away, or to eat in the shop*
**self-service** *just what it says. The food is usually good*

An Italian lunch or dinner normally consists of a '**primo**': pasta, rice or soup, followed by a meat or fish course, '**il secondo**'. A celebration meal or a meal out in a restaurant starts with **antipasto**, then **primo**, then, sometimes, fish, and then the meat course. Bread, **il pane**, is an essential accompaniment. A family meal often finishes with cheese and fruit. A **dolce** is served on special occasions. Feel free to skip a course from time to time in a restaurant. When your hostess has gone to the trouble of cooking it, it is rather more delicate a matter – and often too delicious to resist!

## Alla carta – *vocabulary related to food*

| | | | |
|---|---|---|---|
| **carne** | meat | **pollo** | chicken |
| **vitello** | veal | **tacchino** | turkey |
| **manzo** | beef | **maiale** | pork |
| **agnello** | lamb | **bistecca** | steak |
| **pesce** | fish | **trota** | trout |
| **salmone** | salmon | **calamaro** | squid |

There is a wide variety of fish available. Names are sometimes local – you'll have to to be bold and try!

| | | | |
|---|---|---|---|
| **carote** | carrots | **cipolle** | onions |
| **fagioli** | beans (*dried*) | **fagiolini** | French beans |
| **funghi** | mushrooms | **porcini** | cèpes |
| **melanzane** | aubergine, eggplant | **peperoni** | peppers |
| **piselli** | peas | **peperoncini** | chillis |
| **spinaci** (*Note: pl.*) | spinach | **patate** | potatoes |
| **pomodori** | tomatoes | **zucchini** | baby marrows |
| **insalata mista** | mixed salad | **insalata verde** | green salad |

| | | | |
|---|---|---|---|
| **odori** | herbs | **aglio** | garlic |
| **basilico** | basil | **maggiorana** | marjoram |
| **prezzemolo** | parsley | **rosmarino** | rosemary |
| **salvia** | sage | **timo** | thyme |
| **tartufo** | truffle | | |

| | | | |
|---|---|---|---|
| **panna** | cream | **pepe** | pepper |
| **riso** | rice | **olio d'oliva** | olive oil |
| **aceto** | vinegar | **sale** | salt |

**polenta** — *made with maize flour, once the staple diet of northern Italy, it is a thick, solid paste which is then sliced. Nowadays served with meat or fish dishes*

| | | | |
|---|---|---|---|
| **al forno** | roast, in the oven | **bollito** | stewed |
| **alla griglia** | grilled | **stufato** | a stew |
| **arrosto** | roast | | |

**Alla fiorentina, alla veneziana, alla milanese**, etc. mean prepared Florentine, Venetian or Milanese, etc. style. Menus can be difficult to understand, partly because cooking varies from region to region and partly because imaginative cooks invent dishes. Don't be afraid to ask for explanations.

## Direct object pronouns ('him', 'her', 'it', 'them')

Signora Rossi, hearing Angela order the vegetable soup, says:

**Buona idea. *La* prendo anch'io.**   A good idea. I'll have *it* too.

See also Lesson 5: Joe, choosing a map, said:

**La prendo.**              I'll have it.

Here are some more examples:

**Dov'è il giornale? Non *lo* vedo.**
Where is the newspaper? I can't see *it*.

**Giorgio non vuole venire stasera. *Lo* capisco.**
Giorgio doesn't want to come this evening. I understand *him*.

**Cerco i miei occhiali. Non *li* trovo.**
I'm looking for my glasses. I can't find *them*.

**Mi piacciono molto le lasagne al forno. *Le* prendo.**
I love lasagne. I'll have *them*.

**I miei nonni abitano qui vicino. *Li* vediamo quasi ogni giorno.**

My grandparents live near here. We see *them* nearly every day.

Can you begin to see the way the pronoun works? It depends whether the noun being replaced is masculine or feminine, singular or plural.

|           | *Singular* |          | *Plural* |      |
|-----------|------------|----------|----------|------|
| *Masculine* | **lo**   | him, it  | **li**   | them |
| *Feminine*  | **la**   | her, it  | **le**   | them |

Notice also that the pronoun is placed **before** the verb.

You have already met the *indirect object* pronouns. The difficulty for most English speaking people is to understand the idea of *direct* and *indirect object.* Here are a couple of examples in English. Are the words in italic direct or indirect objects?

He sees *me*.          He speaks *to me*.
They know *her*.       They talk *to her*.

In the first column you have a direct object, in the second, an indirect. The direct object is directly affected by the action of the verb; the indirect object has a preposition before the pronoun. A more complicated case in English would be:

They gave it to me.

What is *it* and what is *to me*, grammatically? They are direct and indirect object respectively. *It* was given. I benefited indirectly – it was given *to me*.

**Exercise 1** You are having a meal in a restaurant. Your host asks you whether you like various dishes. Say you do and that you will have it. *Example:*

HOST:   **C'è prosciutto e melone come antipasto. Le piace?**
YOU:   **Sì, mi piace. Lo prendo.**

HOST:   Come primo ci sono lasagne al forno. Le piacciono?
YOU:   (1) _____
HOST:   Come secondo c'è bistecca alla fiorentina. Le piace?
YOU:   (2) _____
HOST:   E come contorno, ci sono spinaci. Le piacciono?
YOU:   (3) _____

**Exercise 2** Things are being very irritating. You can't see them, you can't find them, you can't understand them – and you are getting into quite a state. You need help (**aiuto**). Here is what you

say, in English. But your Italian friend won't understand if you say
it that way, so say it in Italian:

> Where's Mary's letter? I can't find it. And the magazine? I can't
> see it. Where are the stamps for the postcards? I can't find them.
> Can you see the pen? I can't find it. And this bill (**conto**), I don't
> understand it. Help!

## More about object pronouns

The *indirect object pronouns* are:

| | | | |
|---|---|---|---|
| **mi** | to me | **ci** | to us |
| **ti** | to you | **vi** | to you |
| **gli** | to him | **gli** | to them |
| **le** | to her, to you | | |

**Mi**, **ti**, **ci**, **vi**, are also *direct object pronouns*:

| | | | |
|---|---|---|---|
| **mi** | me | **ci** | us |
| **ti** | you | **vi** | you |

So the problem of difference arises only in the third person:

| | | | |
|---|---|---|---|
| **lo** | him | **gli** | to him |
| **la** | her | **le** | to her |
| | you | | to you |
| **li** | them (*m.*) | **gli** | to them (*m.* and *f.*) |
| **le** | them (*f.*) | | |

*Note:* Confusion between **gli** singular and plural doesn't arise
because you only use a pronoun when you have used a noun
immediately previously. Some grammar books will mention a plural
indirect object pronoun, **loro**, but it is rarely used in speech.

What did you notice about the position of the object pronoun,
whether direct or indirect? It usually goes just before the verb:

|       | | |
|-------|-----|------------------------|
| Carla | mi<br>ti<br>lo<br>la<br>ci<br>vi<br>li<br>le | conosce molto bene. |

| Carla | mi<br>ti<br>gli<br>le<br>ci<br>vi<br>gli | scrive ogni settimana. |

*Note:* When **loro** is used, it must follow the verb: **Carla scrive loro.**

**Exercise 3** Here are some sentences very similar to ones you have met. Translate the pronoun which has been left in English.

1 Mio figlio abita a Toronto. _____ scrive ogni domenica. (*to me*) Quando arriva la lettera _____ leggo sempre tre o quattro volte. (*it*)

2 Il signor Marini _____ conosce bene. (*us*) _____ dà qualche volta delle riviste italiane. (*to us*)

3 (Al telefono) _____ passo subito il Signor Anselmi. (*to you*, formal)

4 Per la riunione _____ va bene giovedì? (*to you*, informal)

5 Anna è una mia carissima amica. _____vedo quasi ogni settimana. (*her*)

6 L'autobus _____ porta in centro. _____ lascia proprio davanti al municipio. (*you*. Try to do each sort: informal singular, formal singular, and the plural – i.e. the object pronouns corresponding to **tu**, **lei**, and **voi**.)

**Exercise 4** How would you say the following to an Italian friend?

1 Signor Galli knows me well. I see him every week. He telephones me often.

2 Do you know Mr and Mrs Fabrizi? Do you like them? I see them every Sunday. I speak to them on the telephone almost every day.

3 I am writing you a letter. I am sending you the photos (**le foto**) of Gianni.

# Dialogue 2

## *La cucina italiana*

*Angela enjoys cooking. She is asking Signora Rossi about Italian food*

> 1 Why, according to Mrs Rossi, is it difficult to talk about Italian cooking?
> 2 Why do they use rice a lot in the Po Plain?
> 3 What does Mrs Rossi say Sicily produces well?
> 4 Why is olive oil not used in the cooking of Lombardy?
> 5 What is used in its place?

SIG.RA R: Veramente parlare di 'cucina italiana' è difficile. Ancora oggi la cucina è diversa da una regione all'altra.

ANGELA: Ah, sì? Come mai?

SIG.RA R: Dev'essere la geografia, penso; cioè il clima e il terreno. Ad esempio, qui nella Pianura Padana, c'è molta acqua e ci sono risaie. Così si mangiano piatti a base di riso, come il risotto alla milanese. Invece, la Sicilia è molto più arida, ma anche più calda. Produce verdure buonissime, frutta, agrumi. Allora si usano questi in cucina.

ANGELA: Certo, capisco. Ci dev'essere una differenza di clima notevole tra la Sicilia e la Lombardia.

SIG.RA R: Sì. Qui abbiamo anche bestiame e naturalmente carne molto buona e latte, panna, formaggi e così via. Ma non abbiamo olive, così nella nostra cucina il burro viene usato più spesso. In quella siciliana si usa quasi esclusivamente l'olio di oliva. Anche in tutta l'Italia centrale si usa l'olio di oliva.

CAMERIERE: (*bringing the pasta course, **il primo***) I passati di verdura? Per chi sono?

SIG.RA R: Per la signora e per me. (*Attention turns to the **primo**.*)

## Vocabulary

| | | | |
|---|---|---|---|
| risaia | paddy, rice field | bestiame | cattle |
| piatti a base di riso | dishes based on rice | così via | and so on |
| agrumi | citrus fruits | il burro | butter |

# Language points

## Come mai?

**Come mai?** means: 'How's that?' 'Why?' 'How come?' The expression implies surprise as well as asking 'why'. A simple 'why' is **perchè?**

## Making your point clear

When we talk or write, we use various words to clarify and structure what we are saying or writing. They catch the ear of the foreign learner since they seem to crop up frequently and he/she wonders what they mean. Such words:

(a) *clarify*. **Cioè**, 'that is', 'i.e.': **Dev'essere la geografia, penso: cioè il clima e il terreno.**

(b) *exemplify*. **Ad esempio**, 'for example'. (The **d** is added to **a** because of the vowel which follows. It is optional, a question of style. The same can be done with **e**, 'and'.)

(c) *contrast*. **Invece**, 'on the other hand'. **Invece** also means 'instead'.

(d) *indicate the consequences*. **Dunque**, 'therefore', 'so'. **Così**, 'so', 'thus': **così si mangiano piatti a base di riso. Così** also means 'in this way' cf. **Così fan tutte**, 'All women behave this way'. (**fan** is an abbreviation for **fanno**.)

Other words of this sort include **comunque**, 'anyway', 'however', often used to introduce a final remark which is seen as concluding the argument:

> **So che non ti piace e che è difficile; comunque il direttore lo vuole così. Non c'è scelta.**
> I know you don't like it and that it's difficult. However the director wants it that way. There's no choice.

Look out for others. They often have very minimal meaning.

## Viene fatto così

When saying how things are generally done, it is common to use
**venire** plus the past participle rather than **essere**. (See Lesson 8
– the passive – but don't forget impersonal **si** – Lesson 4.)

**Il burro viene usato spesso nella cucina settentrionale.**
Butter is often used in northern cookery.

## Va fatto

When saying what should be done it is usual to use: **andare** + past
participle:

**L'ambiente naturale va conservato.**
The natural environment should be preserved.

**Il vino bianco va bevuto fresco.**
White wine should be drunk chilled.

In discussions, you will hear:

**Va ricordato che** ...   It should be remembered that ...
**Va detto che** ...   It should be said that ...

# Dialogue 3

*Una ricetta*

*In the restaurant Angela pursues the topic of Italian food*

> 1 What kind of recipe does Angela ask for?
> 2 What are the ingredients for the dish Mrs Rossi describes?
> 3 What additions does she say would make it more authentically Sicilian?

ANGELA:  Signora Rossi, si vede che lei sa molto sulla cucina italiana. Avrebbe qualche buona ricetta da darmi? Mi piace molto la pasta.

SIG.RA R:  Conosco una ricetta siciliana molto buona. In Sicilia la pasta viene spesso servita mescolata con verdure. Il piatto si chiama 'pasta con i broccoli' o in dialetto siciliano: 'pasta chi vruoccoli'. Io lo preparo così: ci vogliono olio, aglio, broccoli, maccheroni e parmigiano. Butto i broccoli in acqua bollente salata. Una volta cotti, li tolgo dall'acqua e li metto in una zuppiera con olio di oliva, aglio e parmigiano. Metto la pasta nell'acqua dei broccoli. Quando la pasta è cotta, la scolo e la metto sui broccoli, mescolando velocemente. Mmm, buoni, buoni . . .

ANGELA: Grazie. Provo la ricetta appena torno a casa.

SIG.RA R: Per fare un piatto autenticamente siciliano ci vuole anche un po' di peperoncino. Si possono aggiungere anche acciughe o sardine e perfino uva passa e pinoli. Ma così come lo faccio, piace alla mia famiglia.

## Vocabulary

| | |
|---|---|
| **si vede che** | it's clear that (*lit.* 'one can see that') |
| **avrebbe qualche buona ricetta da darmi?** | would you have some good recipes to give me? |
| **mescolata (mescolare)** | mixed (to mix) |
| **parmigiano** | Parmesan cheese. *It goes without saying here that it is grated* |
| **butto** | I throw |
| **acqua bollente salata** | boiling salted water |
| **una volta cotti** | once they are cooked |
| **li tolgo (togliere) dall'acqua** | I take them out of the water |
| **li metto in una zuppiera** | I put them in a soup tureen |
| **scolare** | to drain |
| **mescolando** | tossing, mixing |
| **si possono aggiungere acciughe e sardine** | anchovies and sardines can be added (*Note: plural verb*) |
| **uva passa** | raisins |
| **pinoli** | pine nuts |

# Language point

## Ci vuole, ci vogliono

ci vuole un po' di peperoncino
ci vogliono olio, aglio, broccoli ecc.

The expression means 'you need', 'one needs', but it is impersonal. If what is needed is singular, you use **ci vuole**, if it is plural, **ci vogliono**.

**Per arrabbiarsi ci vogliono 65 muscoli, per sorridere solo 19. Fa' economia, sorridi!**
To get angry you need 65 muscles, to smile only 19. Economize, smile!
(*Handwritten notice commonly seen in offices, etc.*)

**Si può, si possono** work in a similar way – see the conversation above.

# 10 Buone vacanze

## Have a good holiday

**In this lesson you will learn about:**

- Talking about holidays
- Saying where you've been
- The family
- Possessive adjectives ('my', 'his', 'our')
- Saying how old someone is
- Talking about the weather
- Saying something's about to happen
- 'What a silly boy!' – exclaiming

## Dialogue 1 ▣

*Vacanze in Sicilia*

*Enrico bumps into his friend Aldo whom he hasn't seen for a few weeks*

1 Why is Aldo feeling so well?
2 Why is Enrico surprised to learn what he has been doing?
3 What does Aldo recommend to Enrico and why?
4 What are Enrico's holiday plans?
5 Aldo's children seem to intend to spend their holidays very constructively. What are their plans?

ENRICO: Ciao, Aldo, come va? E' un po' che non ti vedo.
ALDO: Infatti, sono appena tornato dalle vacanze. E perciò sto benissimo.

ENRICO: Come mai le vacanze così presto? Siamo solo al 15 maggio. Tu di solito vai all'estero in agosto.

ALDO: Ma quest'anno non siamo andati all'estero, siamo rimasti in Italia. Siamo andati in Sicilia. Per questo siamo partiti così presto, per evitare il gran caldo.

ENRICO: Capisco. Il tempo è stato bello?

ALDO: Si, bellissimo. Non troppo caldo, ma un cielo sempre sereno.

ENRICO: E la Sicilia? Non la conosco.

ALDO: Guarda, è una meraviglia. C'è tanto da vedere, dai templi greci ad Agrigento al duomo di Cefalù. E poi dei paesaggi incantevoli e un mare spettacolare. E si mangia bene, i vini sono ottimi. Dovresti andarci anche tu con Anna.

ENRICO: Forse l'anno prossimo. Anche noi quest'anno rimaniamo in Italia. Andiamo nel Gargano a luglio. E i ragazzi, sono venuti con voi? O sono rimasti qui per la scuola?

ALDO: Per la prima volta non sono venuti con noi. Anche per questo siamo potuti partire presto. Infatti i figli sono grandi ormai e quest'estate vanno via per conto loro. Marco ha 16 anni e va a fare un corso di inglese in Irlanda. Maria invece va in Francia a fare un corso di vela.

## Vocabulary

| | |
|---|---|
| **è un po' che non ti vedo** | I haven't seen you for a while |
| **sono appena tornato** | I've just come back |
| **le vacanze** | holidays |
| **all'estero** | abroad |
| **un cielo sereno** | a clear (cloudless) sky |
| **è una meraviglia** | it's marvellous |
| **paesaggi incantevoli** | enchanting landscapes |
| **dovresti andarci anche tu** | you ought to go there too |
| **ormai** | by now, by this time |
| **per conto loro** | on their own (account) |
| **un corso di vela** | a sailing course |

## Language points

### Talking about where you've been – il passato prossimo

To talk about what you did in the past, or have done recently, you use a tense called the **passato prossimo**, the 'near past', usually called the *present perfect* in English. For verbs which refer to *coming, going, arriving, departing, staying*, the **passato prossimo** is formed with the present tense of **essere** and the past participle:

| | |
|---|---|
| *Sono* appena *tornato* **dalle vacanze.** | I have just come back from holiday. |
| **Non** *siamo andati* **all'estero.** | We didn't go abroad. |
| *Siamo rimasti* **in Italia.** | We stayed in Italy. |
| *Siamo partiti* **così presto.** | We went away so early. |
| **Il tempo** *è stato* **bello.** | The weather was lovely. |
| **Non** *sono venuti* **con noi.** | They didn't come with us. |

*Note:* This is not the same as the passive. Only *transitive* verbs, verbs which can have a direct object, can be used in the passive. (**Scrivo una lettera. La lettera è scritta da me.**) The verbs we are looking at here cannot have a direct object, they are *intransitive*. In Italian it is impossible to say **vado la città**; you have to say **vado alla città** or **in città**. You need a preposition, the object is not a direct but an indirect object. The past participle does however agree with the subject in the same way as in the passive:

| | |
|---|---|
| Enrico è andato | |
| Maria è andata | in Sicilia |
| I bambini sono andati | |
| Le signore sono andate | |

Commonly used verbs which make their past like this are: **andare, venire, arrivare, partire, entrare, uscire, salire, scendere, nascere, morire, rimanere, restare, essere**, all verbs to do with either *movement* or *a state* or *change of state*. The following have irregular past participles:

| | | | |
|---|---|---|---|
| venire | venuto | nascere | nato |
| rimanere | rimasto | morire | morto |

*Warning:* The **passato prossimo** can be translated into English by more than one English tense, according to circumstances, (see the

examples above: 'I have just come back . . .', 'we went away. . .')
The tense systems of Italian and English are different and it is
unhelpful to hope to think from one language to the other on a
'one-to-one' basis. It's not like putting sentences into a code. Cf. the
present tense: **mangio** can mean 'I eat', or 'I am eating'. It is more
helpful to try to understand the way the system of tenses works in
Italian. Remember: the **passato prossimo** is used for a completed
action or event in the past. Here are some more examples:

> **Ieri mattina sono andato a trovare Carla. Il pomeriggio sono
> rimasto a casa e Giorgio è venuto a parlare del nuovo prog-
> etto. La sera io, lui e le nostre mogli siamo andati a vedere il
> nuovo film.**
>
> Yesterday morning I went to see Carla. In the afternoon I stayed
> at home and Giorgio came to talk about the new project. In
> the evening I, he and our wives went to see the new film.

> **– Non siete venuti alla festa sabato?**
> **– No, siamo andati a Parigi e siamo tornati solo ieri sera.**
> – You didn't come to the party on Saturday.
> – No, we went to Paris and we only got back yesterday evening.

> **– Dov'è Giorgio?**
> **– E' sceso in cantina a prendere il vino. Arriva subito – eccolo.**
> – Where's Giorgio?
> – He's gone down to the cellar to get the wine. He'll be here
> straight away – here he is.

*Exercise 1* You've been away for a couple of days and at the
airport on your return, you bump into a friend. Complete the
conversation. To help you where the subject might be unclear the
pronoun has been indicated between square brackets. It would not
normally be used, omit it.

AMICO: Ciao, come stai? Da dove arrivi?
TU: [Io] (1 essere) a Zurigo per affari. E tu?
AMICO: [Io] (2 andare) in Svezia per lavoro.
TU: (3 andare)[tu] da solo?
AMICO: No, (4 andare) [io] con due colleghi. (5 partire) [noi]
insieme ma loro (6 rimanere) a Stoccolma per altri due
giorni.

*Exercise 2* Here is a report of a visit last week by a team from another company. They came to discuss a joint venture the two companies are hoping to undertake together. The visit took place last week. Choose the correct forms for the verbs. They must be in the **passato prossimo**.

La delegazione (1) (*arrivare*) il 20 giugno. L'amministratore delegato (2)(*andare*) all'aeroporto a dare il benvenuto ai membri della delegazione. Poi questi (3) (*andare*) in albergo. Il primo incontro formale (4) (*essere*) molto cordiale ma quando (5) (*arrivare*) alla questione del finanziamento (6) (*venire*) fuori varie difficoltà.

## Vocabulary

### La mia famiglia

| il nonno | grandfather | la nonna | grandmother |
|---|---|---|---|
| il padre | father | la madre | mother |
| il fratello | brother | la sorella | sister |
| il figlio | son | la figlia | daughter |
| lo zio | uncle | la zia | aunt |
| il cugino | cousin (*m.*) | la cugina | cousin (*f.*) |
| il nipote[1] | nephew, grandson | la nipote[1] | niece, granddaughter |
| il marito | husband | la moglie | wife |
| il cognato | brother-in-law | la cognata | sister-in-law |
| il suocero | father-in-law | la suocera | mother-in-law |
| il genero | son-in-law | la nuora | daughter-in-law |

1 Many people use the form: **nipotino, nipotina**, for grandson/granddaughter.

For 'boyfriend/girlfriend' it is usual to use the words **ragazzo/ragazza** which also mean 'boy/girl'. When there is a formal intention to marry, then **fidanzato/fidanzata**, 'fiancé(e)', is used.

*Plurals*

| i nonni | grandparents |
|---|---|
| i genitori | parents |
| i parenti | relations (*not just mother and father, see above*) |
| i fratelli | brothers, *or* brothers and sisters |
| le sorelle | sisters |
| i figli | sons, *or* sons and daughters |
| le figlie | daughters |

| | |
|---|---|
| **gli zii** | uncles *or* uncles and aunts |
| **le zie** | aunts |

What do you notice about the plurals? Yes, the masculine can include the feminine too, e.g. **fratelli** can be 'brothers and sisters' or just 'brothers'. On the other hand **sorelle** can only be 'sisters' (see p.33.)

**Exercise 3** Here is a family tree. Complete the sentences below with the correct word.

(*Note:* **Andrea** = Andrew; **Nicola** = Nicholas; i.e. they are boys' names.)

> *Example:* **Emilio è il figlio di Alberto.**

1 Nicola è _____ di Carla.
2 Andrea è _____ di Rosa.
3 Anna è _____ di Paolo.
4 Margherita è _____ di Aldo.
5 Aldo è _____ di Pietro.

6 Antonietta è _____ di Arturo.
7 Rosa è _____ di Alberto.
8 Paolo è _____ di Arturo.
9 Anna è _____ di Margherita.
10 Aldo è _____ di Silvia.

**Exercise 4** Carlo has drawn his family tree (**albero genealogico**)

Draw your family tree and label it for an Italian friend.

## Possessive adjectives

When Carlo refers to his relations he writes:

> mio fratello    mio nonno    mia sorella    mio padre

This usage is actually an *exception*, used when you are talking about relations in the singular. Here are some examples of how you usually express possession:

| | |
|---|---|
| **La mia famiglia è grande.** | My family is large. |
| **Le mie sorelle sono sposate.** | My sisters are married. |
| **I tuoi nonni, dove abitano?** | Where do your grandparents live? |
| **Il nostro amico, Carlo, è appena tornato da Lisbona.** | Our friend, Carlo, has just come back from Lisbon. |
| **Il suo nuovo direttore è un uomo molto difficile.** | His new manager is a very difficult man. |
| **Dov'è il mio libro?** | Where is my book? |
| **Mi piace la vostra nuova casa.** | I like your new house. |
| **Conoscete i nostri amici?** | Do you know our friends? |

You will note that the *definite article* is used, as well as the possessive. The words used to express possession are adjectives and have to agree with the noun they qualify. The forms are:

| *my* | il mio | la mia | i miei | le mie | (io) |
|---|---|---|---|---|---|
| *your* | il tuo | la tua | i tuoi | le tue | (tu) |
| *his/her/your* | il suo | la sua | i suoi | le sue | (lui/lei) |
| *our* | il nostro | la nostra | i nostri | le nostre | (noi) |
| *your* | il vostro | la vostra | i vostri | le vostre | (voi) |
| *their* | il loro | la loro | i loro | le loro | (loro) |

*Notes:*

(a) You cannot distinguish in Italian between 'his' and 'her'. **E' la sua macchina** means 'it's his/her car', according to the context.

(b) **Il tuo**, etc. is used when talking to someone to whom you say **tu**, a friend, a relation, a colleague, a child: **Usi la tua macchina ogni giorno?**

**Il suo**, etc. is for when you are talking to someone whom you address as **lei**, i.e. someone with whom your relationship is formal: **Signor Martini, lei usa la sua macchina ogni giorno?**

**Il vostro**, etc. is used when talking to more than one person: **Voi usate la vostra macchina ogni giorno?**

(c) **Il loro**, etc. **loro** is invariable. Also, **il loro** is an exception to the rule about omitting the definite article when talking about a relative: **Il loro padre.**

(d) When referring to their family, Italians often call them simply: **i miei**.

(e) The possessives can also be used as *pronouns:*

| | |
|---|---|
| **Non trovo l'ombrello.** | I can't find my umbrella. |
| **Non preoccuparti. Prendi il mio.** | Don't worry. Take mine. |

*Saying:*

**Natale con i tuoi, Pasqua con chi vuoi.**
Christmas with your family, Easter with whoever you like.

**Exercise 5** Gianni is showing you some photos. Ask him if the people are members of his family and if the buildings etc. belong to him.

*Example:* **E' la tua casa?**

1

2

3

4

**5**                                                    **6**

Now imagine that you had only recently met the person showing you the photos, perhaps in a hotel while on holiday. You would use **lei**. How would you change your questions?

## Quanti anni hai? 'How old are you?'

Talking about his son, Aldo says: **Marco ha sedici anni.**

To express age, you use **avere** + the number + years. In answer to the question: **Quanti anni hai?** Marco might say:

    **Ho sedici anni.**         or         **Ne ho sedici.**

**Ne** means 'of them', here referring to years. You need either **anni** after the number or **ne** before the verb.

***Exercise 6*** Work out how you would say

1 your own age
2 that of your children if you have any
3 that of your brothers and sisters
4 and of your grandparents, etc.

You will get sentences like:

    Ho trentaquattro anni.
    Mio figlio, Bill, ha tre anni e mia figlia, Clare, ne ha due.
    Mia sorella ha quarant'anni e mio fratello ne ha trentotto.
    Mio nonno ha novantadue anni.

## Dialogue 2

Il tempo *'the weather'*

*Aldo is telephoning a business colleague who is in Venice. It's January and it is just before lunch*

> 1  Is Aldo's colleague having good weather in Venice?
> 2  Why are the ski buffs likely to be happier in the near future?

ALDO:      Che tempo fa a Venezia?
COLLEGA:   Oggi c'è un bel sole e ora, a mezzogiorno, fa quasi
           caldo. Ieri e lunedì però il tempo è stato brutto: nebbia
           umida, e che freddo! E da te?
ALDO:      Qui fa bello. La notte però la temperatura scende sotto
           zero. In montagna non nevica e gli sciatori si lamen-
           tano perchè non c'è neve. Ma secondo le previsioni, il
           tempo sta per cambiare.

## Talking about the weather

The standard question about the weather is: **Che tempo fa?**
    You can answer in the following ways:

| | | |
|---|---|---|
| **Fa bel tempo** or | **Il tempo è bello** | The weather is fine |
| **Fa brutto tempo** | **brutto** | bad/nasty |
| | **freddo** | cold |
| | **caldo** | hot |

*or*

| | |
|---|---|
| **Fa bello** | It's fine/lovely |
| **brutto** | nasty/bad |
| **freddo** | cold |
| **caldo** | hot |

In other words, either start your sentence with **Fa** and add an adjective or the set phrases **bel tempo**, **brutto tempo**. Or start with **il tempo è** and add adjectives. Other possible answers are:

| | |
|---|---|
| **C'è il sole** | It's sunny/the sun is shining |
| **la nebbia** | foggy |
| **vento** | windy |

| **Piove** | It's raining | **(la pioggia** | rain) |
|-----------|--------------|-----------------|-------|
| **Nevica** | It's snowing | **(la neve** | snow) |

## More weather vocabulary

| le previsioni del tempo | the weather forecast |
|-------------------------|----------------------|
| cielo sereno | clear sky |
| nuvoloso | cloudy |
| mare mosso | rough sea |
| calmo | calm |
| un temporale | a storm |
| il maltempo | bad weather |
| la grandine | hail(stones) |

Every so often you will read the headline in the newspaper:

**Mezza Italia in tilt per il maltempo**
Half Italy in chaos because of the bad weather

and know that heavy snow or rain, high winds, or thick fog has upset road, rail, or air traffic . . .

# Il tempo sta per cambiare 'The weather is about to change'

Use the present of **stare + per** + the infinitive to say 'to be about to', 'to be on the point of', e.g:

| **Stiamo per partire** | We are about to leave/on the point of leaving |
|------------------------|-----------------------------------------------|
| **Il treno sta per arrivare** | The train is about to arrive/on the point of arriving |

The present tense of **stare** is:

| sto | stiamo |
|-----|--------|
| stai | state |
| sta | stanno |

# Che freddo!

**Che** can be used with adjectives or nouns to make exclamations.

| **Che pioggia!** | What rain! |
|------------------|------------|
| **Che scemo!** | What a silly boy/man . . . |

*Exercise 7* The language of weather forecasts tends to be technical but similar to English. There is, however, usually a drawing to help. We have reproduced one below. Study the drawing. Many people's image of Italy is of sunshine and warmth. This was Christmas Eve. Answer the questions.

1  What is the weather going to be like on the coast north of Rome?
2. What are the seas around all of the peninsula going to be like?
3  What is likely to fall on the Alps and the Apennines?
4  What is going to fall in Sardinia? It will also fall in the heel of Italy south of Bari and in the Po Plain.
5  In the instep of Italy (Basilicata) something particularly nasty seems to be in store. What is it?

By courtesy of *La Stampa.*

# Reading 🔊

## Il clima italiano

1 If you are flying to Milan in November, what might be a problem?
2 Why do those who can, leave the northern cities in the summer for the sea or the mountains?
3 In what way is the climate of the Adriatic Coast different from that of the Tyrrhenian coast?
4 If you like really hot weather, where in Italy should you choose for your holiday?

Come per la cucina italiana, così anche per il clima non si può parlare di 'clima italiano'. Varia da regione a regione. Le montagne del nord hanno un clima alpino: inverni freddi, estati calde di giorno ma con notti relativamente fresche. La pianura padana invece ha un clima continentale: inverni freddi, estati molto calde. Un grosso problema in questa zona è l'umidità: d'inverno c'è spesso nebbia e d'estate il tasso d'umidità è alto. In tutta l'Italia le zone costiere godono di un clima mite, grazie all'influenza del mare. Ma c'è una differenza tra la costa adriatica e quella tirrenica: infatti quest'ultima ha un clima generalmente più mite. D'inverno la costa adriatica è battuta qualche volta da venti freddi da nord-est, cioè dall'Europa centrale. Sull'Appennino influisce l'altitudine: d'inverno fa più freddo che sulla costa alla stessa latitudine. E poi, più si va verso sud, più il clima diventa caldo. Naturalmente, dappertutto ci sono momenti in cui il tempo è eccezionale, essendo particolarmente freddo o insolitamente caldo.

## *Vocabulary*

| | |
|---|---|
| **tasso d'umidità** | the level of humidity |
| **costiero** | coastal |
| **godere di un clima mite** | to enjoy a mild climate |
| **quest'ultima** | the latter |
| **battuto** | hit by, beaten by |
| **alla stessa latitudine** | at the same latitude |
| **diventare** | to become |
| **dappertutto** | everywhere |

# 11 Che cosa ha visto?

**What did you see?**

---

**In this lesson you will learn about:**

- **Polizia e carabinieri** – the Italian Police
- Saying what you did/have done
- Saying 'nothing' – **niente, nulla**
- The gerund – 'while going to Rome', 'by selling our house'
- Saying how long something has been going on for
- Diminutives (**casetta**, 'little house') and other suffixes
- Letters to friends

---

## Dialogue 1

### Un giallo

*The apartment next door to Mrs Mancini's has been burgled. She is being interviewed by the Carabinieri*

---

1 Who left home first, Mrs Mancini or her family?
2 Where did she go the first time she went out?
3 Why did she come back again before going to work?
4 What did she notice as she left the house the second time?
5 What did not seem strange to her at the time but does now?
6 Why did she find it strange that her neighbours' door was open?

---

CARABINIERE: Signora, ci racconti che cosa ha fatto questa mattina.

SIG.RA M: Ecco. Mi sono alzata verso le sei e mezzo, come al solito. Ho preparato la colazione per mio marito e i miei figli. Loro sono usciti verso le sette e mezzo e io poco dopo.

| | |
|---|---|
| CARABINIERE | Non ha notato niente di strano in quel momento? |
| SIG.RA M: | No, niente. |
| CARABINIERE: | E poi? |
| SIG.RA M: | E poi sono andata al mercato. Ho fatto la spesa. Siccome ho comprato carne, frutta e verdura, ho portato tutto a casa e ho messo la carne e la verdura nel frigo. E poi sono andata al lavoro verso le nove meno un quarto. |
| CARABINIERE: | E tutto le è sembrato normale? |
| SIG.RA M: | Sì. Ma adesso mi ricordo che ho notato una grande macchina bianca, una Volvo, parcheggiata davanti a casa nostra. Dentro ho visto due uomini. |
| CARABINIERE: | Mi può descrivere questi uomini? |
| SIG.RA M: | Ma questo è il fatto strano: quando sono uscita di casa hanno girato la testa dall'altra parte. Cosi non ho visto la loro faccia. Sul momento non l'ho trovato strano, ma ora ... |
| CARABINIERE; | E poi? |
| SIG.RA M: | E poi sono andata a lavorare e quando sono tornata a casa all'una ho trovato aperta la porta dell'appartamento dei miei vicini. Sono in vacanza all'estero, così ho subito pensato a un furto e ho chiamato i carabinieri. |
| CARABINIERE: | Ha fatto molto bene, signora. Allora, torniamo a quella macchina bianca ... |

## *Vocabulary*

| | |
|---|---|
| **un giallo** | a detective story |
| **carabiniere** | *see below* |
| **ci racconti** | tell us |
| **non ha notato niente di strano?** | you didn't notice anything strange? |
| **siccome** | since (*in the sense of 'because'*) |
| **frigo** | fridge (*short for **frigorifero***) |
| **adesso** | now |
| **mi ricordo** | I remember |
| **dentro** | inside |
| **hanno girato la testa** | they turned their heads |
| **dall'altra parte** | the other way |
| **i miei vicini** | my neighbours |
| **un furto** | theft |

## I carabinieri

The **Arma dei Carabinieri** is a military corps, under the Ministry of Defence. It originated as the Royal Guard of the Kingdom of Piedmont and Sardinia in the days before Italy was unified. Italy also has a police force: **la Polizia di Stato**, set up after the Unification of Italy, under the Ministry of the Interior. There are also other corps such as the **Guardia di Finanza**, under the Ministry of Finance, who deal with tax evasion and smuggling. Each **comune** also has **vigili urbani**.

# Language points

## Saying what you did – more about the passato prossimo

The **passato prossimo** of most verbs is formed with the present tense of **avere** + the past participle:

- Che cosa *ha fatto* questa mattina?
- *Ho preparato* la colazione . . .

Make a list of other examples of the **passato prossimo** in the dialogue. You should have found:

| avere | essere |
|---|---|
| *ha notato* | *mi sono alzata* |
| *ho fatto* la spesa | loro *sono usciti* |
| *ho comprato* | *sono andata* al mercato |
| *ho portato* | *sono andata* al lavoro |
| *ho messo* | tutto le *è sembrato* normale? |
| *ho notato* | *sono uscita* |
| *ho visto* | *sono andata* a lavorare |
| *hanno girato* | *sono tornata* |
| non *ho visto* | |
| non l'*ho trovato* strano | |
| *ho trovato* | |
| *ho* subito *pensato* | |
| *ho chiamato* | |
| *ha fatto* bene | |

You will perhaps have noticed:

(1) that when the **passato prossimo** is formed with **avere** the past participle does *not* agree with the subject.
(2) **messo** is a new past participle to you, from **mettere**, 'to put'.

## The passato prossimo **of reflexive verbs**

The second verb in the conversation, **mi sono alzata**, is not one of the verbs of movement or state which you learned were conjugated with **essere**. It is a reflexive or pronominal verb (Lesson 6). Reflexive verbs also form their **passato prossimo** with **essere**.

## The passato prossimo **of impersonal verbs**

Verbs used impersonally also usually make their **passato prossimo** with **essere**: **Tutto le *è* sembrato normale?** 'Did everything seem normal to you?' (**sembra** means 'it seems').

**Mi *è* piaciuto molto il film.** I liked the film a lot.
**Che cosa *è* successo?**      What's happened?/What happened?

(**Succedere** means 'to happen'; **succede** means 'it happens', 'it is happening'.)

With verbs relating to weather phenomena such as **nevicare**, **piovere**, both **avere** and **essere** are used. **Essere** is considered more correct.

**E' *nevicato* in montagna ieri. Qui *è piovuto*.**
**Ha *nevicato* in montagna ieri. Qui *ha piovuto*.**
It snowed in the mountains yesterday. Here it rained.

**Exercise 1** You and your husband/wife/friend(s) had a busy weekend. Tell someone about it. Here is what you did:

| *Sabato* | mattina | fare la spesa |
| | | comprare un vestito nuovo per me |
| | pomeriggio | andare a una mostra interessante |
| | sera | essere a cena da vecchi amici |
| *Domenica* | | fare una gita con amici che hanno una barca a vela |
| | | andare in mare con questi amici |
| | | pranzare sulla barca |
| | | fare il bagno |
| | | prendere il sole |
| | | cenare in un ristorante sul porto |

**Exercise 2** You are an Italian private detective (*investigatore privato*) and you have been asked to follow a certain lady. Report on what she did yesterday. We give you the verbs in the infinitive.

uscire di casa alle nove e mezzo
salire su un taxi
andare alla Banca Nazionale del Lavoro in Piazza Garibaldi
uscire dalla banca dopo un quarto d'ora
andare a piedi al bar Roma
sedersi all'interno del bar
ordinare un cappuccino
essere raggiunta da un uomo alto, bello, elegante
uscire dal bar con quest'uomo
salire su una Mercedes con lui
andare in un ristorante sul lago
verso le tre lasciare il ristorante, sempre in compagnia dell'uomo

YOUR CLIENT: E poi?

YOU: E poi, niente. Li ho perduti. Ho avuto un incidente con la mia macchina.

YOUR CLIENT: Pazienza. In ogni modo, quell'uomo alto e elegante, che guida una Mercedes, è probabilmente suo fratello.

## Niente/nulla

**Niente** means 'nothing/not ... anything'. The **carabiniere** asks Mrs Mancini:

**Lei *non* ha notato *niente* di strano?**
You didn't notice anything strange?

To use **niente** with a verb, you must have **non** before the verb:

***Non* ho visto *niente*.**
I saw nothing/I didn't see anything.

***Non* capisco *niente*.**
I understand nothing/I don't understand anything.

**Nulla** also means 'nothing' and is used in the same way as **niente**:

***Non* abbiamo visto *nulla*.**
We didn't see anything/we saw nothing.

*Note: Something* is normally **qualcosa**, or a longer form: **qualche cosa**:

**E' successo qualcosa.**       Something has happened.
**Hai visto qualcosa?**       Did you see something/anything?

*Something/nothing* + adjective is **qualcosa/niente/nulla di ...**

**E' successo *qualcosa di* strano.**
Something strange has happened.

***Qualcosa di* bello.**
Something lovely.

***Non* ha detto *nulla di* interessante.**
He didn't say anything interesting.

***Non* so *nulla di* buono di lui.**
I don't know anything good about him.

*Something/nothing* + verb is **qualcosa da/niente da/nulla da ...**

**Vuoi *qualcosa da* mangiare?**
Do you want something/anything to eat?

**Ho *qualcosa da* fare.**
I have something to do.

***Non* ha *niente da* fare.**
He/she has nothing to do/ He/she hasn't anything to do.

***Non* c'è *nulla da* mangiare.**
There's nothing to eat.

***Exercise 3*** Things went badly today. Your husband wants to know about a number of things you intended to do but you had no success, so answers to these questions are negative. Use **non ... niente.**

1   Hai comprato la camicetta che volevi?
2   Hai letto l'articolo di Sergio Romano sul giornale di ieri?
3   Hai finito di scrivere la lettera alla nonna?
4   Hai almeno mangiato bene a mezzogiorno? C'era quel buon prosciutto da finire.
5   Ma insomma, che cosa hai fatto oggi?

   Sono stata poco bene e così (5) _____

# Reading

## *La lettera di un'amica*

*When you write letters to your friends you will often want to talk about what you have been doing. Here is a letter from a friend*

---

1 Marina says a lot has happened since she last wrote. What three events does she write about?
2 Why was 23rd May a special day for Marina?
3 What keeps Marina busy in spite of the fact that she has retired?
4 What did Marina and her husband find difficult when she retired? What has helped them resolve the problem?

---

Cara Sara,
   Ti ringrazio per la tua lettera. Mi scuso per questo lungo silenzio. Sappi almeno che sei spesso stata presente nei miei pensieri.
   Nel frattempo sono successe molte cose. Piero, essendo ormai ben inserito nel suo lavoro di avvocato, si è sposato con la sua ragazza. Si conoscono da quasi dieci anni. Hanno una casa piccola ma fra un mese traslocheranno nella casa che abbiamo comprato vendendo la nostra casetta di Desenzano.
   La seconda grande notizia è stata la nascita di Andrea, figlio di Paola. E' nato il giorno del mio compleanno, il 23 maggio. E' un bambino simpaticissimo con occhi grigio-blu e un carattere allegro. Ora ha nove mesi e tutti gli vogliamo molto bene.
   Terzo avvenimento: sono andata in pensione il primo di settembre. Ma ho molto da fare e non mi annoio. Lavoro sempre come consulente e scrittrice. Poi mi occupo spesso di Andrea mentre Paola lavora. Infine i miei genitori che sono vecchi e deboli hanno bisogno di aiuto. Così sono sempre occupata. Anche mio marito è in pensione: all'inizio è stato difficile ma ormai ci siamo abituati. La nostra casa è grande e ognuno ha il suo studio, il proprio spazio.
   Non mi resta che scusarmi ancora per il ritardo nello scrivere. Con molto affetto, buon lavoro e fatti sentire,

Un abbraccio,

Marina

## *Vocabulary*

| | |
|---|---|
| **ti ringrazio** | I thank you |
| **mi scuso** | I apologize |
| **nei miei pensieri** | in my thoughts |
| **nel frattempo** | in the meanwhile |
| **ben inserito nel suo lavoro** | nicely settled in his work |
| **traslocheranno** | they will move |
| **notizia** | piece of news |
| **la nascita** | the birth |
| **occhi** | eyes |
| **allegro** | happy |
| **tutti gli vogliamo molto bene** | we all love him very much |
| **avvenimento** | event |
| **sono andata in pensione** | I retired |
| **non mi annoio** | I'm not bored (**annoiarsi**, 'to be bored') |
| **mi occupo di Andrea** | I take care of Andrea |
| **mentre** | while |
| **ci siamo abituati** | we have got used to it, we are used to it |

# Language points

## Sappi

The word **sappi** comes from the verb **sapere**. It is the **tu** imperative (command) form. The formal form (**lei**) is **sappia**. Here it has to be translated: 'I want you to know that' ...

## Essendo, vendendo – **the gerund**

Marina writes:

**Piero, *essendo* ormai ben inserito nel suo lavoro di avvocato, si è sposato.**

Piero, now being well settled (since he is now settled) in his work as a lawyer, got married.

**La casa che abbiamo comprato *vendendo* la nostra casetta di Desenzano**

The house we bought by selling our little house at Desenzano

This form is called the *gerund*. In all cases, take the infinitive as the base and remove the ending; **-are** verbs then add **-ando** and all the others **-endo**.

| *-are* | *-ere* | *-ire* | | |
|---|---|---|---|---|
| parlare | decidere | capire | essere | avere |
| parlando | decidendo | capendo | essendo | avendo |

The only verbs which are irregular are: **dire**, **fare**, **bere** and a few others (**produrre** and similar verbs with infinitives ending in **-rre**). All have infinitives which have become shortened (from **dicere**, **facere**, **bevere**, **producere**). The gerund is based on the old infinitive:

dicendo, facendo, bevendo, producendo

Knowing about this older form of the infinitive also helps explain other forms of these verbs.

**Dare** and **stare** behave regularly: **dando, stando**.

The gerund is used:

(1) to explain *how* or *why*, as in the examples in the letter:

**Facendo il lavoro così, lo rendi più difficile.**
(By) doing the work this way, you make it more difficult.

(2) to convey one action happening at the same time as another ('while', 'on', 'as'):

**Andando a Roma, mi sono fermato una notte a Firenze.**
(While) going to Rome, I stopped for a night in Florence.

**Uscendo di casa, Giorgio ha visto l'amico Aldo.**
As he left (on leaving) home, Giorgio saw his friend Aldo.

Do not assume the gerund will always translate the English form ending in '-ing'. The gerund is a verbal form. When the form ending in '-ing' is a noun, in Italian it is more likely to be expressed by an infinitive. For instance, Marina says:

**... il ritardo nello scrivere**     ... the delay in writing

Compare:

**il fatto di essere Italiani**     the fact of being Italian
**Mi piace leggere.**     I like reading.

This is a difficult point. As always, try to imitate what you hear and read. And don't worry too much about mistakes.

**Sbagliando si impara.**     One learns by making mistakes.

*Exercise 4* Below are some pairs of sentences. Combine them using the gerund. This will make the style more interesting. *Example:*

**Faccio passeggiate in campagna. Mi piace guardare i fiori e gli alberi.**

**Facendo passeggiate in campagna, mi piace guardare i fiori e gli alberi.**

A. (These sentences are about Sergio's morning routine.)

1  Sergio va al lavoro ogni mattina. Compra il giornale.
2  E' di Firenze. Compra *la Nazione*.
3  Prende un espresso al bar. Legge il giornale.

*La Nazione* is the Florentine daily.

B. (These sentences are about your friends.)

1  I miei amici hanno una casa in campagna. Passano spesso il fine settimana lì.
2  Il loro giardino è grande. Hanno sempre del lavoro da fare.
3  Hanno un orto (*vegetable garden, kitchen garden*). Hanno sempre frutta e verdura fresca a tavola.

## Si conoscono da dieci anni

When you talk about what you have been doing you use the **passato prossimo**. There is an exception to this: to convey the idea that something has been happening *for* a certain amount of time and is still happening. Marina said Piero and his girlfriend 'have known each other *for* ten years'. Here are some more examples:

**Studio l'italiano da due mesi.**
I have been studying Italian for two months.

**Gianni lavora da due anni in quella ditta.**
Gianni has been working for that firm for two years.

**Non lo vedo da tre anni.**
I haven't seen him for three years.

You say what is going on, using the present tense, and then use **da** plus the amount of time. This is another use of the preposition **da**. You can also use **da** followed by a point in time, 'since' in English:

**E' qui da venerdì.**
He's been here since Friday.

**Abitiamo a Roma da giugno dell'anno scorso.**
We have been living in Rome since June last year.

*Exercise 5* Here are some things Pietro does and the date when
he started doing them. Imagine it is now December 1995. Write
down how long he has been doing these things. Then also write
down how you would say this in English. *Example:*

**Fuma la pipa.**         **1990**
**Pietro fuma la pipa da sette anni.**

1 Suona il pianoforte.     1972
2 Lavora come ingegnere.   1991
3 Conosce Antonio.        1978
4 Studia il francese.       1994, settembre
5 Esce con Alessia.       1985
6 Abita a Milano.         1993

You could, of course, have also said: **Pietro fuma la pipa dal 1990**,
etc.

## La nostra casetta – diminutives and other suffixes

Marina talks about a little house (**una casetta**) in Desenzano (on
Lake Garda) which they have sold to help Piero buy a house.
Rather than saying **una piccola casa** she alters the word **casa** by
adding a suffix (an extra syllable at the end of a word): **-etta**. You
will remember how this device is used with adjectives to convey
the idea 'very': **bello**, **bellissimo**. There are a number of such
suffixes. *Warning:* it takes time for the non-native speaker to get
them right. However, it is useful to be able to recognize them.
Here are some common ones:

• **-etto, -ino** can be added to nouns and adjectives to convey an
idea of smallness.

| | |
|---|---|
| **fratellino** | little brother |
| **orchestrina** | small orchestra (*such as plays for a bar in Piazza San Marco in Venice – see Lesson 1*) |
| **piazzetta** | little square (*indeed the square which lies at right angles to Piazza San Marco and which leads to the waterfront is called la Piazzetta*) |

- **-ino** is also commonly added to certain adjectives and adverbs, modifying their meaning.

| | | | |
|---|---|---|---|
| **caro** | dear | **piano** | softly, slowly |
| **carino** | pretty, cute, sweet | **pianino** | very softly, slowly |

- **-one** indicates bigness. Can be added to nouns, adjectives and the adverb **bene**. When it is added to feminine words they change gender and become masculine.

| | | | |
|---|---|---|---|
| **una donna** | woman | **un libro** | a book |
| **un donnone** | a big woman | **un librone** | a big book |

| | |
|---|---|
| – **Come sta?** | – **Benone.** |
| – How are you? | – Fine. |

- **-accio** indicates the speaker considers the person or object nasty or worthless.

| | | | |
|---|---|---|---|
| **parola** | word | **tempo** | weather |
| **parolaccia** | swear word | **tempaccio** | dreadful weather |
| **parolacce** (*pl.*) | bad language | | |

- **-astro** added to words for colour is equivalent to the English '-ish'.

| | |
|---|---|
| **bianco** | white |
| **biancastro** | whitish |

*Note:* **Fratellastro**, **sorellastra**, **figliastro/a** are used to mean 'step-brother', '-sister', '-son', '-daughter' respectively.

Listen for these suffixes. It is best to use only those you have heard. There are others. Sometimes the words formed come to stand in their own right, for instance **telefonino** is the usual everyday word for a' cellular telephone'; **spago** is 'string', **spaghetti** are long pieces of pasta in the shape of strings.

## Letter writing

When writing to a friend, use **caro**, **cara** and the friend's name. The salutation at the end depends on the intimacy of the relationship: in addition to **un abbraccio** which actually means 'a hug', 'an embrace' but is the equivalent of 'much love', possible endings are:

| | |
|---|---|
| **affettuosamente** | yours affectionately |
| **saluti affettuosi** | affectionate greetings |
| **cari saluti** | warm (*lit.* 'dear') greetings |

When writing to someone you know fairly well but with whom you have a fairly formal relationship, using **lei**, you may start: **Caro Signor Rossi**, and end: **Cordialmente** or **Cordiali saluti**. You should use a capital letter with the **Lei** and related words, e.g:

*La* ringrazio della *Sua* gentile ospitalità.

When writing to someone you do not know or with whom your relationship is very formal, you write:

**Egregio Signore** (to a man)   **Gentile Signora** (to a woman)

You can still end with **cordiali saluti**; or use **distinti saluti** which is more formal.

All that said, these days letter-writing is less and less common. Not only do people prefer to telephone as in English-speaking countries, but Italians have little faith in their postal system which is slow and not very reliable so they tend not to use it much. But even in Italy, the event reported in the news item from *La Stampa*, 14 April 1995, gives rise to surprise. You do not need to understand every word to be able to get the gist.

1  What was the precise date of the letter? (The headline calls it a postcard. Perhaps it was a 'letter-card)'.
2  Was Oreste Brunello on holiday in Germany then?
3  What did he do at the end of the war?
4  Who actually handed the letter to Oreste?
5  Where was Oreste when he received the letter?
6  What happy effect did the letter have on him?

## LE POSTE LUMACHE

*Vicenza: spedita da Beles nel '44, è stata consegnata l'altro ieri.*

La lettera dal lager tedesco arriva con 50 anni di ritardo

VICENZA

In quella lettera spedita alla moglie c'era tutto il suo amore. E forse le sue speranze di ritorno: 'Non preoccuparti se tarderanno a giunger mie notizie ...' Era il 27 agosto 1944 e Oreste Brunello, allora trentaquattrenne, non era in vacanza. Scriveva dal 'Kriegsfagenlager XII D' di Beles, in Germania, un campo di concentramento per prigionieri di guerra. Lui alla fine della guerra è tornato. La lettera no. Fino a lunedì scorso, quando all'ex-deportato hanno messo in mano la cartolina ingiallita misteriosamente uscita da un viaggio di cinquant'anni.

Ha pianto, Oreste Brunello. E con lui la moglie Assunta Moro, 81 anni ... Hanno pianto anche se è finita con una festa nella loro casa di Marostica. ... E' stato Renato Brunello, l'unico figlio della coppia, a portare quel pezzetto di vita passata al padre ricoverato in ospedale. ... Tanta è stata l'emozione di rivedere quella lettera che Oreste si è ripreso. E il giorno dopo i medici l'hanno rimandato a casa.

Alessandro Mognon, *La Stampa*, 14 aprile, 1995 (*adapted*)

## *Vocabulary*

| | |
|---|---|
| **lumaca** | snail (*here used as an adjective to describe the postal service: snail mail*) |
| **consegnare** | to deliver (*a letter, a parcel*) |
| **lager tedesco**[1] | German prison camp |
| **accolto** | received, welcomed |
| **tutto il suo amore** | all his love |
| **le sue speranze** | his hopes |
| **tarderanno a giungere mie notizie** | news of me will be slow (late) in arriving |
| **prigionieri di guerra** | prisoners of war |
| **campo di concentramento** | concentration camp |
| **ex-deportato** | ex-deportee |
| **cartolina ingiallita** | yellowed postcard |
| **misteriosamente** | mysteriously |
| **ha pianto** | he wept |
| **emozione** | emotion |
| **ricoverato**[2] **in ospedale** | in hospital, hospitalized |

1 After Italy signed an armistice with the Allies in 1943 and changed sides in the Second World War, the Germans occupied much of Italy. Under the occupation, Italian men were often sent to do forced labour in Germany.

2 **Ricoverare** is a false friend. It has nothing to do with recovering. It means 'to admit to hospital'. 'To recover' is **guarire**, or (as in the text) **riprendersi**.

*Exercise 6* Write a letter to an imaginary Italian friend telling him/her what you did last weekend. You should try to use some of the expressions in the lesson but of course you are free to try to say whatever you like.

# 12 Ecco la mia casa

## This is my home

**In this lesson you will learn about:**

- How to talk about houses and flats
- Small points: 'My elder sister was born in 1955'
- The various uses of **ci**
- The pronoun **ne** ('of it', 'of them')
- Trends in housing in Italy

## Reading 1

### La cugina italiana

1  Who is Gabriella?
2  Why does Angela go to see her?
3  Does Angela visit Gabriella often?
4  What sort of district is the one Gabriella lives in?

La sorella maggiore della mamma di Angela Smith ha sposato un italiano. Questa sorella è morta qualche anno fa, ma la mamma di Angela ha mantenuto i contatti con i suoi figli, i cugini di Angela. Una in particolare scrive regolarmente. Si chiama Gabriella. La mamma di Angela le ha chiesto di andare a trovare questa cugina. E' la prima volta che Angela va da Gabriella. Gabriella le fa vedere la sua casa, che si trova al quarto piano di un palazzo costruito nel 1967. E' in una zona residenziale nella periferia di Torino, nata negli anni del boom, del 'miracolo italiano', per gente che veniva a lavorare nella grande industria automobilistica. Oggi nella zona ci sono molti palazzi simili ma le strade sono larghe, ci sono alberi e spazio. E' un quartiere tranquillo.

## *Vocabulary*

| | | | |
|---|---|---|---|
| **sorella maggiore** | elder sister | **qualche anno fa** | some years ago |
| **questa sorella è morta** | this sister died | **le fa vedere** | shows her |

## Language points

### Maggiore

As well as meaning 'bigger', **maggiore** is also used to mean 'elder', referring to brothers and sisters. **Minore** means 'younger'.

### Morire

**Morire** (past participle: **morto**) 'to die', is irregular, as is **nascere** (past participle **nato**), 'to be born'. Both verbs form the **passato prossimo** with **essere**:

| | |
|---|---|
| **E' morto il presidente.** | The president has died. |
| **Anna è nata nel 1954.** | Anna was born in 1954. |

### Nel 1967

Notice you say **nel 1967**, 'in 1967'. Similarly in the example above, **nel 1954**. You always do this for 'in' with a year.

***Exercise 1*** Use the information in this family tree to complete the paragraph below.

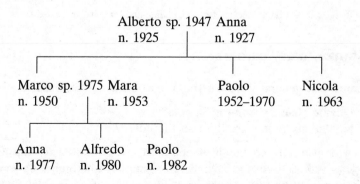

Alberto ha (1) _____ Anna a Napoli (2) _____ 1947. Poco dopo

sono emigrati negli Stati Uniti. Hanno avuto tre figli. Il (3) _____,
Marco, (4) _____ nel 1950. Da studente è tornato in Italia a trovare
i cugini italiani e così ha conosciuto Mara. Si sono sposati nel (5)
_____. Vivono a Chicago e ormai hanno anche loro tre (6) _____,
Anna, (7) _____ nel 1977, Alfredo, nel 1980, e Paolo, nel 1982.
Paolo, il secondo figlio di Alberto e di Anna (8) _____ in un inci-
dente stradale nel 1970. Nicola, il figlio (9) _____ di Alberto e di
Anna, è medico. Per il momento non è (10) _____ e così non ha
figli.

## Vocabulary

### La casa

| | | | |
|---|---|---|---|
| **appartamento** | flat, apartment | **scala** | staircase |
| **palazzo** | apartment | **entrata** | entrance hall |
| | building, block | **stanza** | room |
| | of flats, palace | **soggiorno** | living room, |
| **il pian terreno** | the ground floor | | sitting room |
| **al pian terreno** | on the ground | **sala da pranzo** | dining room |
| | floor | **cucina** | kitchen |
| **il primo piano** | the first floor | **bagno** | bathroom |
| **il secondo piano** | the second floor | **camera (da letto)** | bedroom |
| **il seminterrato** | basement, semi- | **ripostiglio** | boxroom, store |
| | basement | **cantina** | cellar |
| | (*partly below* | **balcone** | balcony |
| | *ground*) | **terrazza/o**[1] | terrace |
| **ascensore** | lift | | |

1 Often used of a large balcony. Both masculine and feminine forms exist.

### Stanza, sala, camera

**Stanza** is a general word for room, particularly in a house.

**Quante stanze ci sono nella casa?**
How many rooms are there in the house?

**Sala** is also a room but in a home its use is limited to **sala da
pranzo**; **sala** is used for spacious rooms in public buildings, e.g. **sala
d'attesa** 'waiting room'; **sala da ballo** 'dance hall'; **sala operatoria**
'operating theatre'. (*Note also:* **saletta** 'little room'; **salone** 'large,

spacious room'.) **Camera** also means 'room', but its use is usually limited, in the context of a home or a hotel, to 'bedroom', sometimes given the longer name of **camera da letto**. **Stanza** is used in **stanza da bagno**, although often the bathroom is just **il bagno**.

## Piano

Floors are counted European-style. **Il primo piano** is one floor up from ground level. **Il pian terreno** is the ground floor at ground level. 'On' a particular floor is **al**:

> **al terzo piano**
> on the third floor (fourth floor American-style counting)

# Dialogue 1 🔲

*Ecco il mio appartamento*

*Gabriella shows Angela her apartment*

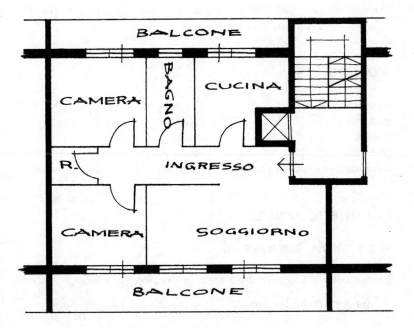

| 1 | What does Gabriella particularly like about her living room? |
|---|---|
| 2 | What does Angela approve of about the kitchen? |
| 3 | Would Gabriella like a second bathroom? |
| 4 | Where is the garage? |
| 5 | What does Gabriella have in the basement? |

GABRIELLA: Questo è il soggiorno. Mi piace perchè dà verso ovest e riceve il sole al tramonto.

ANGELA: E' spazioso e anche molto luminoso.

GABRIELLA: Sì, a causa delle porte-finestre che danno sul balcone. Ed ecco la cucina.

ANGELA: E' bella e grande. Ci si può mangiare senza difficoltà.

GABRIELLA: Sì, serve anche da sala da pranzo. Poi c'è il bagno. E in fondo al corridoio ci sono le camere.

ANGELA: E quella porta lì è un altro bagno?

GABRIELLA: Purtroppo no. Ne abbiamo uno solo. E' un ripostiglio. E' molto utile.

ANGELA: Immagino. Avete anche il garage?

GABRIELLA: Sì. Ma è dietro il palazzo, nel cortile. Abbiamo anche la cantina nel seminterrato.

ANGELA: Hai detto che avete un balcone?

GABRIELLA: Ne abbiamo due, uno davanti e uno più piccolo dietro. Vieni a vedere.

## *Vocabulary*

| | |
|---|---|
| **dà verso ovest** | it looks west |
| **tramonto** | sunset |
| **finestra** | window |
| **porta-finestra** | French door |
| **serve anche da sala da pranzo** | it also acts/serves as a dining room |

## Language points

### A causa di 'because of'

**Perchè** is used followed by a verb; **a causa di** by a noun:

**Mangio perchè ho fame.** I'm eating because I'm hungry.

**Mangio a causa della fame.**   I'm eating because of hunger.

On the other hand if the reason is positive, you can say: **grazie a**:

**Grazie al bel tempo, mangiamo fuori.**
Thanks to the good weather, we are eating outside.

## Ci si può mangiare – uses of ci

'One can eat in it/there'. **Ci** here replaces **nella cucina**. In the letter in the previous lesson, Marina wrote:

*ci* **siamo abituati**                   we are used to it

**Ci** has a number of functions:

(1) As a *pronoun* replacing **in** or **a** + noun. (In English, 'in it', 'to it', 'at it', 'in them', 'to them', 'at them', 'there'.) Used in this way, **ci** may be replaced by **vi** but **vi** is not common in everyday speech. Notice that **ci** goes in front of the verb:

– **Vai spesso a Roma?**        – *Ci* **vado una volta al mese.**
– Do you go to Rome often? – I go there once a month.

**Mi piace molto la campagna.** *Ci* **sto volentieri.**
I like the country. I like being there. (*Lit.* 'I stay in it willingly'.)

(2) *With verbs* which need an **a** before the object, such as **credere** (to believe), **riuscire** (to succeed, to manage), **ci** is used as follows:

**Tu credi *a* quello che dice? Io non *ci* credo.**
Do you believe what he says? I don't believe it.

**Riesci *ad* aprire questa bottiglia? Io non *ci* riesco.**
Can you open this bottle? I can't manage it.

(3) As a *subject* ('there') + **essere**:

*C'***è un libro sul tavolo.**        There's a book on the table.

*Ci* **sono due macchine davanti alla porta.**
There are two cars outside the door.

Again, **vi** can replace **ci** but again it is not common in spoken Italian.

(4) As a *personal pronoun*, direct and indirect object ('us', 'to us'):

**Anna *ci* ha visti al ristorante.**  Anna saw us in the restaurant.

**Maurizio *ci* telefona spesso. (telefonare *a* qualcuno)**
Maurizio telephones us often.

*Note:* The past participle agrees with a direct object pronoun (as in **ci ha visti**).

(5) As a reflexive and reciprocal pronoun:

**Ci divertiamo molto.**
We are enjoying ourselves/enjoy ourselves a lot.

**Ci scriviamo una volta alla settimana.**
We write to each other once a week.

**Exercise 2** Answer these questions using **ci** instead of repeating the place. *Example:*

**Paolo va a Roma sabato?    (domenica)**
**No, ci va domenica.**

1  Anna, da quanto tempo abita a Genova? (due anni)
2  Vai da Giorgio domani? (se ho tempo)
3  Sei stato a New York quest'anno? (due anni fa)
4  I tuoi genitori, quando traslocano nella loro nuova casa? (a maggio)

## Ne abbiamo uno solo

*Lit.* 'we have only one of them'. **Ne** means, according to the context, *of it, of them, some.* It is used in sentences where the speaker is saying how many or how much of something is being referred to. In English the 'of it', 'of them' would normally not be necessary:

– **Quante macchine hai?**          – **Ne ho una sola.**
– How many cars do you have?    – I only have one.

– **Hai dei francobolli?**          – **Si, ne ho due o tre.**
– Have you any stamps?          – Yes, I have two or three (of them).

– **E' buono il gelato?**          – **Sì, ne vuoi un po'?**
– Is the icecream good?          – Yes, do you want a little (of it)?

**Sono belle le mele, ne prendo un chilo.**
The apples are lovely, I'll have a kilo (of them).

- **Ti piacciono gli spinaci?**    – **Sì, ne mangio spesso.**
- Do you like spinach?    – Yes, I eat it often.

***Exercise 3*** Answer 'yes' to the following questions about your family home (imaginary) using the information given. *Example:*

**Avete un bagno?**      **(2)**
**Ne abbiamo due.**

1 Quante camere avete?      (4)
2 Quanti piani avete?      (3)
3 Quante stanze avete?      (7 in tutto)
4 Avete anche un garage?      (1 solo)
5 Avete un giardino?      (2 – uno davanti e uno dietro)

Now give the real answers referring to the house where you actually live.

## Ce n'è per tutti

Sometimes when you are asked whether *there is something*, you need to use both **ci** and **ne**:

- **Mamma, sono qui con i miei amici. C'è qualcosa da mangiare?**
- **Sì, c'è una torta.**
- **E' grande? Siamo in sette.**
- **Non preoccuparti. Ce n'è per tutti.**

- Mum, I've got my friends with me. Is there anything to eat?
- Yes, there's some cake.
- Is it big? There are seven of us.
- Don't worry. There is some/enough (of it) for everybody.

When you have **ci** followed by **ne**, **ci** changes and rhymes with **ne**. In the example, of course, the **ne** was followed by **è** and so shortened.

- **Ci sono delle macchine davanti alla casa? – Si, ce ne sono tre.**
- Are there any cars outside the house? – Yes, there are three (of them).

***Exercise 4*** Overleaf is the plan of some houses being built on the edge of a small town. Land is relatively cheap and the builder is offering small houses built on three floors rather than flats. Study the plans and answer the questions.

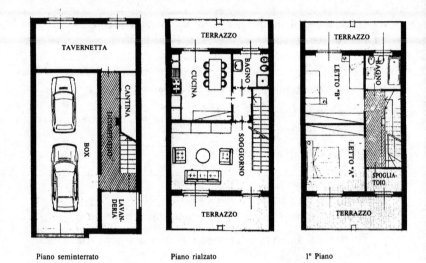

Piano seminterrato       Piano rialzato       1° Piano

*Note:* **Box** is another word for **garage**. **Una tavernetta** is usually furnished simply and used for parties. To have one seems to be something of a status-symbol. **Una lavanderia** is a place for doing the washing. **Uno spogliatoio** is a place where you can take off and leave your clothes, for instance at a gymnasium or a swimming pool. **Piano rialzato** is a floor a little above ground level. *Example:*

– **Quanti bagni ci sono?**      – **Ce ne sono due.**

1  Quanti piani ci sono in questa casa?
2  Nel box quante macchine ci sono?
3  Quanti terrazzi ci sono?
4  Quante camere ci sono?
5  C'è una cantina?

**Exercise 5**  You have enjoyed a holiday in Tuscany. The agent is checking you out of the house as you leave. You ask about a different villa for your stay next year. Explain the following points to him. Keep it simple. You can use: **abbiamo bisogno di** 'we need'; **vorremmo** 'we should like'; or more firmly: **vogliamo** 'we want'.

1  you want to come back next year but not to the same villa
2  next year you want a view over the valley
3  next year your friends, the Simpsons, are going to come with you, so you need four bedrooms
4  you prefer to have two rooms downstairs (i.e. not just one big room, so use **stanza**)

5  you also want two or more bathrooms next year
6  and above all you want a quiet house, away from the road. This year's house has been noisy (**rumoroso**).

*Exercise 6* Write a simple description of your own house and draw a floor plan, labelling the rooms.

# Reading 2

*Dove vivono gli Italiani*

> 1  What is the new trend as far as bathrooms go?
> 2  Which room is sometimes missing?
> 3  What is the latest trend as far as a place to live is concerned?
> 4  How did some families acquire their house in the country?
> 5  What did the many Italians who left the land and moved into the cities in the 1950s and 1960s do there?
> 6  What change in life-style is making it possible to reverse this trend nowadays?

Oggi la maggior parte degli Italiani vive in città e così l'alloggio è un appartamento. In genere gli appartamenti hanno stanze spaziose. Un appartamento tipico comprende un'entrata, un soggiorno, una, due o tre camere, un bagno e una cucina. Sempre di più i costruttori forniscono 'doppi servizi', cioè due bagni. Il secondo bagno di solito non ha la vasca ma solo la doccia. Con una famiglia di due o tre persone è molto pratico. Non c'è sempre la sala da pranzo; piuttosto c'è il tinello, cioè una sala piccola dove si può mangiare ma con un angolo cucina. Generalmente l'appartamento ha un balcone.

Sempre di più però gli Italiani vogliono fuggire dalla grande città per vivere in periferia, in città più piccole o addirittura in campagna. Parecchie famiglie inoltre, pur vivendo in città, possiedono una casa in campagna. Spesso è la casa dei nonni, abbandonata negli anni '50, '60, periodo in cui moltissimi Italiani andavano a lavorare nelle fabbriche in città. Ora, poichè quasi ogni famiglia dispone di una macchina, è possibile tornare a vivere in campagna, o almeno andare in campagna ogni fine settimana e trovare pace e aria pulita.

## *Vocabulary*

| | | | |
|---|---|---|---|
| **la maggior parte** | the majority | **parecchie famiglie** | several families |
| **alloggio** | lodging, place to live in | **inoltre** | furthermore, besides |
| **un costruttore** | a builder | **pur vivendo** | even though they live |
| **fornire** | to provide | | |
| **vasca** | bath tub | **poichè** | since, as |
| **fuggire** | to flee, run away | **pace e aria pulita** | peace and clean air |
| **addirittura** | even | | |

# 13 La vita è cambiata

## Life has changed

---

**In this lesson you will learn about:**

- Talking about what things were like
- Talking about what you used to do
- Saying what was happening at the time of a particular event
- Saying something is going on at this very moment (**stare** + gerund)
- How to say 'no' firmly, more negatives
- Talking about past events which no longer matter
- 'Not even', 'neither'
- Wordpower: ways of guessing meaning

---

## Dialogue 1  ▱

*Nel 1967*

*Having shown Angela her flat, Gabriella offers her a cup of tea. Thanks to her English mother, she knows how to make a good one. They are sitting on the balcony*

---

1 From Gabriella's balcony what can be seen all around?
2 When she first came to live there what did she look out over?
3 What was there opposite the building?
4 What was the road like?
5 There was a factory there, surrounded by fields. How did the workers get to work?
6 Why are there fewer workers at the factory these days?

GABRIELLA: Ecco il tè.

ANGELA: Si sta bene qui. C'è anche posto per mangiare fuori.

GABRIELLA: Sì. Anche se ci sono palazzi tutto intorno, è tranquillo. Ma sai, quando siamo venuti a vivere qui c'era tutta campagna in questa zona, tutti prati.

ANGELA: Davvero?

GABRIELLA: Proprio di fronte, c'era una cascina, con animali, mucche, pecore. La strada non era ancora asfaltata. Io, quando andavo a fare la spesa, mettevo un paio di scarpe vecchie, perchè camminavo sulla terra, sul fango. Poi quando arrivavo sulla strada buona, cambiavo scarpe. Non potevo mica andare in giro con le scarpe coperte di fango. Ma non volevo mettere scarpe belle per camminare su questa strada!

ANGELA: La zona è molto cambiata, allora.

GABRIELLA: Sì, molto. A quell'epoca, la fabbrica era già qui ma era isolata in mezzo ai campi. Gli operai arrivavano con il tram o con pullman privati.

ANGELA: E oggi?

GABRIELLA: Oggi la zona sta cambiando di nuovo. Ora ci sono meno operai alla fabbrica. Usano invece robot. E la gente preferisce vivere fuori, in centri piccoli piuttosto che nella grande città. Ci sono molti appartamenti vuoti nella zona.

## Vocabulary

| | |
|---|---|
| **intorno** | around |
| **vivere** | to live |
| **prati** | meadows |
| **una cascina** | farmhouse, a dairy farm |
| **mucche** | cows |
| **pecore** | sheep (*pl.*) |
| **fare la spesa** | to do the shopping |
| **camminavo sulla terra, sul fango** | I used to walk on earth, on mud |
| **non potevo mica** | I really couldn't (*see below*) |
| **andare in giro** | go around |
| **la fabbrica era già qui** | the factory was already here |
| **gli operai** | the workers (*industrial workers*) |
| **pullman** | motor coach |
| **piuttosto che** | rather than |

# Language points

## Saying what things were like – the imperfect tense

To talk about completed actions in the past you use the **passato prossimo**. But sometimes you want to look at the past in another way. To describe the way things were in the past you use the *imperfect* tense, **l'imperfetto**. The name does not mean there is something wrong with it; it comes from Latin and means 'not finished'. When you use the imperfect, you are not interested in whether the action or event is finished. Gabriella uses it to describe what her district was like when she and her husband first came there as a young married couple:

**Quando siamo venuti a vivere qui c'*era* la campagna.**
When we came to live here, it was the country.

**Di fronte c'*era* una cascina.**   Opposite there was a farm.
**La strada non *era* asfaltata.**   The road wasn't made up.

Notice Gabriella says: **quando siamo venuti** – that was an event which happened at a specific point in time and then was over and done with so she uses the **passato prossimo**.

## Saying what you used to do – the imperfect again

You also use the **imperfetto** for repeated or habitual actions in the past:

**Quando *andavo* a fare la spesa, *mettevo* un paio di scarpe vecchie, perchè *camminavo* sulla terra, sul fango. Poi quando *arrivavo* sulla strada buona, *cambiavo* scarpe.**
When I went shopping, I used to put on a pair of old shoes because I used to be walking on dirt, on mud. Then when I got to the good (made up) road, I used to change shoes.

The **imperfetto** is easy to form: you just take the **-re** off the end of the infinitive and add the endings as shown overleaf:

| *cambiare* | *mettere* | *preferire* |
|------------|-----------|-------------|
| cambia*vo* | mette*vo* | preferi*vo* |
| cambia*vi* | mette*vi* | preferi*vi* |
| cambia*va* | mette*va* | preferi*va* |
| cambia*vamo* | mette*vamo* | preferi*vamo* |
| cambia*vate* | mette*vate* | preferi*vate* |
| cambia*vano* | mette*vano* | preferi*vano* |

The stress falls on the penultimate syllable *except* in the third person plural when, as in the present, it falls on the antepenultimate syllable, the third syllable from the end of the word. Very few verbs are irregular. **Essere**, as you might expect, is; the others are verbs whose infinitives have become shortened in modern Italian from earlier longer forms (see Lesson 11: the gerund).

| *essere* | *fare* | *dire* | *bere* | *produrre* |
|----------|--------|--------|--------|------------|
| ero | facevo | dicevo | bevevo | producevo |
| eri | facevi | dicevi | bevevi | producevi |
| era | faceva | diceva | beveva | produceva |
| eravamo | facevamo | dicevamo | bevevamo | producevamo |
| eravate | facevate | dicevate | bevevate | producevate |
| erano | facevano | dicevano | bevevano | producevano |

Also similar to the gerund are:

> *dare:* davo, davi, dava, davamo, davate, davano
> *stare:* stavo, stavi, stava, stavamo, stavate, stavano

*Note:* When Gabriella said **cambiavo scarpe**, in English she might have said: 'I used to change my shoes', 'I changed my shoes', 'I would change my shoes', all with the same meaning.

The imperfect is also used for actions which were going on when another event occurred.

> **Parlavo con Angela quando il telefono ha suonato. Sapete chi era? Era proprio la mamma di Angela che chiamava.**
> I was talking to Angela when the telephone rang. Do you know who it was? It was Angela's mother calling.

In English we would use: 'I was talking'. As was said in relation to the **passato prossimo** it is wiser and more profitable to try to avoid thinking of English and to see the Italian tense system in its own terms. You have two past tenses, one for actions viewed as completed and the other for setting the scene, describing, and also for habitual actions or events. (English has five!)

*Exercise 1* Last summer you attended an enjoyable party at the country house of some friends of yours. Here you are recalling some of it. We have helped you, except that you have to put the verbs into the correct tense. Since you are describing the day and your friends, you will need to use the tense for descriptions: the imperfect.

Il tempo (1 essere) così bello. (2 Fare) caldo ma non troppo. La campagna (3 avere) ancora il bel verde della primavera. I fiori (4 avere) un profumo delicatissimo. Tutti gli amici (5 essere) lì. Anna (6 portare), come al solito, un vestito molto elegante. Il colore, un giallo chiaro, le (7 andare) benissimo. Aldo (8 avere) una maglia fatta a mano, molto grande. (9 Sembrare) strano e preoccupato. Infatti abbiamo saputo che la sua ditta (10 avere) dei problemi. Meno male che c'(11 essere) anche Roberto che gli ha parlato e ha potuto aiutarlo. Anche per questo la festa è stata bella, un grande successo.

## Vocabulary

| | |
|---|---|
| **i fiori** | the flowers |
| **un profumo** | a perfume, a smell |
| **le andava benissimo** | it suited her very well |
| **abbiamo saputo** | we learned (*note how the tense of **sapere** tells us that this happened at a precise time, hence the translation*) |
| **la sua ditta** | his firm, company |
| **meno male** | thank goodness, just as well, luckily |

*Exercise 2* Describe, in writing, a happy scene you have been part of in the last year. This is of course a free exercise.

*Exercise 3* When you were a child, were things very different? Mario is talking about his childhood around 1960. Complete what he says; be careful: often he is including his brothers and sisters or all the family in what he says, so he will say 'we' . . .

Quando ero bambino, le cose (1 essere) diverse. Mio nonno (2 essere) pescatore. Noi (3 abitare) in Liguria. Mio padre invece

(4 lavorare) in un bar. Noi bambini (5 guardare) la TV nel bar, non a casa. A casa non (6 avere) la TV. Mia madre (7 fare) la casalinga. (8 Essere) cinque fratelli e la mamma (9 avere) molto lavoro da fare. Non (10 mangiare) spesso la carne ma naturalmente mio nonno (11 portare) a casa molto pesce. Mia madre (12 fare) i nostri vestiti. Non (13 essere) ricchi come la gente oggi. Ma (14 divertirsi) molto. (15 Essere) felici.

**pescatore**   fisherman      **fare la casalinga**   she was a housewife

**Exercise 4** Has life changed a lot since you were a child? Write down some of the things you used to do; and things which people did then and they no longer do today. Another open-ended exercise.

**Exercise 5** There's been an accident. Nothing serious, thank goodness, but two cars have hit each other at the traffic lights and the drivers are looking for witnesses to support their views of what happened. There's a bar on the corner so they ask the customers: **Che cosa ha visto?** Complete the answers:

| | |
|---|---|
| SIGNORE ANZIANO: | Ma, non ho visto niente. (1 Leggere) il giornale. |
| DUE GIOVANI INNAMORATI: | Non abbiamo visto niente. (2 Parlarsi) e (3 guardarsi). |
| CAMERIERE: | Non ho visto niente. (4 Essere) al bar. (5 Aspettare) il barista che (6 fare) due cappuccini. |
| SIGNORA CON BAMBINO: | Scusi, non ho visto niente. (7 Aiutare) il bambino a mangiare il gelato. |
| AUTOMOBILISTA: | Ma possibile, tutta questa gente e non hanno visto niente! |

**due giovani innamorati**      two young people in love

Do you feel now that you understand better the three uses of the imperfect? In Exercise 1 it was used to describe what things were like on one particular day in the past; in Exercise 3 it was used partly for that and partly to say what people habitually did in the past. In Exercise 5 it was used to say what people were doing at a point in time in the past.

## La zona sta cambiando – **the present continuous**

Gabriella talks about what her district was like when she and her husband first moved there. She goes on to say that the area is changing again: **la zona sta cambiando**. When there is a need to emphasize that something is happening now, at this moment, Italian uses **stare** + gerund, the *present continuous*. This seems similar to the English present continuous: 'the area is changing'. But it is not used as much as the English version. It is used *only* when you want to emphasize that the action is taking place now.

| | |
|---|---|
| – **Dov'è Carlo?** | – **E' in cucina,** *sta preparando* la cena. |
| – Where is Carlo? | – He's in the kitchen, he's getting supper ready. |
| – **Che cosa** *stai facendo?* | – *Sto cercando* di riparare la macchina. |
| – What are you doing? | – I am trying to repair the car. |

*Exercise 6* The telephone rings and you answer it. The caller would like to speak to almost anyone in the household except you but they are all busy. Explain what they are doing:

1 Vorrei parlare con Paolo. (*Tell the caller Paolo is having a shower.*) Non può venire al telefono.
2 E Aldo? (*Tell the caller Aldo is making a bechamel sauce* (**una besciamella**).) Non può venire al telefono in questo momento.
3 E Maria? (*She's reading a story* (**un racconto**) *to little Anna.*)
4 E Margherita? (*She's out. She's doing the shopping.*)
5 E il nonno? (*He's asleep.*)

*You:* **Senta. Dico a tutti che lei ha chiamato e la faccio richiamare appena possibile.**
(Look, I'll tell everyone you called and I'll get them to call you back as soon as possible.)

## Stare **+ gerund – postscript**

**Stare** + gerund can also be used to say what was going on at a certain point of time in the past when there is a need to emphasize that the action was in progress.

**Ho chiamato Giorgio ma stava facendo la doccia. Così ho lasciato un messaggio a sua moglie.**
I called George but he was having a shower. So I left a message with his wife.

**Scusa, ti ho interrotto. Cosa stavi dicendo?**
I'm sorry, I've interrupted you. What were you saying?

## Non ... mica

**Non potevo mica andare in giro con le scarpe coperte di fango**, said Gabriella. 'I couldn't go round in shoes covered in mud'. You learned (Lesson 3) that to make a sentence negative you simply put **non** immediately before the verb. In Lesson 11 you met **non ... niente/nulla**. Gabriella uses here a form commonly heard: **non ... mica**. It is used to strengthen the negative. (In English you might say: 'I couldn't go round in shoes covered in mud, could I?') Other ways of emphasizing the negative are **non ... affatto**, **non ... per niente**, **non ... per nulla**. **Mica** belongs very much to the spoken language. The other forms are more acceptable in writing.

| | |
|---|---|
| *Non* è *mica* vero/*non* è *affatto* vero. | It's not true at all. |
| *Non* lo conosco *mica*/*non* lo conosco *affatto*. | I don't know him at all. |
| *Non* lo conosco *per niente*. | I don't know him at all. |
| *Non* è *per nulla* vero. | It isn't true at all. |

## The remote past

There is another past tense called, in Italian, the **passato remoto**. It is little used in spoken Italian in the north; in the centre of Italy, it is more common and it is used a lot in the south. Strictly its use is for completed events and actions in a remote past which has no link with the present, i.e. it is similar to the **passato prossimo** but for a remote not a recent past. Because story-telling implies a remoteness from the events being recounted, it is usually used in novels and of course history books. Some Italians use it when recounting something which has happened to them but which they now regard as finished. They become story-tellers temporarily. Many native speakers hardly ever use the **passato remoto** and the foreign learner can safely defer learning it until he is an advanced student. For completeness and for recognition when necessary, the forms are given in the Grammar summary.

# Reading  📼

Gabriella talked about the changes in her neighbourhood since she moved there in 1967. Every country in the world has seen tremendous changes in the second half of the twentieth century, but many Italians find the consideration of this period of change particularly poignant and sad. 1995 marked the fiftieth anniversary of the end of the Second World War, the last part of which had seen much of Italy occupied by German forces and then painfully fought over and finally liberated. In 1945 Italians had an opportunity to build their country afresh. In 1995 that time of hope and optimism seemed very distant. Italy was undergoing a long political crisis: the political system set up after the war, popularly known as the First Republic, was in disarray following revelations of widespread corruption in politics and business. At the end of 1994 the first government of the Parliament elected on 27 March 1994, which many had hoped would usher in a Second Republic, had fallen. On 2 January 1995, *La Stampa* announced a series of articles looking back over the period since the end of the war and considering the reasons for the crisis. The series was introduced with an article by a well-known journalist, Lietta Tornabuoni. Below are extracts, published with her kind permission.

Read the passage carefully, more than once, listening to the recording if you have it. Many of the words are guessable and you should find you can answer the questions below after two or three readings, if not sooner. Then read the notes and finally come back to the passage again. At that stage you can look up any words you haven't managed to work out.

1 What sort of year does the writer anticipate the coming one will be?
2 What one thing did Italy, in the opinion of the writer, have for the first time ever at the end of the second World War?
3 List at least three material goods which Italians did not have at that time.
4 The writer says fewer than 7 per cent of Italians had all of three basic amenities. What were they?

5 What did almost 2 million Italians do between 1946 and 1957? Why?

6 What do you learn about the Italian language at the end of the second World War?

7 What values does Lietta Tornabuoni say guided people and how does she find them in contrast with today's values?

8 In the third paragraph, the writer lists a number of aspects of life which have improved and one which has not. What is that?

Album dei 50 anni: l'Italia 1945–1995

# Con gli occhi aperti

MEZZO secolo di democrazia in Italia, 1945–1995. L'anniversario cade all'inizio di un anno difficile e rischioso di transizione, in un momento politico di novità e incertezza ... e di infiniti interrogativi (sul Paese, su noi stessi) ...

Cinquant'anni fa, finita la seconda guerra mondiale, c'era in Italia, per la prima volta, la democrazia. Non c'erano la televisione, la lavatrice, la plastica, l'automobile come veicolo di massa, la pubblicità come linguaggio collettivo, l'elettronica coi suoi computers. Non c'era granchè da mangiare, nelle macerie belliche mancavano gli alloggi: e neppure il sette per cento delle famiglie aveva in casa elettricità, acqua potabile e gabinetto insieme. Non c'era lavoro, bisognava andarselo a cercare fuori, tra il 1946 e il 1957 quasi due milioni di persone emigrarono per lavorare nelle Americhe o in Europa: erano gli unici viaggi degli italiani e per chi restava i salari erano miseri. Non c'era una lingua comune, davvero usata, quotidiana: al di là dei libri, della scuola, delle leggi o dei documenti, l'italiano rimaneva un' astrazione, si parlavano i dialetti. Non c'era la pratica del consumo, ma l'etica del risparmio; non la pratica dell'edonismo, ma l'etica del sacrificio. Paese rurale, l'Italia era pure un Paese sottosviluppato.

In cinquant'anni, la nostra vita è immensamente cambiata, migliorata. Meno fame, meno fatica, meno freddo, meno malattie, più benessere, più libertà, più diritti, più informazione, più divertimento: sono dati indiscutibili ... Certo è che all'evoluzione del modo di vivere non ha corrisposto l'evoluzione del sistema politico. ...

Lietta Tornabuoni, *La Stampa*, 2 gennaio, 1995.

## *Vocabulary*

| | |
|---|---|
| **lavatrice** | washing machine |
| **veicolo di massa** | a vehicle for mass use |
| **non c'era granchè da mangiare** | there wasn't much to eat |
| **macerie belliche** | rubble, ruins left by the war |
| **mancavano gli alloggi** | there was a housing shortage |
| **gabinetto** | lavatory |
| **bisognava andarselo a cercare fuori** | it was necessary to go off and find it for oneself outside (Italy) |
| **le Americhe** | the Americas, North and South |
| **misero/a** | paltry, poor, wretched |
| **al di là di** | beyond, outside |
| **risparmio** | saving |
| **sottosviluppato** | underdeveloped |

## Language points

### Coi suoi computers

**Coi** is **con** + **i**. Some speakers and writers join **con** to **il** (**col**) and **i** (**coi**). It is quite acceptable to say and write **con il** and **con i**.

### Neppure

**Neppure** means 'not even', 'neither'. **Neanche** and **nemmeno** mean the same and work the same way.

> *Non* ho *neppure* 10.000 lire.
>     *neanche*
>     *nemmeno*

As with **niente**, **nulla**, **mica**, **affatto**, there needs to be a **non** before the verb. (See also Lesson 15.)

### Emigrarono

**Emigrarono** means 'emigrated'. This is a **passato remoto**, 3rd person plural. The writer considers the phenomenon of mass emigration as belonging to the past, as indeed it does. Italy is now experiencing *immigration* from poorer countries, particularly in North Africa and Eastern Europe.

## Wordpower

The passage looks superficially difficult. This is partly because to an eye brought up on the English language, words of Latin origin seem erudite. Italian however has grown from Latin, with various other influences mixed in. Words of Latin origin are part and parcel of the normal everyday vocabulary of the man or woman in the Italian street. So rule number one when faced with a passage in Italian is: expect Latinisms.

The passage also contains quite a high proportion of abstract words and this gives the reader a feeling it is difficult. But such words are particularly guessable. Intelligent guessing is invaluable when dealing with a foreign language. Using a dictionary takes time and you may not always have one handy. When faced with a word you have not met before you should try to guess. Here are three possible approaches:

(1) Does it look like a word I know in English? **Democrazia** was an easy one of this sort. **Inizio** perhaps less so, but didn't it remind you of 'initial'? Initial means 'occurring at the beginning'. So a good, indeed a correct guess for **all'inizio di un anno** would be 'at the start of a year' ...

(2) Sometimes you may not be able to make the link with an English word but you may recognize part of the word as being similar to an Italian word you know. For instance, **lavatrice** contains **lava-** and you may be able to link that with **lavare**, 'to wash', and then guess that a **lavatrice** is some sort of person or machine which washes. **Novità** may not in your mind immediately suggest 'novelty' but it may make you think of **nuovo**. Or, to return to strategy no. 1, maybe that would take you to 'innovation' and from there to 'something new'. In the case of **sottosviluppato**, you have met **sotto**, 'under', and **sviluppo**, 'development'. And **benessere** is **bene** + **essere**, 'to be well'. What would **malessere** mean?

(3) Occasionally neither of these approaches works but you may be able to guess from the context. For instance you have not so far met the word **gabinetto**, used in '**elettricità, acqua potabile e gabinetto insieme**'. You will realize from the rest of the sentence that the author is saying that certain basic conveniences which we today take for granted were not all three available together in their homes to most Italians in 1945. So you might be able to guess that the third of the trio was a *flush lavatory*. This type of guessing is however to be used with caution as it can lead the guesser astray.

# 14 Alla salute!

## Here's to your health!

**In this lesson you will learn about:**

- 'Have a nice day!' – the difference between **giorno/giornata**
- Object pronouns
- **Il corpo umano** – the human body
- Saying you are not well

## Dialogue 1

### Una distorsione alla caviglia

*Enzo had planned to go to the cinema yesterday evening with his friends Piero and Elena. However he had a bad cold, so he stayed at home. Now he is telephoning them to hear what they thought of the film*

1 How is Enzo's cold today?
2 Did Piero and Elena enjoy the film?
3 What must Elena avoid doing for a week?

ENZO:   Pronto. Ciao Piero, sei tu? Come stai?
PIERO:  Io bene, grazie, e il tuo raffreddore?
ENZO:   Un po' meglio oggi, grazie. Scusa se non sono venuto con voi ieri. Stavo proprio male. E il film? Come l'avete trovato? Vi è piaciuto?
PIERO:  Ma non ci siamo andati.
ENZO:   Come mai? Che cosa è successo?
PIERO:  Beh, uscendo di casa Elena è caduta e si è fatta una brutta

distorsione alla caviglia. Così invece di andare al cinema, abbiamo passato la serata al pronto soccorso.

ENZO: Oh, mi dispiace. Come va adesso Elena?

PIERO: E qui, accanto a me, sdraiata, con il piede su un cuscino. Non deve assolutamente mettere il piede a terra per sette giorni. Vuoi parlarle? Te la passo. Ciao.

## *Vocabulary*

| | |
|---|---|
| **una brutta distorsione alla caviglia** | a nasty ankle sprain |
| **pronto soccorso** | hospital emergency service |
| **sdraiata** | lying down |

## Language points

### La serata/la sera

**Sera** refers to the evening as a point in time, i.e. as opposed to the morning or the afternoon.

> **Vuoi andare dalla nonna questa *sera* o domani *pomeriggio*?**
> Do you want to go to grandmother's this evening or tomorrow afternoon?

> **Lavorare dalla *mattina* alla *sera*.**
> To work from morning to night (evening).

You use **serata** when thinking about the evening as a period of time, about how the evening is spent. Hence:

> **Abbiamo passato la *serata* al pronto soccorso.**
> We spent the evening at the hospital emergency department.

> **le lunghe *serate* invernali**
> the long winter evenings

Compare also **giornata/giorno**. **Giorno**: the day as a point in time:

> – **Che *giorno* è oggi?**     – **E' mercoledì.**
> – What day is it today?     – It's Wednesday.

> **Ci sono sette *giorni* in una settimana.**
> There are seven days in a week.

You use **giornata** when you are thinking about how the daylight hours are spent, the conditions and events in them:

**E' stata davvero una *giornata* bellissima.**
It really was a lovely day (*meaning* 'the weather was wonderful',
*or* 'we had a marvellous time').

People wish you **Buona giornata!** 'Have a nice day!', and **Buona
serata!** 'Have a nice evening!' as opposed to **buongiorno, buona
sera**, which are simply greetings without thought about how the
day or evening might be spent. The same distinction is true but
less commonly met for: **mattina, mattinata** and **anno, annata**.
**Un'annata buona** is used in agricultural circles when talking about
a 'good year' referring to the quality of the crop that year. When
making a rather imprecise appointment you might say:

**Passo da te in mattinata/in serata/in giornata.**
I'll call on you during the morning/the evening/the day.

## More about personal pronouns, object form

Here are three points about the position of pronouns:

(1) You will remember you were told these pronouns are placed
immediately before the verb, but Piero says:

**Vuoi parlar*le*?**        Do you want to talk to her?

When used with an infinitive, the object pronoun follows the infinitive with the final **e** removed and is written joined to it:

**Carlo sta suonando il pianoforte. Mi piace *sentirlo*.**
Carlo's playing the piano. I like to hear him.

**Dicono che il nuovo film è molto bello. Andiamo a *vederlo*
stasera.**
They say the new film is very good. Let's go and see it this evening.

**Pronto, Carla? Ciao. Senti, è arrivato Bernardo. Perchè non vieni
a *trovarlo* domani da noi?**
Hello, is that Carla? Hi. Bernardo's arrived. Why don't you come
and see him at our house tomorrow?

Usually the infinitive will follow another verb as in the above
examples, but not necessarily:

***Dargli* la mia macchina? Neanche per sogno.**
Give him my car? Never in a thousand years (*lit.* 'not even in
a dream').

When the first verb is one of that useful trio: **volere**, **dovere**, **potere**, the pronoun may be put either before that verb or after the infinitive:

> – **Hai telefonato a Giorgio?**
> – **Non ancora. *Gli* devo telefonare oggi. /Devo telefonar*gli* oggi.**
> – Have you telephoned Giorgio?
> – Not yet. I must ring him today.

> – **Hai finito il libro che stavi leggendo?**
> – **No. *Lo* vorrei finire oggi. /Vorrei finir*lo* oggi.**
> – Have you finished the book you were reading?
> – No. I'd like to finish it today.

> – **Quando può fare questa riparazione?**
> – ***La* posso fare domani. /Posso far*la* domani.**
> – When can you do this repair?
> – I can do it tomorrow.

It is simpler for the learner to stick to the second model, thus treating all verbs the same way, but be prepared for the other usage.

(2) *Ecco.* The direct object pronouns are also attached to **ecco**:

| | |
|---|---|
| **Ecco*mi*.** | **Ecco*ci*.** |
| Here I am. | Here we are. |

| | |
|---|---|
| – **Dov'è Giorgio?** | – **Sta arrivando. Ecco*lo*.** |
| – Where's Giorgio? | – He's coming. Here he is. |

**Dove abbiamo lasciato la macchina? Ah, ecco*la*.**
Where did we leave the car? Ah, there it is.

(3) *Imperatives.* The object pronouns, including reflexive pronouns, are attached to the end of imperatives with one exception.

**Scusa*mi*, Maria. Ti ho fatto male?**
Forgive me, Maria. Did I hurt you?

**Non preoccupar*ti*.**
Don't worry.

(In this case you have an imperative which is formed with the infinitive.)

| | |
|---|---|
| **Di*mmi*, Gianni, cosa pensi?*** | Tell me, Gianni, what do you think? |
| **Dite*lo* coi fiori.** | Say it with flowers. |

| | |
|---|---|
| **Accomodate*vi*.** | Take a seat. |
| **Divertiamo*ci*.** | Let's enjoy ourselves. |

\* The doubling of the **m** in **dimmi**, is a small point. The verbs in which this happens are **andare (va')**, **dare (da')**, **dire (di')**, **fare (fa')** and **stare (sta')**. The **tu** form of the imperative of these verbs is a monosyllable. The initial consonant of any object pronoun doubles when it is attached to these monosyllables. This applies to all the object pronouns *except* **gli**. However, the one most commonly heard is **mi**:

| | |
|---|---|
| **Fa*mmi* vedere la foto.** | Show me the photo (make/let me see the photo). |
| **Fa*cci* un piacere.** | Do us a favour. |
| **Da*mmi* la tua valigia.** | Give me your suitcase. |
| **Da*mmi* la mano.** | Give me your hand. |
| **Da*gli* la mia chiave.** | Give him my key. |

The *exception* to the rule that the object pronoun is attached to the end of the imperative is the formal, third person imperative. In this case the pronoun precedes the verb:

| | |
|---|---|
| ***Mi* scusi, signore. Le ho fatto male?** | I am sorry, sir. Did I hurt you? |
| ***Mi* dica.** | Tell me. (*see below*) |
| ***S'*accomodi.** | Take a seat/ sit down. |

It helps to use commonly heard forms as models for these rather tricky points. You will hear:

| *From your friends (**tu** form)* | *From people you do not know well (**lei**)* |
|---|---|
| Scusa*mi* | *Mi* scusi |
| Di*mmi* | *Mi* dica |
| Siedi*ti* | *Si* sieda |
| | *S'*accomodi |

**Dimmi/mi dica** are often heard. When you claim a friend's attention by saying his/her name, the response will very often be: **dimmi** or **dimmi tutto**. And it is very common for a waiter, a shop assistant, etc. to say: **mi dica** to indicate he/she is ready to listen to you.

**Exercise 1** Finish these remarks as indicated. You will need to use a pronoun.

*Example:* **Ho finito di leggere il giornale.** (*Do you want to see it?*)

*Answer:* **Vuoi vederlo tu?/Lo vuoi vedere tu?**

1 Gianni è un amico molto caro. (*He comes to see us often.*)
2 Sabato è il compleanno di Andrea. (*I'd like to invite him to supper.*)
3 Hai già scritto al Signor Lombardi? (*No, I must write to him today.*)
4 Buongiorno, signora. (*Can I help you?*)
5 Sei mai stato a Parigi? (*No, I hope to go there this year.*)

**Exercise 2** Answer the following using **ecco** and a pronoun:

1 Dove sono i bambini?     2 Ha il passaporto, signore?
3 Dove sei?     4 Mi dà le chiavi, per piacere?

**Exercise 3** How would you say the following (A) to a person you did not know well – i.e. using **lei** – and (B) to a friend:

1 Enjoy yourself!     2 Do me a favour.
3 Give me the key, please.     4 Tell him to come tomorrow.

## Combining pronouns

You saw in Lesson 12 that when **ci** and **ne** occur in the same sentence, **ci** comes first and changes to **ne**: *Ce ne sono tre*.

This also happens with **mi**, **ti**, **ci** (us, to us), **vi**, and the reflexive pronoun **si**. Piero says:

**Te la passo.**               I'll pass her to you.

Similarly:

**Me lo dici?**                Are you going to tell me? (*lit.* 'Are you telling me?')
**Ce li manda.**              He's sending them to us.

The order is always:

(1) **mi**, **ti**, **si**, **ci**, **vi**, **si**, followed by:
(2) **lo**, **la**, **li**, **le**, **ne**.

(*Note:* **Ci** in any of its uses, subject or object.)

What about **gli**, **le** singular and **gli** plural? All three become: **glie** and precede **lo**, **la**, **li**, **le**. The resulting sound group is written as one word:

***Glielo*** **dico domani.**  I'll tell ⎡ you ⎤ (it) tomorrow.
  him
  her
  them

Without a context the Italian phrase could mean any of the English versions. How are you going to learn this? Find some model sentences. A once popular song with the '**orchestrine**' in Venice went:

**Me lo dai? me lo dai? me lo dai un bel bacin?**
Will you give me . . . a nice little kiss?

(**Bacin** is a diminutive of **bacio**, 'a kiss'.) The line from the song could be transformed:

**Me la dai? Me li dai? Me le dai? Me ne dai?**
Will you give it/them/some of them to me?

**Te lo do. Te la do. Te li do. Te le do. Te ne do.**
I am giving (will give) it/them/some of them to you.

**Glielo do. Gliela do. Glieli do. Gliele do. Gliene do. ecc.**
I am giving it/some of it to him/her/them. etc.

***Exercise 4*** Complete the following using a double pronoun:

*Example:* – **Pronto. C'è il Signor Rossi?**
(*I'll put you through straight away*)
*Answer:* – **Glielo passo subito.**

1 – Hai fatto quel lavoro per me?
   (*I'll do it for you tomorrow.*)
2 – Scusi, signorina. Non capisco questo modulo.[1]
   (*I'll explain it to you.*)
3 – Ho comprato un nuovo frigo.
   (*They are bringing it to us tomorrow.*)
4 – Sai che Alberto ha un nuovo lavoro?
   (*Yes, he told me about it[2] on Saturday*)

1 **modulo**          form (*to fill in*)

2 use **parlare di**

## *Vocabulary*

Il corpo umano **'the human body'**

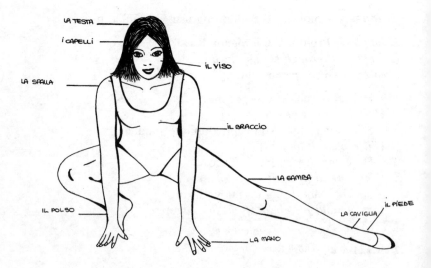

*Altre parole utili:*

| la gola | throat | il cuore | heart |
|---------|--------|----------|-------|
| lo stomaco | stomach | la pelle | skin |
| il sangue | blood | i polmoni | the lungs |
| i reni | the kidneys | il fegato | the liver |

It is usual not to use the possessive adjective with parts of the body unless it is necessary to make clear whose body the part belongs to! i.e. in rather unusual circumstances.

Elena è accanto a me con il piede su un cuscino.
Si è fatta una brutta distorsione alla caviglia.

There is no doubt whose foot is on the cushion – Elena's. And the same goes for the ankle. Similarly:

**Mi lavo le mani.**          I am washing/wash my hands.

# Dialogue 2 ▧

*Dal medico*

---

1 What are the patient's symptoms?
2 What is the doctor's diagnosis?
3 What treatment does he recommend?

---

MEDICO:    Buon giorno, signore.
PAZIENTE:  Buon giorno, dottore. Ho mal di gola, e mal di testa e mi fa anche male lo stomaco, non ho appetito e mi sento stanco da morire.
MEDICO:    Vediamo un po'. (*He takes the patient's temperature and examines him.*) Lei ha la febbre alta. Dovrebbe essere a letto.
PAZIENTE:  Che cosa è, dottore?
MEDICO:    E solo questa brutta influenza che c'è in giro quest'anno. Le do delle pastiglie e uno sciroppo ma è molto importante tornare a casa, mettersi a letto e riposarsi bene. Bisogna anche bere molto: acqua, tè leggero, eccetera. Niente alcool. E non deve tornare a lavorare se non quando non avrà più la febbre.

## *Vocabulary*

| | |
|---|---|
| **mi sento stanco da morire** | I feel dead tired |
| **vediamo un po'** | let's see, let's have a look |
| **lei ha la febbre alta** | you have a high temperature |
| **questa brutta influenza che c'è in giro** | this nasty influenza which is going round |
| **niente alcool** | no alcohol |
| **se non quando non avrà più la febbre** | until you no longer have a temperature |

## Saying you are not well

| | | |
|---|---|---|
| **stare male** | | to be unwell |
| **sto meglio** | | I feel/am better |
| **sto bene** | | I'm well |
| **sentirsi bene/male** | | to feel well/ill |
| **non mi sento bene** | | I don't feel well |
| **si sente male** | | he feels poorly |
| **ti senti meglio?** | | do you feel better? |
| **ho mal di** | **testa** | I have a   headache |
| | **stomaco** | stomach ache |
| | **schiena** | back ache |
| | **denti** | tooth ache |
| | **gola** | sore throat |
| **mi fa male la caviglia** | | my ankle hurts |
| **mi fanno male gli occhi** | | my eyes hurt |

'Eyes' are of course plural, hence also the plural verb.

The word for 'pain' is **dolore** *(m.)*. 'A prescription' is **una ricetta**. And you have already met the false friend: **essere ricoverato/a**, 'to be admitted to hospital'. **Ricoverare qualcuno d'urgenza** means 'to admit someone to hospital as an emergency case'.

## Language point

### Non ... più 'no longer, not any more'

**quando *non* avrà *più* la febbre**
when you no longer have a high temperature

(**Avrà** is the future of 'have' – see Lesson 16.)

> **Una volta Paolo mi scriveva regolarmente ma da un po'** *non* **mi scrive** *più.*
> At one time Paolo used to write to me regularly but for a while he hasn't written any more.

As with the other negatives, you must put **non** before the verb. With a **passato prossimo** the **più** goes before the past particple:

> **Non ha più detto niente.**
> He didn't say anything (any) more.

**Exercise 5** You are being asked by your doctor about your habits. Answer saying you used to do all these things but you don't any more.

*Example:* **Mangia cioccolata?**
*Answer:* **Una volta, sì, ne mangiavo ma ora non ne mangio più.**

1 Fuma?
2 Beve molto?
3 Mangia carne rossa?
4 Dorme male?

**Exercise 6** Things have changed. Write a new sentence based on the one given saying that it's not happening any more. Say what the resulting sentence means.

*Example:* **Ci parlavamo spesso.**
*Answer:* **Non ci parliamo più.**
> We don't talk to each other anymore.

1 Lo vedevo spesso.
2 Mi scriveva spesso.
3 Lo aiutavo.
4 Ci telefonavamo.

# 15 Buona fortuna!

## Good luck!

In this lesson you will learn about:

- Saying what you would do if . . .
- How to say 'never', 'not yet', 'no one' and 'neither . . . nor'
- Offering to do something, insisting on doing something
- The subjunctive and moods of the verb
- Saying if something were the case . . .
- Ways of saying 'perhaps' and the other meaning of **magari**
- 'If only' . . . how to say what you would have done if . . .

## Dialogue 1

### La lotteria

*In Italy there are various lotteries, some of which have very big prizes. One is the **lotteria gratta e vinci** – scratch and win. You buy your ticket at a newsagents' and scratch the silver area with a coin. And you see immediately whether or not you have won. Three friends, Edoardo, Filippo e Elisa, are enjoying a coffee on the terrace outside a bar . . .*

1 Does Filippo often buy lottery tickets?
2 What would he do if he won?
3 And Elisa?

EDOARDO:   Compriamo dei biglietti della lotteria?
FILIPPO:   Io non vinco mai niente alla lotteria.
ELISA:     Compri spesso i biglietti?

| | |
|---|---|
| FILIPPO: | Raramente. |
| ELISA: | Per questo non vinci mai. Come vuoi vincere se non compri biglietti? Dai, compriamo dei biglietti. |
| FILIPPO: | Va bene. |
| EDOARDO: | Vado io a prenderli. |
| ELISA: | Che cosa faresti se vincessi? |
| FILIPPO: | Mah, non lo so. Comprerei una macchina nuova. Magari vi porterei a fare il giro del mondo. E tu Elisa? |
| ELISA: | Comprerei una casa al mare. Ci metterei un pianoforte a coda. Prenderei delle lezioni di piano e passerei le mie giornate a suonare. Inviterei anche gli amici. Quando non suonassi, starei in cucina a preparare dei buoni piatti. Sarebbe una festa continua ... |
| EDOARDO: | Allora, ecco il tuo biglietto, Elisa. E il tuo, Filippo. Gratta e vedi se hai vinto. |
| FILIPPO: | Sì, ho vinto! |
| ELISA: | Oh, che bello. Facciamo il giro del mondo! |
| FILIPPO: | Macchè giro del mondo! Ho vinto cinquantamila lire! |

## Vocabulary notes

**dai** go on, come on. *From* **dare** *and used to encourage someone to do something*
**vado io a prenderli** I'll go and get them
**ho vinto** I've won. (**vincere** *has an irregular past participle:* **vinto**)
**macchè** *roughly* You're joking! (*It expresses strong contradiction of what has just been said.*)
**cinquantamila lire** *at the time of writing this would not buy a restaurant meal for two although it might cover quite a good one for one person. It would barely fill the tank of a small car (supermini type) with petrol*

## Language points

### Saying what you 'would do if ...' – the conditional

You have met this quite often: **vorrei**, **dovrei**, **potrei**, **mi piacerebbe** ... And now you have heard people talk about what they *would* *do* if they won money in a lottery. The base for the conditional is the infinitive without the final **-e**. Here are several verbs; pick out the ending:

| dire | fare | dare | prendere | partire |
|------|------|------|----------|---------|
| dir*ei* | far*ei* | dar*ei* | prender*ei* | partir*ei* |
| dir*esti* | far*esti* | dar*esti* | prender*esti* | partir*esti* |
| dir*ebbe* | far*ebbe* | dar*ebbe* | prender*ebbe* | partir*ebbe* |
| dir*emmo* | far*emmo* | dar*emmo* | prender*emmo* | partir*emmo* |
| dir*este* | far*este* | dar*este* | prender*este* | partir*este* |
| dir*ebbero* | far*ebbero* | dar*ebbero* | prender*ebbero* | partir*ebbero* |

The stress falls on the penultimate syllable, except in the third person plural when it falls on the antepenultimate syllable (**ebbero**). *Note:* In the first person singular, the **-e-** of the **-ei** ending is a syllable.

A complication is that **-are** verbs make an additional change. The **a** in the infinitive ending becomes an **e**, so that they work like **-ere** verbs:

### comprare

| | |
|------|------|
| compr*erei* | compr*eremmo* |
| compr*eresti* | compr*ereste* |
| compr*erebbe* | compr*erebbero* |

**Essere**, predictably, is irregular:

| | |
|------|------|
| sarei | saremmo |
| saresti | sareste |
| sarebbe | sarebbero |

A handful of other verbs, some of which you have already met and got used to, are irregular. They fall into three groups:

(1) Verbs like **potere** which forms **potrei**. The **e** between the **t** and the **r** has disappeared. Other common verbs like this are:

| | |
|---|---|
| dovere → dovrei | vedere → vedrei |
| andare → andrei | sapere → saprei |
| vivere → vivrei | avere → avrei |

(2) Other verbs, like **volere** which forms **vorrei**, not only have the shortened form but the first consonant changes and becomes the same as the second, giving **-rr-**. Common are: **rimanere → rimarrei**; **venire → verrei**. **Bere** is a bit of an oddball and can be thought of as being in this group: **berrei**.

(3) The verbs **dare, fare, stare**, make their conditional form thus:

    **dare → darei   fare → farei   stare → starei**

The conditional is used to:

- express what *you would do* if . . .
- ask politely, make requests seem less assertive, make suggestions in a way that is more polite, even charming, as you have already seen:

| | |
|---|---|
| **Dovresti riposarti domani.** | You ought to rest tomorrow. |
| **Saresti molto gentile se . . .** | You would be very kind if you . . . |
| **Potresti aiutarmi?** | Could you help me? |

*Exercise 1* This is what Marco would do if he won a really big prize in a lottery. Write it in Italian:

*Example:* He would go to Australia.
*Answer:* **Andrebbe in Australia.**

1 He would move house. (*cambiare casa*)
2 He would buy a house with a garden.
3 He would marry Anita. (*sposarsi con*)
4 They would learn to play golf.
5 He would not give up work. (*smettere di lavorare*)

*Exercise 2* Well, what would *you* do if you won the big prize in a lottery? This is an open-ended exercise.

## Non vinco mai – saying 'never', 'not ever'

Here is another negative. As with **niente, mica, più**, you must have **non** before the verb:

*Non* escono *mai* la sera. A loro non piace lasciare i bambini con una babysitter.
They never go out in the evening. They don't like leaving the children with a babysitter.

*Non* beve *mai* alcool.
He/she never drinks alcohol.

*Non* ho *mai* capito perchè.
I never understood/have never understood why.

*Exercise 3* You are being asked whether you do certain things. They are things you would never dream of doing! Say so using **mai**.

1  Lei fuma?
2  Beve vodka?
3  Va spesso in discoteca?
4  Compra cibi surgelati (*frozen food*)?
5  Cammina per la strada a piedi nudi?

## Other negative expressions

You have now met several negatives. The remaining ones are:

• **non ... ancora** 'not yet'

*Non* abbiamo *ancora* mangiato. Perchè non viene a mangiare con noi?
We haven't eaten yet. Why don't you come and eat with us?

*Non* sono *ancora* pronto. Puoi aspettare?
I'm not ready yet. Can you wait?

*Note:* **Ancora** without **non** means 'still':

| E' *ancora* molto giovane. | He's still very young. |
| C'è *ancora* tempo. | There's still time. |

or it can be used thus:

| Vuoi *ancora* dell'insalata? | Do you want some more salad? |
| C'è *ancora* del caffè? | Is there still (any more) coffee? |

• **non ... nessuno** 'no one', 'nobody', 'not ... anyone'

| *Non* conosco *nessuno* a Napoli. | I don't know anyone in Naples. |
| *Non* abbiamo visto *nessuno*. | We didn't see anyone. |

It can also precede the verb, in which case **non** is not used:

*Nessuno* fa le lasagne al forno come mia madre.
No one makes lasagne like my mother.

**Nessuno** can be used with a noun, i.e. as an adjective. It then behaves like **un**. When there is a verb and **nessuno** comes after it, **non** must precede it:

*Non* si vende in *nessun* negozio in questo paese.
It's not sold in any shop in this village.

- **nè ... nè** 'neither ... nor', 'not ... either ... or'

  *Non* **conosco** *nè* **la Signora Biondi** *nè* **suo marito.**
  I know neither Mrs Biondi nor her husband/ I don't know either
  Mrs Biondi or her husband.

  *Nè* **Mario** *nè* **Carla possono venire.**
  Neither Mario nor Carla can come.

Notice in the second case, since the **nè . .. nè** precede the verb,
**non** is not necessary. This is always the case when the negative
expression precedes the verb.

Most negatives can be used alone:

  – **Sei andato negli Stati Uniti?** – *Mai.*
  – Have you been to the United States? – Never.

  – **Chi ti ha aiutato a fare tutto il lavoro?** – *Nessuno.*
  – Who helped you do all the work? – No one.

  – **Che cosa hai imparato alla conferenza?** – *Niente.* **Non ho capito!**
  – What did you learn at the lecture? – Nothing. I didn't under-
    stand!

*Reminder:* When used with the **passato prossimo**, **niente**, **nulla** and
**nessuno** go after the past participle. The other negatives go before
the past participle.

  *Non* ho mangiato *niente.*
  *Non* ho visto *nessuno.*

But: *Non* **ho**
| mai |
| più |
| ancora |
**visto il presidente.**

With **nè** the negative word goes in front of what it is negating:

  *Non* ho *nè* mangiato *nè* bevuto.
  *Non* ho mangiato *nè* carne *nè* pesce.

*Exercise 4* Say the opposite of the following:

1 Vado spesso al cinema.
2 Vedo molta gente nella piazza.
3 A Maria piace tanto la musica rock.
4 Carlo ha molti amici.

5 Mangio sempre al ristorante.
6 Il direttore beve molto.
7 Ho molto da fare.
8 E' già arrivato il professore.

## Offering to do something, insisting on doing something

How does Edoardo offer to get the lottery tickets? **Vado io a prenderli**. One of the cases in which you use the pronoun **io** rather than omitting it, is when you are offering to do something. In English you would stress the 'I' with your voice. In Italian you put it after the verb:

| | |
|---|---|
| **Lo faccio io.** | I'll do it. |
| **Pago io.** | I'm paying. |

## Dialogue 2 📼

### Se fossi in te

*Aldo, whose Sicilian holiday we heard about, is troubled. He has been asked by the company he works for to move to the USA for two years to oversee a new development the company is planning. It is a promotion and a challenge he would love to accept. But his wife has her career and the children are in high school (liceo). Enrico spots him looking glum in the canteen and gets him talking*

---

1 Is Patrizia, Aldo's wife, pleased at the prospect of two years in the USA?
2 Why does Aldo think it may be difficult for Maria to go?
3 Enrico thinks it may offer exciting possibilities for Patrizia. In what way?
4 Why does Enrico think it's an opportunity for the children?

---

ENRICO: Bravo, congratulazioni. E' un'occasione meravigliosa. Patrizia dev'essere molto contenta.

ALDO: Magari! Non ho ancora avuto il coraggio di parlargliene. Se fosse casalinga ... Ma ha il suo lavoro che non lascerebbe mai.

ENRICO: Ah, capisco.

ALDO: Poi ci sono i ragazzi. Maria è all'ultimo anno di liceo. Ha la maturità quest'anno e dovrebbe iscriversi all' università in autunno.

ENRICO: Guarda, Aldo. Se fossi in te, ne parlerei subito con Patrizia. Tenerti tutto per te non risolve niente. E poi, chissà? Potrebbe essere un'opportunità anche per lei. Può darsi che possa avere un anno o due di aspettativa. Forse potrebbe lavorare anche negli Stati Uniti o magari fare un master. Lì sono all'avanguardia nel suo campo.

ALDO: Non avevo pensato a questo. E' vero. Se potesse aggiornarsi in un'università, ne avrebbe vantaggi per il suo lavoro. Ma i ragazzi, come potrei convincerli? Se avessero 4 o 5 anni, se facessero ancora le elementari. Ma hanno la loro vita, le loro amicizie. Alla loro età è difficile partire.

ENRICO: Ma Aldo, non lo sai? Due anni negli Stati Uniti e il loro inglese sarebbe perfetto. Oggi è tanto importante per un giovane conoscere bene l'inglese. E anche per loro ci sono possibilità nel campo degli studî.

ALDO: In effetti, hai ragione.

ENRICO: Se fossi in te, presenterei la cosa come una decisione collettiva da prendere insieme nell'interesse dell'intera famiglia.

## Vocabulary

| | |
|---|---|
| **se fossi in te** | if I were you. *You can say* **se fossi te***, but* **in** *is often used.* **Fossi** *is explained below* |
| **magari!** | *here* if only she were! (*see text*) |
| **liceo** | high school |
| **maturità** | the high school leaving certificate in Italy, necessary to enrol in a university |
| **aspettativa** | leave from work |
| **aggiornarsi** | to get up to date |
| **le elementari** | elementary or primary school (*'classes' is understood*) |

## 'If I were you . . .' – the imperfect subjunctive

When you express an idea needing the conditional in the main clause, in the 'if' clause you need the *imperfect subjunctive*. The idea you are expressing is that *if* something were the case, then certain things would follow. You are talking about the improbable or even impossible.

**Se io fossi in te, direi tutto a Patrizia.**
If I were you, I would tell Patrizia everything.

**Se avessi tempo, lo farei volentieri ma oggi non posso.**
If I had time I would happily do it but today I can't.

**Se potesse, ci aiuterebbe.**
If he/she could, he/she would help us.

Language learners tend to panic at the word *subjunctive*. They should try not to. What follows is technical but is given to try to clarify what the subjunctive is. Italian grammarians classify verbs into **modi**. This is usually translated into English by the word 'mood' but 'mode' might convey the sense better since the word refers to the *manner* in which the speaker presents the action or state of the verb. The **modi** are:

**A Modi finiti**, which have tenses and different forms for each person.

(1) The *indicative* (**indicativo**) – the mood for presenting facts, straightforward statements:

**Carlo *mangiava*.**          Charles was eating.

(2) The *imperative* (**imperativo**) – the mood for giving orders:

***Sta'* zitto!**          Be quiet!

(3) The *conditional* (**condizionale**) – the mood for actions which depend on a condition being fulfilled:

**Se venisse, gli *parlerei*.**          If he came, I would speak to him.

(4) The *subjunctive* (**congiuntivo**) – the mood for expressing an element of subjectivity vis à vis the action. For instance, doubt about it, desire that it should take place, etc. In the case we have been dealing with the speaker is expressing lack of probability.

**Se *fosse* casalinga, le cose sarebbero diverse.**
If she were a housewife, things would be different.

*B* **Modi non finiti** – these do not have different forms according to the person.

(1) The *infinitive* (**infinito**) – this can be present or past:

*essere* **o non** *essere*          to be or not to be
*– present*

*avere amato* **e** *avere perduto*   to have loved and lost
*– past (for verbs which use* **avere** *for the* **passato prossimo***)*

*essere andato*          to have gone
*– past (for verbs which use* **essere** *for the* **passato prossimo***)*

(2) The *participle* (**participio**) – the ending can be changed as if it were an adjective:

*finito/a/i/e*          finished

(3) The *gerund*:

*andando* **a Roma**          going to Rome

To come back to the subjunctive, it has four tenses. You can use the imperfect subjunctive without knowing all this but for some learners it helps to get the full picture clear. The form of the imperfect subjunctive is not difficult. Take the same root as for the imperfect indicative (Lesson 13). Any verb which had a special root for the imperfect (e.g. **fare**) will have the same special root in the imperfect subjunctive, with three exceptions, (see below). The endings are as follows:

| *parlare* | *decidere* | *partire* | *fare* |
|-----------|-----------|-----------|--------|
| parl*assi* | decid*essi* | part*issi* | fac*essi* |
| parl*assi* | decid*essi* | part*issi* | fac*essi* |
| parl*asse* | decid*esse* | part*isse* | fac*esse* |
| parl*assimo* | decid*essimo* | part*issimo* | fac*essimo* |
| parl*aste* | decid*este* | part*iste* | fac*este* |
| parl*assero* | decid*essero* | part*issero* | fac*essero* |

The stress is irregular in the first and third person plural, falling on the antepenultimate syllable.

The three verbs which are irregular are:

| *essere* | *dare* | *stare* |
|----------|--------|---------|
| fossi | dessi | stessi |
| fossi | dessi | stessi |
| fosse | desse | stesse |
| fossimo | dessimo | stessimo |
| foste | deste | steste |
| fossero | dessero | stessero |

The stress irregularity occurs in the same places as with the regular verbs.

In the dialogue you met the most common use of the imperfect subjunctive. There are those who say the subjunctive is dying in Italian but this usage is very much alive.

**Exercise 5** How would you say in Italian:

1  If we went to Rome we would see Marco.
2  If he wrote to me I would answer.
3  If we had the money, we would help him.
4  If you won the lottery, Anna, what would you do? (**tu**)
5  If you won the lottery, Prof. Turco, what would you do?
6  If they knew, they would be pleased.

## What 'would you have done if they had . . . '?

Look at these sentences:

>   **Se *avessi saputo*, non *avrei parlato* così.**
>   If I had known, I would not have spoken in that way.

>   **Se *fossimo partiti* un quarto d'ora prima, *saremmo arrivati* in tempo.**
>   If we had set off a quarter of an hour before, we would have arrived in time.

The events have taken place, they are past, but *if only the clock could be put back* . . . In order to express that idea, both tenses have been put into the past, using **avere** plus a past participle in the case of verbs which form their **passato prossimo** with **avere**, and **essere** for those which make it with **essere**. The names given to these tenses are:

*Pluperfect subjunctive*: **avessi saputo,** fossimo partiti

*Past conditional*: **avrei parlato,** saremmo arrivati.

**Exercise 6** Did you ever play the game of consequences? Here are some actions and their consequences. If one thing hadn't happened neither would the other. Or if someone had done something, something else would not have occurred. Can you say this?

*Example:* **Sono arrivata in ritardo. Mio marito si è arrabbiato.**
*Answer:* **Se non fossi arrivata in ritardo, mio marito non si sarebbe arrabbiato.**
(*If I hadn't arrived late, my husband would not have got angry.*)

1  Non mi ha detto che era stanco. Non l'ho aiutato.
2  Ha bevuto tanto. Si è sentito male.
3  E' andato veloce. Ha avuto un incidente.
4  Sono andata alla festa da Giulia. Ho incontrato Tommaso.
5  Ho comprato un biglietto della lotteria. Ho vinto un premio.

*Note:* In colloquial speech this idea can be expressed by two imperfect tenses:

> **Se mi diceva che era stanco, lo aiutavo.**
> If he had told me he was tired, I would have helped him.

> **Se non andavo alla festa di Giulia, non incontravo Tommaso.**
> If I hadn't gone to Giulia's party, I wouldn't have met Tommaso.

This is a way of avoiding the subjunctive which some Italians prefer to take – and you might too.

## Ways of saying 'perhaps'

While talking of the unlikely and what one would do if circumstances allowed, you often need to say: 'perhaps', 'maybe'. Italian has more than one word:

### Forse

**Forse** is problem-free. It expresses doubt, uncertainty, hesitation or possibility, including the idea of hope:

> **Forse viene domani.**
> He/she may be coming tomorrow, perhaps he/she'll come tomorrow.

> **E' stato forse un errore.**
> Maybe it was a mistake.

*Può darsi . . .*

**Può** is of course the third person singular of the verb **potere,** 'to be able'. You can also say **può essere**. Used by itself **può darsi** is very common and no problem but to introduce a clause it becomes **può darsi che** and needs to be followed by a subjunctive:

> **Può darsi che** *possa* **avere un anno o due di aspettativa.**
> Maybe she'll be able to have a year or two's leave.

This form and use of the subjunctive will be dealt with in Lesson 17.

## Magari

**Magari** has two meanings; the tone of voice tells you which.

(a) 'Perhaps' (like **forse**):

| | |
|---|---|
| **Magari viene domani.** | He may be coming tomorrow. |
| **Magari è stato un errore.** | Perhaps it was a mistake. |

(b) 'Would that it were so', expressing strong desire or hope:

| | |
|---|---|
| – **Hai vinto?** | – **Magari!** |
| – Did you win? | – I wish I had! |

| | |
|---|---|
| – **Patrizia deve'essere contenta . . .** | – **Magari!** |
| – Patrizia must be pleased . . . | – I wish she were! |

In this use it can be used with the imperfect subjunctive:

> **Magari fosse vero!**     Would to God it were true!

## Chissà?

This literally means 'who knows'? and can also be written **chi sa?** It is also used to express doubt, uncertainty or vague hopefulness:

> **Ci rivediamo, ma chissà quando.**
> See you again, but goodness knows when.

# Reading

### *Napoli oggi è tutta da scoprire*

*For years Naples had a bad reputation. Recently efforts have been made to make the city safer, cleaner and generally more attractive to visitors. The city was of course, until the unification of Italy, the capital of the Kingdom of the Two Sicilies and has much to offer the visitor in terms of relics of its former glory, beauty of setting, climate, etc.*

---

1  What is happening which hasn't happened for years until now?
2  Why have tourists not been able to enjoy the artistic beauties of Naples in recent years?

---

Era sporca e caotica. Ora torna a respirare. A vivere. A mostrare la sua antica bellezza. Grandi restauri, riaprono i musei e i turisti affollano gli alberghi, come non accadeva da anni. Un miracolo? Macchè, stavolta San Gennaro non c'entra. Vedere per credere. . . .

L'immagine del nuovo sono i turisti che nelle vacanze di Pasqua hanno riempito gli alberghi, ma anche i musei che in quegli stessi giorni sono rimasti aperti, come non accadeva da anni. Perchè a Napoli le bellezze ci sono, ma per troppo tempo sono rimaste dietro a un cancello sbarrato. Come se non esistessero. Invece la città ora ha scoperto che aprire le porte del suo patrimonio è un'impresa possibile . . .

From an article by Fulvio Bufi, *Anna*, 13 maggio, 1995.

## *Vocabulary*

| | |
|---|---|
| **sporco** | dirty |
| **torna a respirare** | it is beginning to breathe again |
| **affollare** | to flock to |
| **accadere** | to happen |
| **stavolta** | this time (*questa volta*) |
| **San Gennaro non c'entra.** | San Gennaro has nothing to do with it. (*San Gennaro is the patron saint of Naples*) |
| **Vedere per credere.** | Seeing is believing. |

| | |
|---|---|
| **riempire** | to fill |
| **un cancello sbarrato** | a barred gate *i.e. permanently closed* |
| **patrimonio** | heritage |
| **un'impresa** | an undertaking, an enterprise |

# 16 Progetti e previsioni – che sarà, sarà

**Plans and predictions – what will be, will be**

---

**In this lesson you will learn how to:**

- Talk about what you intend to do: the future
- Understand business letters
- Say you can manage something – or not manage
- Say you said you would do something
- Make the past participle agree when necessary

---

## Dialogue 1

### *Benissimo. Possiamo firmare*

*Angela Smith had come to Italy to talk about a new project, you may remember. Her company has bought robots for welding from Mr Rossi's company in the past and now plans to update its equipment over the next two years. Here she is with Mr Rossi. Everything has been discussed, the robots have been demonstrated and Angela is satisfied they will meet her firm's needs. She and Mr Rossi are confirming the agreement verbally before signing the contract for the first consignment*

---

1 How many robots is Angela ordering at this stage?
2 What discount has Mr Rossi's company offered?
3 What percentage of the total price will be withheld until one month from the date of installation?
4 Who will see to the installation?

> 5 What does Mr Rossi promise to do during his next visit to England?

ANGELA: Allora, siamo d'accordo. Prendiamo il modello Merlino X390B specifico per saldatura.

ROSSI: Ne avete bisogno di quattro, vero?

ANGELA: Per ora, sì. Ci fate uno sconto del 15%?

ROSSI: Sì, è inteso. Il pagamento si farà come concordato, cioè: il 30% alla firma dell'ordine, il 60% alla consegna e il restante 10% a 30 giorni. La consegna si farà come promesso, cioè fra due mesi. Al momento della consegna verrà un nostro tecnico che provvederà all'installazione dei robot.

ANGELA: Benissimo. Possiamo firmare il contratto, così le verso anche l'assegno.

ROSSI: La ringrazio. Sono sicuro che si troverà bene come sempre anche con questo nuovo modello.

ANGELA: Sicuramente. Spero che venga a vedere dove verranno installati. Così si renderà conto di come stiamo crescendo.

ROSSI: Grazie, mi farebbe piacere. Verrò senz'altro durante il mio prossimo viaggio in Inghilterra.

## *Vocabulary*

| | |
|---|---|
| **firmare** | to sign |
| **saldatura** | welding |
| **pagamento** | payment |
| **la consegna** | delivery, handing over |
| **le verso l'assegno** | I will pay you the cheque (*versare is used in banking to mean 'pay in', 'remit'*) |
| **spero che venga** | I hope you will come (*present subjunctive – Lesson 17*) |
| **si renderà conto di come stiamo crescendo** | you will realize how we are growing |
| **senz'altro** | without fail, of course |

# Language points

## Talking about what you intend to do – the future

**Il pagamento si *farà* come concordato.**
Payment will be made as agreed.

***verrà* un nostro tecnico che *provvederà* all'installazione**
one of our technicians will come and he will take care of the
installation

**Sono sicuro che *si troverà* bene come sempre ...**
I am sure you will be pleased as always ...

***si renderà* conto ...**
you will realize, understand ...

***Verrò* senz'altro durante il mio prossimo viaggio.**
I'll come without fail during my next trip.

**dove *verranno* installati**
where they will be installed

(**Venire** is used here to form the passive – see Lesson 9.)
The future tense is formed on the same base as the conditional,
the infinitive, minus the final **-e**. Here are the future forms of each
type of regular verb and of three irregular verbs. **Essere** is unique;
**avere** and **venire** represent the two types of irregular verbs we
showed you when dealing with the conditional.

| *comprare* | *prendere* | *partire* | *essere* | *avere* | *venire* |
|---|---|---|---|---|---|
| comprer*ò* | prender*ò* | partir*ò* | sar*ò* | avr*ò* | verr*ò* |
| comprer*ai* | prender*ai* | partir*ai* | sar*ai* | avr*ai* | verr*ai* |
| comprer*à* | prender*à* | partir*à* | sar*à* | avr*à* | verr*à* |
| comprer*emo* | prender*emo* | partir*emo* | sar*emo* | avr*emo* | verr*emo* |
| comprer*ete* | prender*ete* | partir*ete* | sar*ete* | avr*ete* | verr*ete* |
| comprer*anno* | prender*anno* | partir*anno* | sar*anno* | avr*anno* | verr*anno* |

*Notes:*

(1) As with the conditional, the vowel in the **-are** infinitive ending
becomes **e**.

(2) There is a one-letter difference in spelling between the first
person plural of the future and the same part of the conditional.
It reflects a difference of pronunciation:

| Future | | Conditional | |
|---|---|---|---|
| **saremo** | we shall/will be | **saremmo** | we should/would be |
| **prenderemo** | we shall/will take | **prenderemmo** | we should/would take |
| **verremo** | we shall/will come | **verremmo** | we should/would come |

It is vital to distinguish the single **m** of the future from the double **m** of the conditional. Pronouncing one **m** or two changes the meaning.

**Exercise 1** Translate these sentences into Italian. They concern the visit of Mr Rossi's technician to install Angela Smith's robots.

1 Our technician will arrive at East Midlands airport at 16.00 on 17 July.
2 He will start the installation on the 18th.
3 He will finish by (**entro**) the end of the month.
4 He will need a room in a hotel.
5 Will it be possible to meet him at the airport? (*meet*: use **prendere**)
6 Will you be able to give him a car for the period?
7 He will explain the robots to your technicians during the installation.

**Exercise 2** You are tired. Someone is asking you whether you have done certain things or whether you are going to do them now. Promise to do each tomorrow.

*Example:* **Sei andato a fare la spesa?**
*Answer:* **Andrò domani a fare la spesa.**

1 Hai spedito le cartoline?
   No, le _____ domani.
2 Vuoi finire questo lavoro oggi?
   No, lo _____ domani.
3 Telefoni a Mario oggi?
   No, gli _____ domani.
4 Vuoi ritirare oggi i biglietti per il nostro viaggio?
   No, li _____ domani.
5 Mi puoi aiutare adesso a fare la traduzione?
   No, ti _____ domani.

## Business letters

Business letters are more difficult than those between friends. It is usual to address a firm or organization as: **Spettabile**, usually abbreviated to: **Spett.le**, and to put the address the letter is going to at the top. **Alla cortese attenzione di** indicates whose attention the letter is for. The subject of the letter is set out in the heading, preceded by the word: **oggetto**. Often a stylized business Italian is still used. Here are two examples of the type of letter Mr Rossi's company (Robotica Milanese) writes and receives:

1 Whose attention is this letter for?
2 Can you guess what ns. and Vs. mean?
3 What is the letter about?

---

Spett.le Ace Motori. S.r.l.
Via Gramsci 121,
Collegno (TO)

Alla cortese attenzione dell'Ing. Mansuco

Cinisello Balsamo, 20/03/95

Oggetto: NS. OFFERTA N. 2430/95

Con la presente, siamo lieti di sottoporVi la ns. migliore offerta per l'impianto di Vs. interesse.

Rimanendo a disposizione per qualunque chiarimento tecnico commerciale, porgiamo distinti saluti.

M. Rossi
Area Manager
Robotica Milanese S.p.A.

---

Note the addressee's name is put at the top right. And with the date of the letter, the place of writing is often stated.

On the next page is an incoming letter:

1 What is the letter asking for?
2 Robotica Milanese will not be surprised to get this request. Why?

---

Spett.le Robotica Milanese,
Via Leonardo da Vinci 10,
Cinisello Balsamo (MI)

Bologna, 10/6/95     Alla C. A. Ing. Tondelli

NS. Rif: 140/95/C

OGGETTO : RICHIESTA DI INTERVENTO

Come già comunicato telefonicamente in data
odierna, con la presente richiediamo con urgenza
il Vs. intervento tecnico su impianto robotizzato
ARTU' da Voi vendutoci.

RingaziandoVi per la collaborazione, con l'occasione porgiamo distinti saluti.

N. Bortolotti
Meccanica Panigale S.p.A.

---

## *Vocabulary*

| | |
|---|---|
| **in date odierna** | of today's date |
| *Common abbreviations are:* | |
| ns. | nostro |
| Vs. | Vostro |
| C.A. | cortese attenzione |
| u.s. | ultimo scorso (*last month*) |
| p.v. | prossimo venturo (*next month*) |
| c.m. | corrente mese (*this month*) |
| gg. | giorni |
| S.r.l. | società a responsabilità limitata (*limited company*) |
| IVA | imposta sul valore aggiunto (*VAT – value added tax*) |

*Openings:*
*To a firm:*             Spett.le ditta/società
*To a man:*            Egregio dott. Manzini
*To a woman:*        Gentile dott.ssa Vasino

*Common closing salutations:*
Porgiamo distinti saluti.
Cogliamo l'occasione per porgerVi i nostri più distinti saluti.
RingraziandoVi anticipatamente, con l'occasione porgiamo distinti saluti.

Note the practice of capitalizing **Voi, Vi** and **Vostro**. It is regarded as a courtesy.

# Dialogue 2

## Un invito

*Angela's visit to her cousin proved to be the start of a friendship. Gabriella had promised to take Angela to spend a day at the farmhouse she and her husband are restoring in the country. On one of Angela's trips to Italy, Gabriella telephones her at her hotel*

---

1 How is Angela going to get to the farmhouse?
2 When must she be ready?

---

GABRIELLA:    Pronto. Angela? Ciao. Sono Gabriella. Come va?
ANGELA:    Gabriella, ciao! Che piacere! Io sto benissimo grazie. E tu?
GABRIELLA:    Anch'io, bene, grazie. Senti, questo fine settimana andiamo in campagna. Ti ricordi che abbiamo una vecchia cascina? Avevamo detto che ti avremmo portata a passare una giornata lì. Vuoi venire con noi questa volta?
ANGELA:    Sì, mi farebbe molto piacere. A che ora partite?
GABRIELLA:    Ci piacerebbe partire presto. Se passiamo a prenderti all'albergo sabato alle otto, ce la fai?
ANGELA:    Certo che ce la faccio. Sarò pronta alle otto.
GABRIELLA:    Allora, arrivederci a domenica.

**avevamo detto**            we had said (*some time in the past*)

## Ce la fai? Farcela 'to manage'

This is a much used idiomatic expression. The two object pronouns, **ce la**, do not refer to anything specific and do not change.

| | |
|---|---|
| **ce la faccio** I am managing | **ce la facciamo** |
| **ce la fai** | **ce la fate** |
| **ce la fa** | **ce la fanno** |

| | |
|---|---|
| **Ce la fai?** | Can you manage (it)? |
| **Non ce la faccio** | I can't manage (it). |
| **Ce l'ho fatta.** | I did it/I've done it. |

Two other common expressions use combined pronouns. In these the first pronoun is a reflexive pronoun and changes with the subject of the sentence.

*Andarsene* 'to go (away), to leave'

| | |
|---|---|
| **me ne vado** I'm going (away) | **ce ne andiamo** |
| **te ne vai** | **ve ne andate** |
| **se ne va** | **se ne vanno** |

*Cavarsela* 'to get by'

| | |
|---|---|
| **me la cavo** I get by | **ce la caviamo** |
| **te la cavi** | **ve la cavate** |
| **se la cava** | **se la cavano** |

## 'We said we would take you ...'

**Avevamo detto che ti avremmo portata ... Avevamo detto** is the imperfect of the auxiliary plus the past participle, corresponding to the English 'we had said'. It puts the saying further back in the past than 'we said', **abbiamo detto**. No problems here. But when reporting words which were originally in the future (**ti porteremo** 'we will take you'), in Italian they are not in the conditional but in the *past conditional*. This is made using **avere** or **essere** according to the verb, plus the past participle. Here are some examples with first the actual words followed by a reported version:

**Arriverò prima delle otto.**
**Ha detto che sarebbe arrivato prima delle otto.**
He said he would arrive before eight.

**Ti aiuterò di sicuro.**

**Mi ha risposto che mi avrebbe aiutato di sicuro.**
He answered that he would certainly help me.

**Andremo al mare domenica.**
**Hanno detto che sarebbero andati al mare domenica.**
They said they would go to the seaside on Sunday.

## Ti avremmo portata . . .

It is usual to make the past participle when used with **avere** agree with a direct object pronoun preceding it. The agreement is also made with **ne**:

**La mela? L'ho mangiata.**
The apple? I've eaten it.

| | |
|---|---|
| **– Dove sono i bambini?** | **– Non lo so, non li ho visti.** |
| – Where are the children? | – I don't know, I haven't seen them. |

*Exercise 3* Complete the past participle in the following sentences:

1 E' arrivata tua mamma? Non l'ho vist _____
2 Hai visto i miei occhiali? Li ho smarrit _____
3 E' buona questa torta. Ne hai mangiat _____
4 Hai assaggiat _____ anche il gelato?

| | |
|---|---|
| **smarrire** | to mislay (**oggetti smarriti** – *lost property*) |
| **assaggiare** | to taste, try (*food, drink*) |

Don't forget that when the verb is conjugated with **essere** the participle agrees with the subject.

**Anna è andata a comprare il pane.**
Anna has gone to buy bread.

## More about the future

When talking about the future the *present tense* is often used, as indeed it is in English:

**Andiamo in campagna questo fine settimana.**
We are going to the country this weekend.

**Andate al cinema stasera?**
Are you going to the cinema this evening?

**Lo faccio subito.**
I'll do it immediately.

It is not *wrong* to use the future in these cases. The future tends to emphasize intention or advance planning, so Angela says:

**Sarò pronta.**
I'll be ready.

**Quest'estate andremo in California.**
This summer we are going (i.e. we have plans to go) to California.

The future can be used when contrasting a *near future* with a more distant future:

Questa sera non usciamo; venerdi però andremo a teatro.

The following expressions are often associated with the future:

| | |
|---|---|
| **entro giovedì** | by Thursday (*by a certain time*) |
| **entro domani** | by tomorrow |
| **fra due ore** | in two hours' time |
| **fra due giorni** | in two days' time |
| **fra poco** | in a little while |
| **la settimana prossima** | next week |
| **l'anno prossimo** | next year |
| **lunedì prossimo** | next Monday |
| **domani** | tomorrow |
| **dopodomani** | the day after tomorrow |

A common use of the future is to suggest something is *possible*, implying it is likely but you can't confirm it as fact:

| | |
|---|---|
| – **Dov'è Giorgio?** | – Where's Giorgio? |
| – **Sarà in ufficio.** | – He'll be in his office/he's likely to be in his office. |

**Anna è partita questa mattina. Sarà già a Roma.**
Anna left this morning. She's probably already in Rome.

Following from this, you will notice the *past conditional* used in journalism, particularly when the journalist is reporting what is thought to have happened rather than a fact:

**Il conducente della macchina si sarebbe addormentato al volante.**
The driver of the car appears to have fallen asleep at the wheel.

**Il ministro avrebbe promesso una nuova riunione con il sinda-
cato per domani.**
It seems the Minister promised a new meeting with the union
tomorrow.

**Exercise 4** Italians, like so many other advanced Western peoples,
enjoy – and indeed often have faith in – horoscopes. Here is a
selection from the women's magazine *Anna*. However, written as
it is, it is not a forecast but a statement of fact, since the verbs are
in the present. Put them into the future (as they were in the
original) to indicate that this is a prediction for the coming week.

## *Cancro*

**Amore:** Chi sta con te non (1 *si annoia*) di sicuro. (2 *Inventi*) a getto
continuo progetti sociali, turistici e culturali insoliti e stimolanti.

**Denaro:** (3 *Hai*) intuizioni fortunate che (4 *rafforzano*) la tua
posizione finanziaria o professionale. Ma dovresti cambiare idea
meno spesso.

**Salute:** (5 *Hai*) i nervi a fior di pelle: nel vero senso della parola, per
il rischio di nevralgie, o perchè (6 *sei*) emotivamente poco stabile.

## *Pesci*

**Amore:** Ti (7 *fai*) guidare dalle emozioni e (8 *prendi*) qualche
iniziativa in campo sentimentale. Ma non (9 *hai*) le idee molto
chiare.

**Denaro:** (10 *Te la cavi*) meglio nei momenti difficili che in quelli
normali. La fortuna (11 *è*) dalla tua parte, con qualche oscillazione.

**Salute:** (12 *Sei*) in buona forma, ma attenta a possibli disturbi alle
gambe a causa delle vene. Se noti dei sintomi, curati subito.

(Guido Montpellier, *Anna* 15–21 aprile, 1995)

## **Vocabulary**

| | |
|---|---|
| **a getto continuo** | in a continuous stream (***getto*** *is a jet of water*) |
| **rafforzare** | to strengthen |
| **i nervi a fior di pelle** | nerves on edge (*lit.* 'on a level with your skin') |
| **curati subito** | see a doctor immediately (***curarsi*** *means 'to get/follow medical treatment'*) |

# 17 Un vestito per un matrimonio

## A dress for a wedding

In this lesson you will learn about:

• Clothes
• Saying what you think, what you want, what you need etc.:
  the present subjunctive

## Dialogue 1

### Desidero che mi dia un consiglio

*Angela has been invited to a wedding and she thinks it would be fun to buy an outfit to wear to it in Italy. However, she doesn't know the shops well and so she telephones Signora Rossi to ask her advice. She starts by asking how Signora Rossi is*

1 Who is getting married?
2 What type of outfit does Angela say she wants?

ANGELA:     Mi scusi se la disturbo. La chiamo perchè desidero
            che mi dia un consiglio.
SIG.RA R:   Ma molto volentieri se posso.
ANGELA:     Ecco: la figlia della mia cugina di Torino si sposa
            a settembre. Mi piacerebbe comprare un abito per
            la cerimonia in Italia ma non so dove si possa
            trovare un vestito adatto che non sia troppo impeg-
            nativo. Infatti, bisogna che sia elegante ma se
            possibile che si adatti anche ad importanti occa-
            sioni di lavoro. Dunque voglio che sia semplice e
            anche che abbia un buon taglio e un bel tessuto.

SIG.RA R:     Non c'è nessun problema, anzi mi farebbe molto
              piacere accompagnarla in qualche negozio. Penso
              che sia possibile trovare qualcosa che le piaccia. E'
              libera domani?

## Vocabulary notes

**ecco** *here, Angela is indicating she is about to give an explanation, a common use of* **ecco**
**vestito** clothes, a dress, an outfit. *The word can be applied to
clothes for men or women*
**abito** a dress (*for a woman*), a suit (*for a man*). (*Add:* **da uomo**
*or* **da donna** *when necessary*)
**impegnativo** exacting, binding. *Angela doesn't want to buy something which will be suitable only for the wedding. There is also
the idea that it should not cost too much.* **Un impegno** *is 'a
pledge'; also 'an engagement'.* **Sono impegnato/a** *means 'I have
an engagement'*
**taglio** cut
**tessuto** fabric, material (*also* **stoffa**)

## Language point

### Saying what you think, what you want, what is needed, etc. – the present subjunctive

We explained in Lesson 15 that the subjunctive is used when there
is an element of subjectivity in the way the action is being
presented. In the dialogue above a number of present subjunctives
occur. Be warned: they do not always translate neatly into a similar
English structure.

**Desidero che mi *dia* un consiglio.**
I want you to give me some advice.

**Bisogna che *sia* semplice ma che *si adatti* anche ad importanti
occasioni di lavoro.**
It needs to be elegant but it must adapt to important working
occasions as well.

**Voglio che *sia* semplice e che *abbia* un buon taglio ...**

I want it to be simple and to have a good cut ... (to be well cut) ...

**Penso che *sia* possibile trovare qualcosa che le *piaccia*.**
I think it is possible to find something you will like.

## Form

The form is not difficult. There are two types: (1) verbs in **-are**, and (2) the rest. In the singular, there is one form for all persons. For this reason the subject pronouns are often used with the subjunctive. The **-ire** group subdivides: verbs which had **-isc-** in the present indicative also have it in the present subjunctive. You will also notice one form which is the same as that of the present indicative for all verbs. Which is it? Also, as you look, think whether one of the parts reminds you of another mood you have met.

| (io) | parl*i* | vend*a* | cap*isca* | part*a* |
|------|---------|---------|-----------|---------|
| (tu) | parl*i* | vend*a* | cap*isca* | part*a* |
| (lui/lei) | parl*i* | vend*a* | cap*isca* | part*a* |
| (noi) | parl*iamo* | vend*iamo* | cap*iamo* | part*iamo* |
| (voi) | parl*iate* | vend*iate* | cap*iate* | part*iate* |
| (loro) | parl*ino* | vend*ano* | cap*iscano* | part*ano* |

The stress in the third person plural is always, as in many other moods and tenses, on the antepenultimate syllable: parlino, capiscano, etc.

Yes, the first person plural, the **noi** form, is the same as for the present indicative. And the singular form is the same as that of the formal imperative (**-are**: **scusi**, other verbs: **senta**, **dica**). Verbs which are irregular in the formal imperative are also irregular in the subjunctive. Common irregular subjunctives are:

| *essere* | *avere* | *andare* | *fare* | *dare* | *dire* | *venire* |
|----------|---------|----------|--------|--------|--------|----------|
| sia | abbia | vada | faccia | dia | dica | venga |
| sia | abbia | vada | faccia | dia | dica | venga |
| sia | abbia | vada | faccia | dia | dica | venga |
| siamo | abbiamo | andiamo | facciamo | diamo | diciamo | veniamo |
| siate | abbiate | andiate | facciate | diate | diciate | veniate |
| siano | abbiano | vadano | facciano | diano | dicano | vengano |

The *perfect subjunctive* is formed with **avere** or **essere** and the past participle:

**Credo che *abbia* finito di piovere.**
I think it has stopped raining.

## Uses

When is the present subjunctive used? This is more difficult to grasp than the form and a comprehensive treatment is beyond the scope of this introductory book. The subjunctive is used mostly in subordinate clauses, and is usually preceded by **che**. The most frequent uses are the following:

(1) After verbs expressing an *opinion*, or perhaps casting doubt: **penso che . . .**, **credo che . . .**; the negative, in particular casts doubt: **non penso che . . .**, **non so se . . .**

> *Penso che* sia possibile ...
> *Credo che* abbia finito ... (I think so, but I am not sure)
> *Non so se* sia possible ...

Compare **secondo me**, a way of saying what you think without needing a subjunctive – or indeed a verb.

(2) After verbs expressing desire, will, regret, fear and some other emotions. The most common is *desire*, wanting.

> *Desidero che* mi dia un consiglio.
> *Voglio che* sia semplice.

*Note:* If the same person is the subject of both verbs you can use the infinitive:

> **Desidero darle un consiglio.**
> I want to give you some advice.
> (*I want* and *I am giving* the advice.)

(3) After a number of *impersonal verbs*: **occorre che, bisogna che, è necessario che, è possibile che, può darsi che, sembra che, pare che, basta che, è meglio che**, etc.

> *Bisogna* che *sia* elegante ma ... che si *adatti* anche ad importanti occasioni di lavoro.
> It must be elegant but it must be usable for important professional occasions too.

(4) After a *relative pronoun* when the clause is referring to a type rather than the particular:

**... qualcosa che le *piaccia***
... something which you like

**Ci vuole *un governo che sappia modernizzare il paese*.**
What is needed is a government which knows how to modernize
the country.

*Note:* If you are describing a particular government, not a type of
government, you would say:

**Abbiamo un governo che sa quello che fa.**
We have a government which knows what it is doing.

(5) The subjunctive is also used after a number of *conjunctions*
including: **benchè** ('although'), **poichè** ('since', 'as' – causal), **perchè**
('so that' – not when meaning 'because'), **prima che** ('before').

**Benchè *abbia* ormai sessant'anni, è sempre molto giovane di
spirito.**
Although he (she) is now sixty, he (she) is very young in spirit.

**Facciamolo prima che *cambi* idea.**
Let's do it before he (she) changes his (her) mind.

All this is probably more than you can absorb in one reading.
However, it needs to be said that the present subjunctive belongs
to fairly formal, careful speech and there is a tendency in spoken
Italian to avoid it. The choice depends on the person speaking and
how careful he wants his way of speaking to be. Many educated
people, however, look down on someone who does not use the
subjunctive: a recent Minister of Education, for instance, was the
subject of some mockery because of his failure to use it.

As you can see the forms are very similar to the indicative so,
as a foreign speaker of Italian, you should not worry unduly. It is
not necessary to master all the intricate details in the relatively
early stages of language learning. The use of the subjunctive which
you learned in Lesson 15 will probably prove more useful to you.
At this stage, you should be noting subjunctives as you meet them.
You will gradually, with practice, understand and be better able to
get them right. Nevertheless, here is some practice for you.

**Exercise 1** In the following exchanges the second speaker is uncertain about the facts. Can you supply the correct form of the verb
to convey this uncertainty:

*Example:* – **Devo andare in banca.**

**– Non credo che (essere) _____ aperta a quest'ora.
Sono già le diciassette. (sia)**

1 – Aldo dice che Giorgio viene alla festa domani. E' vero?
  – Non penso che (venire) _____. Non sta molto bene.
2 – E' partita Anna?
  – Non credo che (essere partita) _____. Mi ha telefonato questa mattina.
3 – Invece di andare a New York, perchè non andiamo a Sydney?
  – Non credo che si (potere) _____ cambiare la destinazione adesso. Il viaggio è tutto prenotato.
4 – Giorgio arriva stasera, vero?
  – Non penso che (arrivare) _____ stasera. Arriva forse domani.
5 – Luisa ha comprato una nuova macchina?
  – Non penso che ne (avere comprata) _____ una. Però la sta cercando.
6 – Aldo è andato in Francia questo fine settimana?
  – Non credo che (essere andato) _____. Voleva andare ma ha avuto dei problemi.

**Exercise 2** Your holiday villa has a maid – what bliss! Tell her what you want her to do this morning.

Voglio che _____.

1 fare i letti.
2 pulire la cucina.
3 lavare questi vestiti.
4 stirare la biancheria lavata ieri.
5 preparare il pranzo per l'una.

**Exercise 3** You are shopping for various things. How would you say 'I'd like . . .':

1 a blouse which is easy to iron.
2 a sweater which can be washed in the machine.
3 a handbag in which there is space for a book.

**Exercise 4** You're talking politics with a friend. Explain what you think are the qualities needed in a Prime Minister: in Italy, **Presidente del Consiglio (dei Ministri)**.

Bisogna che (1 capire) _____ i problemi della gente comune. Nello stesso tempo è necessario che (2 avere) _____ una visione larga del suo lavoro. Ci vuole una persona che (3 sapere) _____ resistere alle pressioni. Naturalmente occorre che (4 essere) _____ molto paziente. Sarà possibile trovare una persona adatta?

# Dialogue 2

## *Alla boutique*

*Signora Rossi and Angela go to a shop where Signora Rossi has often bought clothes for important occasions. She introduces Angela to the owner and explains what Angela is looking for*

---

1 Why does the owner of the shop ask when the wedding is?
2 Angela likes the first outfit she tries on but there is a small problem.
3 Why is Angela pleased with her shopping expedition?

---

NEGOZIANTE: Buongiorno Signora Smith. Sono sicuro che c'è quello che cerca. In che mese è il matrimonio?

ANGELA: Ai primi di settembre.

NEGOZIANTE: Allora andrebbe bene un vestito di seta. A settembre non farà freddo. Venga a vedere qui. Che misura ha?

ANGELA: 44, penso.

NEGOZIANTE: Ci sono tailleur come questi. C'è anche la camicetta ma naturalmente in un'altra occasione la può sostituire. Oppure potrebbe prendere un vestito con giacca, come questi.

ANGELA: Posso provare questo?

*Shortly Angela appears from the changing room wearing the outfit*

SIG.RA R: Che bello! Veramente le sta molto bene questo colore.

ANGELA: Mi piace molto. E' proprio quello che volevo. Ma non è un po' larga la gonna?

NEGOZIANTE: Sì, ha ragione ma gliela possiamo stringere leggermente. Ma non vuole provare un altro vestito? Guardi questo abito a fiori, lo provi. Può darsi che le piaccia di più.

ANGELA: No, veramente mi piace molto questo. Se mi potete stringere la gonna senza che si noti, lo prendo.

*The purchase concluded, Angela and Signora Rossi go for a coffee
in a nearby bar*

| | |
|---|---|
| SIG.RA R: | Il vestito che ha comprato è proprio bello ma come mai non ha voluto provarne ancora uno o due? |
| ANGELA: | Mi è subito piaciuto quello e così abbiamo risparmiato tempo. Mi ero presa tutta la mattinata libera. Che ne dice, Signora Rossi? Andiamo a visitare un museo? |
| SIG.RA R: | Che bella idea! Ma diamoci del tu. E' più facile. |

## *Vocabulary notes*

**boutique** *French word, used to indicate a smart dress shop*

**sono sicuro che ...** I am sure that ... *Since the shop owner is sure, there is no subjunctive here*

**ai primi di settembre** in the first (few) days of September

**andrebbe bene un vestito di seta** a silk dress would be very suitable

**misura** size

**tailleur** suit (*jacket and skirt or coat and dress, for women only*) – *the word is borrowed from French*

**le sta bene** it suits you (***stare bene*** and ***andare bene*** *mean the same*)

**non è un po' larga la gonna?** isn't the skirt a little big (*lit.* 'wide')?

**stringere** (*of clothes*) to take in. ***Stringere*** *means 'to make tight', 'to squeeze';* ***stringere la mano a qualcuno*** *is 'to shake hands'*

**senza che si noti** without it showing. ***Senza che*** *requires a subjunctive*

**abbiamo risparmiato tempo** we've saved time

**che ne dice?** what do you say about it? (*i.e.* do you like the idea?)

**diamoci del tu** let's use 'tu'. *In English: 'let's use first names'. When you use 'tu' you also use first names*

## Ha ragione **'you're right'**

You met this in Lesson 5 and again in Lesson 15. A number of common ideas which in English are expressed using 'to be' and an adjective, in Italian are conveyed by **avere** and a noun:

| | | | |
|---|---|---|---|
| **avere ragione** | to be right | **avere torto** | to be wrong |
| **avere caldo** | to be hot | **avere freddo** | to be cold |
| **avere fame** | to be hungry | **avere sete** | to be thirsty |
| **avere fretta** | to be in a hurry | **avere bisogno di** | to need |
| **avere sonno** | to be sleepy | **avere 17 anni** | to be 17 |

**Ho fame, andiamo a mangiare. C'è un ristorante qui vicino?**
I'm hungry, let's go and eat. Is there a restaurant near here?

**Mi scusi, ho fretta. Devo partire con il treno delle undici. Devo scappare.**
Forgive me, I'm in a hurry. I have to catch the eleven o'clock train. I must fly.

**Ho bisogno di un nuovo vestito.**
I need a new dress/suit.


## Vocabulary

Il vestiario *'clothing'*

| | | | |
|---|---|---|---|
| **biancheria (personale)** | underwear | **impermeabile** | raincoat |
| | | **cappello** | hat |
| **giacca** | jacket | **gonna** | skirt |
| **pantaloni** | trousers | **calze** (*sing.* **calza**) | stockings |
| **camicia** | shirt (man's) | **calzini** | socks |
| **camicetta** | blouse | **collant** | tights |
| **golf** | cardigan, knitted jacket | **tailleur** | (woman's) suit |
| | | **vestito** | (man's) suit, (woman's) dress |
| **cappotto** | overcoat | | |
| **(di) lana** | wool | **largo** | wide, loose |
| **(di) seta** | silk | **stretto** | narrow, tight |
| **(di) cotone** | cotton | **corto** | short |
| **stare/andare bene a (qualcuno)** | to suit (someone) | | |

The world of fashion is one in which imaginations are more than usually lively in the use of words and where foreign words have a particular glamour. Reading the fashion pages you will find writers appear to try to avoid the standard words. It will add to your fun when you read – and you may well find quite a lot of English words which of course sound exotic in Italian!

**Exercise 5** We are now at the end of our course. You have studied the main structures of Italian grammar, been introduced to many of the situations you are likely to find yourself in in Italy and met a very large number of words. The second set of dialogues above contained many of the grammar points you have studied. Can you pick out examples of the following:

1  the conditional?
2  the imperfect?
3  the perfect (**passato prossimo**)?
4  the future?
5  the imperative?
6  personal pronouns, direct and indirect object?
7  combined pronouns?
8  relative pronouns?

And what should you do, especially if you didn't pick them out correctly? Yes, revise those points. Revision allied to seeing and hearing as much Italian as you can, will help you gradually to become more and more at ease with the language.

You are now ready to visit Italy and try out your Italian. Be prepared for surprises, disappointments but also fun and moments to treasure. Here is an invitation.

# Reading 🔘

### Un weekend per due

*You have heard how Naples in the 1990s has become more inviting for the tourist. So, would you like a weekend in Naples? The questions on this final reading passage are in Italian: See how you get on*

1  Per quanti weekend è valida l'offerta speciale Alitalia?
2  In che giorni si parte? Da quali città?
3  Dove si trova l'Hotel Vesuvio?
4  Quale albergo propone un prezzo in cui sono incluse le escursioni nel centro storico?
5  Quale albergo offre una cena a lume di candela?
6  Lei, quale albergo sceglierebbe?
7  E quale escursione le interessa di più?

Sole, mare, arte. E prezzi superscontati! Sognate un romantico weekend a Napoli? Partite subito. L'occasione è da cogliere al volo: per quattro fine settimana, con la tariffa speciale Alitalia 'Napoli Maggio dei Monumenti', il biglietto aereo Milano/Napoli (andata e ritorno) costa solo 200 mila lire (più 12 mila lire di tasse) a persona. Si viaggia in due: partenza il venerdì o il sabato, ritorno la domenica. Il biglietto Roma/Napoli invece costa 100 mila lire.

Dove dormire? In riva al mare, all'Hotel Vesuvio, quattro stelle, proprio di fronte al Castel dell'Ovo. Per due notti in camera doppia, compresa la prima colazione (fatevela portare in camera e sorseggiate il caffè ammirando il Vesuvio e il golfo) si spendono 330 mila lire a persona.

Un weekend di due notti all'Hotel Miramare costa 310 mila lire a persona, incluse le escursioni nel centro storico, le prime colazioni e una cena offerta, venerdì sera, in un ristorante tipico. Dalla collina di Posillipo l'Hotel Paradiso domina il golfo di Napoli. Il prezzo? 220 mila lire a persona per due notti, prima colazione, una cena a lume di candela nel ristorante dell'albergo.

Escursioni e gite. La giornata è bellissima? Saltate sul primo aliscafo in partenza da Mergellina. Destinazione Capri, per un aperitivo in piazzetta e una passeggiata per giardini e stradine, fino ai Faraglioni. Bellissima anche l'isola di Ischia e la piccola Procida, con le sue caratteristiche casette bianche e rosa. Da non perdere gli scavi di Pompei. Raggiungerli è facile: basta prendere, alla Stazione Centrale, la circumvesuviana, e scendere a Villa dei Misteri.

*Anna*, 12 May, 1995.

## Vocabulary

| | |
|---|---|
| **superscontati** | with big discounts |
| **da cogliere al volo** | to seize straight away, *lit.* 'to pluck while in flight' (*there is an element of play on words here, since the offer is of a flight – un volo*) |
| **fatevela portare** | have it brought to you |
| **sorseggiate** | sip |
| **lume di candela** | candle light |
| **aliscafo** | hydrofoil |
| **da non perdere** | not to be missed |
| **la circumvesuviana** | name of a railway line round Vesuvius |

*Places:* curiosity may be aroused by the names:

> **Il Castel dell'Ovo** *this castle is in Santa Lucia, the little port made famous by the song*
> **Posillipo** (*stress on the first* **i**) *an attractive residential neighbourhood*
> **i Faraglioni** *a group of rocky islets with strange shapes off Capri*

**Buon viaggio e buona fortuna!**

# Grammar summary

When grammar points are dealt with in a single lesson, the reader is referred to that chapter. This section contains summaries of points which are scattered over two or more lessons.

## Nouns and articles

| Masculine singular | | | Masculine plural | |
|---|---|---|---|---|
| *Definite article* | *Indefinite article* | *Noun* | *Definite article* | *Noun* |
| il | un | vino<br>padre | i | vini<br>padri |
| l' | un | albergo<br>ambiente | gli | alberghi<br>ambienti |
| lo | uno | spuntino<br>zio<br>studente | gli | spuntini<br>zii<br>studenti |

| Feminine singular | | | Feminine plural | |
|---|---|---|---|---|
| la | una | casa<br>madre<br>stella | le | case<br>madri<br>stelle |
| l' | un' | azienda<br>estate | le | aziende<br>estati |

*Note:* The indefinite article does not have a plural. The partitive article would convey the idea with a plural noun ('some') and can also be used with a single non-count noun, e.g. **pane** 'bread'. The form is **di** + definite article, see *Prepositions with the definite article* below.

## Adjectives

In Italian adjectives must agree with (match) the noun they describe in gender (*m.* or *f.*) and number (*sing.* or *pl.*). There are two main types: (1) those with a masculine singular ending in -**o** and (2) those with a singular ending (both *m.* and *f.*) in -**e**.

|  | Masculine Singular | Plural | Feminine Singular | Plural |
|---|---|---|---|---|
| *Type 1* | ross*o* | ross*i* | ross*a* | ross*e* |
| *Type 2* | verd*e* | verd*i* | verd*e* | verd*i* |

## Adverbs

See Lesson 8.

## Prepositions with the definite article

See Lesson 6. Some common, short prepositions combine with the definite article. Here is the complete table:

|  | *a* | *di* | *da* | *su* | *in* |  |
|---|---|---|---|---|---|---|
| il | al | del | dal | sul | nel | libro |
| l'(*m.* and *f.*) | all' | dell' | dall' | sull' | nell' | { albergo azienda |
| lo | allo | dello | dallo | sullo | nello | studio |
| la | alla | della | dalla | sulla | nella | casa |
| i | ai | dei | dai | sui | nei | negozi |
| gli | agli | degli | dagli | sugli | negli | { alberghi studi |
| le | alle | delle | dalle | sulle | nelle | { case aziende |

In older Italian, **con** and **per** were combined with the definite article, giving **col** and **pel**, etc. This is unusual today, although in speaking **con** is combined with the definite article by some speakers. Learners need not worry about this. In the case of **al**, **del**, etc., where there is a double consonant in the spelling it is because a double consonant is pronounced.

## Pronouns

Summary of the information on personal pronouns given in Lesson 1, 5, 6, 8, and 9.

| Subject | | Direct object (unstressed) | | Indirect object (unstressed) | | Reflexive | | Stressed | |
|---|---|---|---|---|---|---|---|---|---|
| io | I | mi | me | mi | to me | mi | (to) myself | me | me |
| tu | you | ti | you | ti | to you | ti | (to) yourself | te | you |
| lui | he | lo | him | gli | to him | si | (to) himself | lui | him |
| lei | she | la | her | le | to her | si | (to) herself | lei | her |
| lei* | you | la* | you | le* | to you | si* | (to) yourself | lei* | you |
| noi | we | ci | us | ci | to us | ci | (to) ourselves | noi | us |
| voi | you | vi | you | vi | to you | vi | (to) yourselves | voi | you |
| loro they (m.) | | li | them | gli | to them | si | (to) themselves | loro | them |
| loro they (f.) | | le | them | gli | to them | si | (to) themselves | loro | them |

* formal form

*Note:* There exist the subject forms **egli** and **ella**, 'he' and 'she'; also **esso**, **essa**, 'it' and **essi**, **esse**, 'they', 'them', usually used referring to objects or concepts, not people, and in writing rather than speech.

### Stressed or strong pronouns

**Me**, **te**, **lui**, **lei**, **lei** (formal 'you'), **noi**, **voi**, **loro** are used:

(1) after a preposition:

> **Sta parlando di te.**  He's talking about you.
> **Venite con me.**  Come with me.

(2) for emphasis:

> **Ama me, non te.**  He loves me, not you.

## Negatives

Summary of the information in Lessons 3, 13, 14 and 15.

(1) Simple negative: **non** placed before the verb:

***Non* sono italiano.**    I am not Italian.

(2) Stronger:

**non ... mica**        **non ... per niente**
**non ... affatto**     **non ... per nulla**

(3) Other negative expressions:

| | |
|---|---|
| **non ... ancora** | not yet |
| **non ... mai** | never, not ever |
| **non ... niente** ⎫ | nothing, not anything |
| **non ... nulla** ⎬ | |
| **non ... nessuno** | no one, not ... anyone |
| **non ... più** | no longer, not any more |
| **non ... nemmeno** ⎫ | not even |
| **non ... neanche** ⎬ | |
| **non ... neppure** ⎭ | |
| **nè ... nè** | neither... nor, not ... either ... or |

There must be a negative word before the verb. Most of the expressions in (3) above may be placed at the beginning of the sentence. Then the **non** is not necessary:

***Nessuno* sa dov'è andato.**    No one knows where he has gone.

With a compound tense, **niente**, **nulla**, **nessuno** and **nè ... nè** come after the past participle:

**Non ho capito *niente*.**    I didn't understand anything.
**Non ho visto *nessuno*.**    I didn't see anyone.
**Non ha detto *nè* sì *nè* no.**    He didn't say yes or no.

*But:*

**Non ha *mai* lavorato tanto.**    He has never worked so much.
**Non ha *ancora* deciso.**    He hasn't made his mind up yet.
**Non ha *nemmeno* finito**    He hasn't even finished eating.
**di mangiare.**

Most of the negatives can be used without a verb or can stand alone:

– **Ti piace?** – *Affatto.*    – Do you like it (him)? – Not at all.
– **Chi hai visto?** – *Nessuno.*    – Who did you see? – No one.
– **Hai visto Gianni e Paolo?**    – Did you see Gianni and Paolo?
– *Nè* l'uno *nè* l'altro.    – Neither the one nor the other.

## Interrogatives

These are words (pronouns or adjectives) for asking questions:

**Che**[1], **che cosa**, **cosa? What?**
**Quale** (**qual** + vowel – no apostrophe)/**quali? Which?**
**Chi? Who?**
**Come?**[1] How?
**Come mai** means 'why' but introduces a note of surprise into the question.
**Dove? Where?**
**Quando? When?**
**Quanto?**[1] How much?
**Perchè?**[2] Why?

1 **Come, quanto,** (plus verb) and **che** (plus noun or adjective), can also be used as exclamatives:

| | |
|---|---|
| **Come sei elegante!** | How smart you are! |
| **Quanto sei elegante!** | How smart you are! |
| **Che bello!** | How lovely! |
| **Che paura!** | What a fright! |
| **Che fortuna!** | What luck! |

2 **Perchè** also means 'because'.

## Relative pronouns

- **Che** 'who', 'whom', 'which', – can refer to a person or an object and be subject or object of the clause it introduces. See Lesson 4 for detailed treatment.

- **Cui**, not **che**, is used after a preposition:

  **La signora con cui ho parlato è stata molto gentile.**
  The lady who I talked with was very nice.

- **Il cui, la cui, i cui, le cui** mean 'whose'; the article must be the one which would go with the object possessed:

  **Il Signor Rossi, la cui figlia vuole studiare negli Stati Uniti ...**
  Mr. Rossi, whose daughter wants to study in the United States ...

  **L'autore, i cui libri hanno un enorme successo, ha accettato il nostro invito.**

The author whose books are having a great success has accepted
our invitation.

- **Il quale**, **la quale**, **i quali**, **le quali** – 'who', 'which' – can replace
**che** or **cui** and are especially useful to avoid ambiguity:

  **La figlia di mio cugino, la quale lavora in Francia, . . .**
  My cousin's daughter, who works in France, . . .

  **La quale** makes it clear that it is the daughter, not the cousin,
  who works in France.

- **Chi** – 'he who', 'some . . . others', – is used in proverbs and
sayings and sentences such as those below:

  **Chi va piano, va sano e va lontano.**
  He who goes slowly, goes safely and a long way.

  **C'è chi pensa che . . .**
  There are those who think . . .

  **Erano molto allegri: chi cantava, chi ballava, chi rideva . . .**
  They were very happy: some were singing, some dancing, some
  laughing . . .

- **Ciò che, quello che** – 'what' – refers not to specific nouns, rather
to ideas:

  **So quello che bisogna fare.**
  I know what it is necessary to do.

  **Dimmi ciò che pensi.**
  Tell me what you think.

- **Tutto ciò che, tutto quello che** mean 'everything that/which' . . .

  **So tutto ciò che è successo.**
  I know everything that happened.

## Possessives

These ('my', 'your', etc.) are dealt with fully in Lesson 10.

## Demonstratives

- **Questo** 'this', 'this one' has regular forms in **-o, -a, -i, -e**. See Lesson 5.
- **Quello** 'that', 'that one' has a regular form when it is a pronoun. When used as an adjective before the noun its endings are those of the definite article: **quel, quell', quello, quei, quegli, quella, quelle**. See Lesson 5.
- **Ciò** means 'that'. It refers to ideas, phrases, not specific people or objects. It is mostly used with **che** as a relative pronoun:

**Trovo interessante *ciò che* dice.**
I find what (that which) he says interesting.

But it will be found without **che**:

***Ciò* vuol dire che non hai capito.**
That means you haven't understood.

## Indefinites

Reference list of indefinite adjectives (*adj.*) and pronouns (*pr.*):

**uno** (*pr.*) one, someone (*used in the same way as impersonal **si***)
**qualcuno** (*pr.*) someone;
**ogni** (*a.*) every, each (+ *sing.*)
**tutti i . . ./tutte le . . .** (*adj.*) every, each, all (+ *pl.*)
**tutti/e** (*pr.*) everyone (*used without a noun and followed by plural verb*)
**tutti e due/tutte e due** (*pr.*) both. *Note: Used as an adjective the article is needed: **Tutte e due le sorelle** 'Both sisters'*
**ognuno** (*pr.*) each person, everyone (*sing. only*)
**ciascuno/a** (*pr.*), **ciascun/a** (*adj.*) each, each one (*sing. only*)
**qualcosa, qualche cosa** (*pr.*) something
**qualche** (*adj.*) some (+ *sing. noun*) – *refers to a few, not a large number*
**alcuni/e** (*adj. and pr.*) some (*pl.*)[1]
**alcun/a** (*adj. sing.*) *can be used with **non** to form a negative: **Non ho alcun'idea**, I don't have any idea*
**altro/a/i/e** (*adj. and pr.*) other, another[2]
**qualsiasi, qualunque** (*adj.*) any, whatever
**chiunque** (*pr.*) anyone (it doesn't matter who)
**molto, molti/e** (*pr.*); **molto/a/i/e** (*adj.*) much, many

**poco, pochi** (*pr.*); **poco/a/hi/he** (*adj.*) few, little
**un poco, un po'** a little (a bit)
**troppo** (*adj. and pr.*) too much
**tanto** (*adj. and pr.*) so much
**parecchio** (*adj. and pr.*) some, several, a good many, a good deal
**tale/i** (*adj.*) such
**un tale** (*pr.*) *is used to convey* 'someone or other'
**certe persone** some (people)

1 The partitive, **del**, also conveys 'some' but the amount is more open. **Qualche** and **alcuni** mean 'a few'.

2 (a) **Ho comprato altri due libri.** 'I bought two other/more books.' **Altri tre, altri quattro**, etc. (b) **Certe persone pensano questo, altri no.** 'Some people think this, others not.' **Ecco i pomodori. Altro?** 'Here are the tomatoes. Anything else?'

(See also the section on *Negatives*)

# Verbs

## Non-finite moods

See Lesson 15.

### The infinitive

*Present*

There are three main types, ending in (1) **-are**, (2) **-ere**, or (3) **-ire**. For reflexive verbs the reflexive pronoun is attached to the infinitive: **divertirsi**, 'to enjoy oneself'. In a sentence the reflexive pronoun must be the appropriate one for the subject of the verb preceding the infinitive:

    **Vogl*iamo* divertir*ci*.**      *We* want to enjoy *ourselves*.

*Notes:* (a) In group (2), some of the infinitives have a regular stress, on the **e** of **-ere**, while others have the stress on the preceding syllable. e.g. **temere** but **vendere**. The verbs do not differ in form or stress at any other point of the conjugation. (b) Some verbs have infinitives which have become contracted over the centuries, e.g. **bere, produrre, porre**. In some tenses they function from the older infinitive: **bevere, producere, ponere**.

### Past or perfect infinitive

Formed using **avere** or **essere,** according to which of these the verb is conjugated with (see *Compound tenses*), and the past participle (see below).

**avere mangiato** to have eaten  **essere arrivato** to have arrived

*Note:* With reflexive verbs the appropriate reflexive pronoun is attached to the infinitive:

**Sono contento di essermi divertito.**
I am happy to have enjoyed myself.

### The gerund

See Lesson 11.

### The past participle

See Lesson 8.
  Common *irregular* forms are:

#### -ere *verbs*

| | | | |
|---|---|---|---|
| chiudere | chiuso | spendere | speso |
| decidere | deciso | prendere | preso |
| includere | incluso | uccidere | ucciso |
| rimanere | rimasto | scrivere | scritto |
| leggere | letto | chiedere | chiesto |
| vedere | visto *or* veduto | rispondere | risposto |
| perdere | perso *or* perduto | mettere | messo |
| nascere | nato | | |

#### -ire *verbs*

| | | | |
|---|---|---|---|
| aprire | aperto | coprire | coperto |
| offrire | offerto | | |

#### Irregular verbs

| | | | |
|---|---|---|---|
| essere | stato | venire | venuto |
| fare | fatto | dire | detto |
| stare | stato | morire | morto |
| dare | dato | | |

*Note:* These have a *regular* past participle:

| | | | |
|---|---|---|---|
| avere | avuto | potere | potuto |
| volere | voluto | dovere | dovuto |

| | | | |
|---|---|---|---|
| andare | andato | uscire | uscito |
| sapere | saputo | | |

## Finite moods

See Lesson 15.

### The indicative – simple tenses

*Present*

(summary of information in Lessons 1–5)

**Regular verbs** *Note:* Verbs in **-ire**, divide into (1) those which have an extra syllable, **-isc-**, in some parts of the present tense and (2) those which form their present tense exactly like verbs in the **-ere** group.

| -are | -ere | -ire (1) | -ire (2) |
|---|---|---|---|
| parlo | vendo | capisco | parto |
| parli | vendi | capisci | parti |
| parla | vende | capisce | parte |
| parliamo | vendiamo | capiamo | partiamo |
| parlate | vendete | capite | partite |
| parlano | vendono | capiscono | partono |

In the third person plural of all these verbs the stress falls on the antepenultimate syllable.

**Spelling** (1) Verbs ending in **-care**, **-gare**, **-ciare**, **-giare**, **-sciare**. The sound does not change and the spelling is adapted to show this. The first two types (**-care**, **-gare**) insert an **h** before **i** in the ending; the others (**-ciare**, **-giare**, **-sciare**) omit the **i** of the stem before **i** or **e**. This is also true in other tenses.

cerco, cerchi, cerca, cerchiamo, cercate, cercano
pago, paghi, paga, paghiamo, pagate, pagano
comincio, cominci, comincia, cominciamo, cominciate, cominciano
mangio, mangi, mangia, mangiamo, mangiate, mangiano
lascio, lasci, lascia, lasciamo, lasciate, lasciano

(2) Verbs ending in **-cere**, **-ggere**. With verbs in the **-ere** group

the opposite happens: the spelling does not change because the sound does:

vincere: vinco, vinci, vince, vinciamo, vincete, vincono
leggere: leggo, leggi, legge, leggiamo, leggete, leggono

## Imperfect

For a table of regular forms see Lesson 13. Few verbs are irregular and they are fully dealt with in Lesson 13.

## Future

For a table of regular forms see Lesson 16. The following verbs are *irregular* in the future tense:

(a) **Essere: sarò, sarai, sarà, saremo, sarete, saranno.**

(b) Verbs which lose the vowel of their infinitive. The endings follow the regular pattern: **andare: andrò, andrai, andrà, andremo, andrete, andranno; avere: avrò; dovere: dovrò; sapere: saprò; vedere: vedrò; vivere: vivrò.**

(c) Verbs which lose the vowel and also have the final vowel of the stem of the infinitive changed to become the same as the second, giving **-rr-: rimanere: rimarrò; venire: verrò; volere: vorrò.**

(d) **Bere: berrò.**

(e) **Dare: darò; fare: farò; stare: starò.**

The first and third person singular are stressed on the final vowel which is written with an accent to indicate this.

## Past definite

This tense has not been presented in the text, but its use is explained briefly in Lesson 13.

| | | |
|---|---|---|
| parl*ai* | vend*ei (etti)* | cap*ii* |
| parl*asti* | vend*esti* | cap*isti* |
| parl*ò* | vend*è (ette)* | cap*ì* |
| parl*ammo* | vend*emmo* | cap*immo* |
| parl*aste* | vend*este* | cap*iste* |
| parl*àrono* | vend*èrono (ettero)* | cap*ìrono* |

*Notes:* (a) The stress falls regularly except in the third person singular, where the accented vowel is stressed, and the third person plural where the stress falls on the antepenultimate syllable.

(b) In the **-ere** group of verbs there are alternative forms for the first and third person singular and third person plural. Many verbs in this group are irregular in this tense. They are irregular in the first and third person singular and the third person plural, but regular in the other parts. Therefore if you know the first and second person singular you can form the remaining parts. **Bere**, **dire**, **fare** form the **passato remoto** from their older infinitives. Below are some examples:

> avere: ebbi, avesti, ebbe, avemmo, aveste, ebbero
> dire: dissi, dicesti, disse, dicemmo, diceste, dissero
> fare: feci, facesti, fece, facemmo, faceste, fecero
> vedere: vidi, vedesti, vide, vedemmo, vedeste, videro

Given the first and second person the others may be formed on these models.

| | |
|---|---|
| bere: bevvi (bevetti), bevesti | nascere: nacqui, nascesti |
| chiedere: chiesi, chiedesti | prendere: presi, prendesti |
| chiudere: chiusi, chiudesti | rimanere: rimasi, rimanesti |
| conoscere: conobbi, conoscesti | rispondere: risposi, rispondesti |
| decidere: decisi, decidesti | sapere: seppi, sapesti |
| leggere: lessi, leggesti | scendere: scesi, scendesti |
| mettere: misi, mettesti | uccidere: uccisi, uccidesti |

Also irregular are:

| | |
|---|---|
| essere: fui, fosti, fu, fummo, foste, furono | |
| dare: diedi, desti | stare: stetti, stesti |
| venire: venni, venisti | vivere: vissi, vivesti |
| volere: volli, volesti | |

### The indicative – compound tenses

### Present perfect

(See also Lessons 10, 11, 15. 16.) This is formed with the present tense of **avere** or **essere** and the past participle.

**A** Verbs conjugated with **essere** include:

(1) Verbs of motion: **andare, venire, arrivare, partire, entrare, uscire, salire, scendere, tornare, passare da** ...

(2) Verbs indicating a change of state: **ingrassare, dimagrire, diventare, divenire, aumentare, diminuire, migliorare** ...

(3) **Essere, stare, nascere, morire, piacere.**

(4) Verbs used reflexively.

(5) Verbs used impersonally, e.g. **è sembrato** ('it seemed').

(6) Verbs relating to weather conditions can be conjugated with **essere**, but they will also be found with **avere**: **è nevicato** and **ha nevicato**.

The past participle must agree with the subject:

| | |
|---|---|
| sono andato/a | siamo andati/e |
| sei andato/a | siete andati/e |
| è andato/a | sono andati/e |
| | |
| mi sono divertito/a | ci siamo divertiti/e |
| ti sei divertito/a | vi siete divertiti/e |
| si è divertito/a | si sono divertiti/e |

**B** All other verbs are conjugated with **avere**:

| | |
|---|---|
| ho finito | abbiamo finito |
| hai finito | avete finito |
| ha finito | hanno finito |

The past participle does not agree with the subject. If there is a direct object pronoun preceding the verb, it agrees with that: **I biscotti? Li ho finiti.**

Other compound tenses can be formed, with **essere** or **avere** according to the verb:

*Pluperfect*

The imperfect of **avere** or **essere** plus the past participle:

**avevo finito** I had finished    **ero andato/a** I had gone

*Future perfect*

The future of **avere** or **essere** plus the past participle:

**avrò finito** I shall have finished **sarò andato/a** I shall have gone

## The conditional

See Lesson 15.

### Conditional perfect

**avrei parlato** I would have spoken
**sarei andato/a** I would have gone, *etc.*

## The imperative

(Summary of Lesson 6.) There is no first person singular for the imperative; and the third person plural is rarely used since the formal plural, **loro**, is rarely used. The plural 'you' is normally **voi**. As in the present indicative, the **-ire** group subdivides. An example of each type is given.

| | | | |
|---|---|---|---|
| parl*a* | vend*i* | cap*isci* | part*i* |
| parl*i* | vend*a* | cap*isca* | part*a* |
| parl*iamo* | vend*iamo* | cap*iamo* | part*iamo* |
| parl*ate* | vend*ete* | cap*ite* | part*ite* |
| parl*ino* | vend*ano* | cap*iscano* | part*ano* |

The stress is regular except that in the third person plural form it falls on the antepenultimate syllable.

## The subjunctive

(1) *Present* – see Lesson 17.

(2) *Perfect subjunctive* – this is formed using the present subjunctive of **avere** or **essere** and the past participle:

abbia parlato                   sia andato/a

(3) *Imperfect* – see Lesson 15.

(4) *Pluperfect* – this is formed with the imperfect subjunctive of **avere** or **essere** and the past participle:

avessi parlato                  fossi andato/a

# The passive

All the verbs above are *active*. Those which can take a direct object can be made passive using **essere** and the past participle, or sometimes **venire** or **andare** and the past participle (see Lessons 8 and 9).

| | |
|---|---|
| *Present:* | **Il lavoro è fatto a mano.**<br>The work is done by hand. |
| *Perfect:* | **Il lavoro è stato fatto a mano.**<br>The work has been/was done by hand. |
| *Imperfect:* | **Il lavoro era fatto a mano.**<br>The work was being done/used to be done by hand. |
| *Future:* | **Il lavoro sarà fatto a mano.**<br>The work will be done by hand. |
| *Future perfect:* | **Il lavoro sarà stato fatto a mano.**<br>The work will have been done by hand. |
| *Conditional:* | **Il lavoro sarebbe fatto a mano.**<br>The work would be done by hand. |
| *Conditional perfect:* | **Il lavoro sarebbe stato fatto a mano.**<br>The work would have been done by hand. |
| *Present subjunctive:* | **Occorre che il lavoro sia fatto a mano.**<br>The work must be done by hand. |
| *Imperfect subjunctive:* | **Voleva che il lavoro fosse fatto a mano.**<br>He wanted the work to be done by hand. |

# Verbs and other expressions followed by an infinitive

To express certain ideas, we frequently need to use a verb, an adjective, or a noun followed by a verb. In this case this following verb is in the infinitive. The precise structure necessary will depend on the first word.

- No preposition is required after: **dovere, potere, volere, lasciare, piacere, preferire, sapere, vedere; basta, bisogna, facile, difficile, possibile, impossibile, necessario; bene, meglio.**

| | |
|---|---|
| **Mi piace ballare.** | I like dancing/to dance. |
| **Basta telefonare.** | All you need to do is telephone. (*lit.* 'It is enough to telephone.') |

**E' difficile sapere che cosa fare.**
It's difficult to know what to do.

- The preposition **a** is required after a number of verbs including: **andare, abituarsi, cominciare, imparare, provare, venire**; and certain *adjectives*; **abituato, pronto**:

| | |
|---|---|
| **Vado a sciare domenica.** | I am going skiing on Sunday. |
| **Comincia a piovere.** | It's beginning to rain. |
| **Sei pronto a fare il bagno?** | Are you ready to bathe/have a bath? |

- The preposition **di** is required after many *verbs*, e.g. **credere, decidere, dimenticare, ricordarsi**; *adjectives* such as: **contento, felice**, and *nouns*, usually used with **avere: avere paura di, avere bisogno di**.

| | |
|---|---|
| **Credo di farcela.** | I believe I can manage it. |
| **Ha deciso di partire domani.** | He has decided to leave tomorrow. |
| **Sono contento di sapere che stai meglio.** | I am pleased to know you are better. |
| **Ho paura di fare un errore.** | I am afraid of making a mistake. |

Students are advised to consult a good dictionary when in doubt.

# Key to exercises

## Lesson 1

**Al bar** Aranciata – this is a fizzy orange drink; Coca-Cola.

**Prima colazione** 1 Maria has a bun; Piera has a pastry. 2 Maria drinks a white coffee, Piera black.

**Exercise 1** **un** vino rosso, **un** gelato, **una** birra, **un** caffè, **un'** acqua minerale, **una** spremuta, **un** succo di frutta, **un** tè, **un** vino bianco, **un'** aranciata.

**Exercise 2** 1 un cappuccino 2 un'aranciata 3 una spremuta di arancia 4 una birra

**Exercise 3** (1) 7, (2) 9, (3) 400, (4) 803, (5) 2.500, (6) 1.300, (7) 10.000, (8) 6.100

**Exercise 4** 1 Cinquemilanovecento lire 2 Quattromiladuecento lire 3 Duemiladuecento lire 4 Milletrecento lire 5 Seimila lire 6 Cinquemilasettecentolire 7 Seimilaottocento lire

**Un appuntamento con il signor Rossi** 1 to wait a moment and to sit down 2 S'accomodi

**Un incontro per la strada** Because the teacher has to go, presumably he's hurrying somewhere.

**Exercise 5** – Buongiorno, signor Rossi, come va? – Bene grazie. E lei? – Bene. Devo andare. Arrivederla. – Arrivederla (Buongiorno).

***Exercise 6*** In ***Al bar:*** 1 Prego. *lit.* I beg, request. 2 Va bene. *lit.* It goes well. It's fine, OK. In ***Prima colazione:*** 3 Desidera? *lit.* You desire? i.e. What would you like? In ***Un appuntamento con il signor Rossi:*** 4 Sono Angela Smith. I am A.S. 5 Come va? How are you? In ***Un incontro per la strada:*** 6 Ha un raffreddore. He has a cold. 7 Mi dispiace. *lit.* it is displeasing to me. I'm sorry. 8 Sta bene. He's well. 9 Lavora molto. He's working a lot. 10 Devo andare. I have to go.

***Bar famosi*** 1 In 1720. 2 Sparkling white wine and peach juice. 3 Yes. The food is very good, but the bill would be substantial. 4 Arrigo Cipriani.

***Exercise 7*** You should find it easy to make the list and the lesson gives you help with all the meanings.

# Lesson 2

***Sono americano, e lei?*** 1 In Boston. 2 In Rome. 3 His mother is Italian, from Siracusa in Sicily. 4 His brother lives in Los Angeles and he finds the US friendly and interesting. 5 Yes. He likes Bologna: it is friendly and interesting.

***Exercise 1*** 1 Gérard Depardieu è francese. 2 Placido Domingo è spagnolo. 3 Sofia Loren è italiana. 4 Brigitte Bardot è francese. 5 Robert de Niro è americano. 6 Meryl Streep è americana. 7 Roma è una città italiana. 8 New York è una città americana. 9 Rio de Janeiro è una città brasiliana. 10 Toronto è una città canadese. 11 Sydney è una città australiana. 12 Tokio è una città giapponese.

***Exercise 2*** Chiara studia. Lucia canta. Paolo fuma. Luigí balla. Anna telefona. Marco lavora.

If you were doing them you would say: 1 Canto. 2 Fumo. 3 Lavoro. 4 Telefono. 5 Ballo. 6 Studio.

***Exercise 3*** Mi chiamo Charlie Hardcastle. Sono sudafricano. Abito a Johannesburg. Parlo inglese e francese. Mia madre è francese, di Bordeaux. Bordeaux è una città simpatica.

***Exercise 4*** 1 Mi piace lavorare. 2 Mi piace New York. 3 Mi piace

cantare. 4 Mi piace Roma. 5 Mi piace parlare italiano. 6 Mi piace
Luciano Pavarotti.

**Exercise 5** 1 Devo telefonare. 2 Devo lavorare. 3 Devo venire.
4 Devo studiare.

**Mi chiamo Paolo Bianchi** 1 His name is Paolo Bianchi. 2 From
Milan. 3 In Milan. 4 In a hospital in Milan. 5 He is tall and fair-
haired. 6 Yes. 7 He likes playing tennis and he also likes classical
music.

**Exercise 6** 1 sono 2 sono 3 abito (*or* lavoro) 4 lavoro 5 sono

**Exercise 7** Mi chiamo Giorgio. Sono italiano. Abito a Napoli. Mia
madre abita a Roma con mio fratello. Sono medico in un ospedale
a Napoli. Mi piace il mio lavoro. Sono sportivo e mi piace giocare
a golf e a tennis. Mi scusi, devo scappare. Mi dispiace. Arrivederci.

**Mi chiamo Luisa Lucchini** 1 History and geography. 2 Yes, she
likes tennis and golf. 3 Because it is a big, lively city, interesting
and stimulating. *You may also have said*: She likes opera and in
Milan there is La Scala opera house.

**Exercise 8** *Possible combinations are:* una birra: bionda, australiana; una signora, una madre, una signorina: romana, bionda,
australiana, vivace, interessante, romana; un signore, un marito, un
fratello, un professore: alto, simpatico, interessante, americano,
sportivo, vivace, sposato; un vino: bianco, americano, vivace, interessante, simpatico; un lavoro, un paese: interessante, simpatico; una
città: interessante, australiana.

**Suo marito, come si chiama?** 1 He is a good pianist. 2 No, he
is Scottish. 3 He works in a bank. (He is an accountant or financial adviser.) 4 No. He's mad about do-it-yourself. 5 In Toronto,
Canada, presumably, since that is where Bill works.

**Exercise 9** 1 Sono australiana. Sono alta e bionda. Sono sposata.
Lavoro a Sydney. 2 Sono canadese. Sono sposato. Mia moglie è
inglese. Abito a Milano. 3 Sono italiano, sono siciliano, di Palermo.
Mi chiamo Salvatore. Abito a Bologna. Lavoro in una banca. Sono
sposato e mia moglie è scozzese. E' insegnante. 4 E' australiana,
alta e bionda, sposata e lavora a Sydney. 5 E' canadese. E' sposato.

Sua moglie è inglese. Abita a Milano. 6 E' italiano, siciliano, di
Palermo. Si chiama Salvatore. Abita a Bologna e lavora in una
banca. E' sposato e sua moglie è scozzese. E' insegnante.

## Lesson 3

*A Perugia* 1 It's the town hall. 2 Along Corso Vannucci, the main
street. 3 To see the view over the valley towards Assisi.

*Exercise 1* You should have found: (*in Dialogue 1*) Lei è
americano? E lei? Lei è in Italia per lavoro? E lei? E' a Bologna
per lavoro? (*in Dialogue 2*) E suo marito, come si chiama? Che
lavoro fa? (*twice*) E come passa il suo tempo libero? E' sportivo,
ama lo sport?

*Exercise 2* 1 il 2 il 3 la 4 la 5 il

*C'è una banca qui vicino?* 1 He asks whether there is a bank
nearby. 2 Because he thinks the bank is shut at that time.

*Exercise 3* 1 C'è un ristorante qui vicino? 2 C'è una farmacia qui
vicino? 3 C'è un albergo qui vicino? 4 C'è una fermata
dell'autobus qui vicino? 5 C'è un supermercato qui vicino?

*Scusi, dov'è il consolato americano?* The passerby doesn't
know where it is and suggests the tourist asks at the town tourist
office.

*Exercise 4* 1–V (vero), 2–V, 3–F (falso), 4–F, 5–V. Only you can
answer 6–12.

*Exercise 5* 1 No, non lavoro qui. 2 No, non abito in questa città.
3 No, non sono qui in vacanza. 4 No, non sono americano/a. 5
No, non parlo francese.

*Exercise 6* 1 La Mole Antonelliana (*the symbol of the city of
Turin, in the way the Leaning Tower is for Pisa*). 2 Piazza San Carlo
(*a lovely square*). 3 Il Duomo (*where the Turin Shroud is kept*).

*Exercise 7* open

*Exercise 8* 1 vedo 2 Dipende 3 chiedere; abito 4 Prenda 5 Chiedo 6 abita 7 piace 8 chiama 9 lavora 10 vedi; prendi

**A Roma** 1 It used to be the residence of the Venetian ambassadors. (Venice was an independent republic until 1797. Rome was, until 1870, the capital of a state whose head was the Pope.) 2 Because it is a monument to the first king of the united Italy, Victor Emmanuel II, who was the figurehead and rallying point of the movement for unification. 3 It was the religious centre. 4 Because it runs through the area of the imperial forums/fora. 5 Between Piazza Venezia and Piazza del Popolo.

# Lesson 4

*Devo andare a Torino* 1 Almost hourly. 2 Two, Novara and Vercelli. 3 45.000 lire with the supplement for the express train.

*Exercise 1* 1 diciotto 2 settantasette 3 cinquantadue 4 trentanove 5 sessantuno

*Exercise 2* 1 millesessantasei 2 milleduecentoquindici 3 millequattrocentonovantadue 4 millesettecentoottantanove 5 milleottocentoquarantotto 6 millenovecentodiciotto

*Exercise 3* 1 Sono le quattro e un quarto. 2 Sono le due e mezzo. 3 E' mezzogiorno meno cinque (*or you may have thought it was nearly midnight:* E' mezzanotte meno cinque). 4 Sono le tre e dieci. 5 Sono le due meno un quarto.

*Exercise 4* open

*Exercise 5* 1–e, 2–f, 3–d, 4–c, 5–a, 6–g, 7–b.

You would say: 1 Ballo ... 2 Visito ... 3 Prendo ... 4 Guardo ... 5 Leggo ... 6 Scrivo ... 7 Parto ...

*Exercise 6* 1 E' 2 Abita 3 lavora 4 deve 5 parte 6 arriva 7 torna 8 finisce 9 dorme 10 preferisce 11 decide (lui)

*Vorrei andare in Piazza Castello* 1 No. 2 She has to get off behind the cathedral. She then has to take a little street which will take her into Piazza Castello. 3 The 15.

***Come si fa a prendere l'autobus?*** From a tobacconist, a newsagent, in a bar, or wherever there is a sign saying tickets are sold there. 2 In cities, generally one pays the same price for all journeys regardless of distance. 3 Because you are in touch with people and you avoid parking problems.

***L'aeroporto*** 1 Because English is much used in airports (and in the air). 2 When the flight is going to an English-speaking country.

# Lesson 5

***Vorrei una guida*** 1 A small, pocket one. 2 No. The shop has only one sort at the moment.

***Exercise 1*** 1–F, 2–V, 3–V, 4–F, 5–F.

***Exercise 2*** Alberto is a very polite (well brought-up) boy. At the moment he is at high school. He is a very good student. He likes reading and often goes to bookshops to look at and buy books.

***Exercise 3*** 1–b, 2–d, 3–a, 4–e, 5–c.

***Exercise 4*** 1 Vorrei andare a Roma. 2 Mi dispiace, non posso andare a Roma. 3 Potrei vedere il libro? 4 Puoi (*formal* può) giocare a tennis domani? Mi dispiace, non posso. Devo andare a Milano. 5 Non voglio partire domani. 6 Si può partire per Roma stasera? Mi dispiace, non si può. 7 Vorrei una birra. 8 Si può pagare con la carta di credito? 9 Si può vedere l'Etna da qui?

***Cinque cartoline per favore*** 1 Ten, five small and five large. 2 The USA.

***Exercise 5*** 1 No, tre caffè. 2 ... quattro aranciate. 3 ... cinque birre. 4 ... sei acque minerali. 5 ... sette spremute di arancia. 6 ... otto cappuccini.

***Exercise 6*** 1 L'albergo ... 2 La città ... 3 I ragazzi ... 4 Le cartoline ... 5 I francobolli ... 6 Lo studente ... 7 Gli uffici ... 8 Il monumento ... 9 Gli scontrini 10 Le città ...

***Exercise 7*** 1 Quell'albergo ... 2 Quella città ... 3 Quei ragazzi ... 4 Quelle cartoline ... 5 Quei francobolli ... 6 Quello studente

... 7 Quegli uffici ... 8 Quel monumento ... 9 Quegli scontrini. 10 Quelle città ...

**Exercise 8** 1 Preferiamo 2 Arriviamo 3 Comprano 4 Capite 5 Partono 6 Prendono

**Exercise 9** (A) 1 andiamo 2 guardiamo 3 leggiamo 4 invitiamo 5 vogliamo (B) 1 lavorano 2 cominciano 3 tornano 4 mangiano 5 Finiscono 6 vogliono 7 devono

**Il mercato in Italia** 1 Because each little town and each district in the big towns has one at least once a week. 2 Because people come in from the surrounding areas to meet each other.

# Lesson 6

**Vorrei parlare con il signor Rossi** 1 Next week, when she will be in Italy. She suggests Wednesday at 9 a.m. 2 He invites Angela to have dinner with him and his wife.

**Exercise 1** 1 il mese prossimo 2 il mese scorso 3 l'anno prossimo 4 l'anno scorso 5 ogni anno 6 domani mattina 7 ieri pomeriggio

**Exercise 2** 1 Il primo maggio 2 Il venticinque dicembre 3 Il quattordici luglio 4 L'undici giugno 5 Il venticinque aprile 6 Il venti settembre

**Exercise 3** (1) 115 (2) 118 – or perhaps 113, general emergency number (3) 113 (4) 12 (5) 161

**Andiamo al cinema** 1 Monday and Wednesday. 2 At Marisa's house.

**Exercise 4** ... Biblioteca *sulla* salute e *sullo* sport ... La possibilità *nella* bella stagione di allenarsi *all'* aperto ... *dal* lunedì *al* venerdì *dalle* ore 9.00 *alle* ore 21.15, il sabato *dalle* ore 10.00 *alle* ore 12.30
    ... pranzo *nel* corso *dell'* intervallo ... che segue *allo* shopping, ... prima *dello* spettacolo ... sala *del* centro, ... l'altra *nella* città ...

*Exercise 5* More logical order: 5, 2, 4, 6, 1, 3 (*or perhaps:* 3, 1)

*Exercise 6* 1 Si sveglia alle sette. 2 Si alza. 3 Fa la doccia. 4 Si veste. 5 Si pettina. 6 Fa colazione. 7 Si prepara ad andare a lavorare.

*Exercise 7* 1–d, 2–h, 3–g, 4–e, 5–a, 6–c, 7–b, 8–f

*Exercise 8* 1 prendi 2 gira 3 va' 4 andare 5 gira 6 sta' 7 girare 8 rallenta 9 prendi 10 cerca 11 facciamo

*Exercise 9* 1 Mi dica 2 Mi dia 3 Abbia pazienza 4 Mi scusi 5 Si accomodi 6 Aspetti

*La domenica in Italia* 1 Because, while many adults do not work, the children are at school in the morning. 2 Having relations to lunch; going for a walk – in the park, through the streets of the town, or in the country; going to the cinema; watching a football match, or listening to the radio commentary while out walking with the family; skiing. 3 To the sea or to the country.

# Lesson 7

*All'albergo (1)* 1 Two double rooms. 2 They should have bathrooms and be quiet. They don't mind whether the beds are double or single. 3 She asks to see the rooms.

*Exercise 1* 1 due giorni 2 due settimane 3 due mesi interessanti 4 due nuovi progetti 5 due banche 6 due giornali 7 due cappuccini 8 due birre 9 i nuovi film 10 gli spettacoli 11 i giornali interessanti 12 i supermercati francesi 13 le nuove gallerie 14 le strade che vanno in città 15 gli adulti responsabili 16 i vini rossi

*All'albergo (2)* 1 Taxes and service are included; breakfast is not. 2 Behind the hotel, at the end of the courtyard.

*Exercise 2* The order should be: 8, 1, 10, 2, 13 (*or:* 8, 2, 13, 1, 10), 4, 14, 3, 5, 9, 7, 12, 15, 6, 11

*Vorrei un po' di frutta* 1 They are very sweet, good for juicing. 2 She wants bananas, grapefruit and apples. 3 1,000 lire (½ kilo at 2,000 a kilo).

**Exercise 3** Quanto costano: le albicocche? le ciliegie? i limoni? i meloni? le pesche? le prugne? le arance? le fragole? le mele? le pere? i pompelmi? le susine? *but* Quanto costa l'uva?

**Ho bisogno di formaggio** 1 300 grammes. 2 Ham, cured ham, not cooked.

**Exercise 4** 1 Trentaduemila (lire) al chilo. 2 Trentanovemila (lire) al chilo. 3 Seimilacinquecento il pecorino. 4 Tremilaotto il prosciutto. 5 Diecimilatrecento in tutto.

**Exercise 5** Vorrei 1 dei limoni, 2 dei francobolli, 3 del caffè, 4 del formaggio, 5 dell'uva, 6 dell'acqua minerale, 7 delle arance, 8 delle pesche, 9 del pane.

**Ci sono altri colori?** 1 For his wife. 2 A green one. 3 Because his sister likes to wear her sweaters big.

**Exercise 6** 1 (a) compri (b) compro (c) comprate (d) compriamo 2 (a) leggo (b) legge (c) leggono 3 (a) preferisco (b) preferisce 4 (a) parlano (b) parlo (c) parla (d) parli 5 (a) vivono (b) viviamo

**Che cosa pensano gli Italiani?** 1 That she is the most beautiful woman in the world. 2 70%. 3 Not many go regularly: 46% go once a year; 12% go less often; 9% never go to confession at all. 4 Being Italian. 5 Food and music.

# Lesson 8

**Un po' di geografia** (V = vero, F = falso) 1–F. 2–F – they are to be found in the Alps. 3–F – quite the opposite: three quarters is mountain or hill. 4–V. 5–F – they both have a long history of industrial development. 6–F – the Appenines are. 7–F – it is still active. 8–F. 9–V.

**Exercise 1** 1 Il fax deve essere spedito questa mattina. 2 La riunione può essere organizzata per lunedì. 3 L'albergo può essere prenotato per telefono. 4 La prenotazione può essere confermata per fax. 5 I biglietti devono essere ritirati a mezzogiorno. 6 Roma può essere informata via fax. 7 Il taxi può essere chiamato fra dieci minuti.

*Fare il ponte nel Bel Paese* 1 Because Andrea knows Italy well. 2 Spending too much time in the car. 3 He likes small, quiet places, she likes cities. 4 Verona. 5 Asolo.

*Exercise* **2** 1 Bellissimo. 2 Simpaticissima. 3 Tranquillissimo. 4 Elegantissime. 5 Piacevolissimo.

*Exercise* **3** 1 automaticamente 2 allegramente 3 velocemente 4 lentamente 5 bene 6 regolarmente

*Exercise 4* 1 Mi piace Roma. 2 Mi piacciono le montagne. 3 Mi piace visitare monumenti storici. 4 Mi piacciono le isole piccolissime. 5 Mi piacciono questi spaghetti.

*Exercise 5* (a) 1 Ti piacciono i vini italiani? 2 Ti piace Venezia? 3 Ti piace studiare l'italiano? (b) 1 Le piacciono i vini italiani? 2 Le piace Venezia? 3 Le piace studiare l'italiano? (c) 1 Vi piacciono i vini italiani? 2 Vi piace Venezia ? 3 Vi piace studiare l'italiano?

*Exercise 6* The choice is yours!

*Exercise 7* 1 C'è il lampadario etrusco. *C'è* also for numbers 2, 4, 6. *Ci sono* for numbers 3, 5, 7.

*Nord–Sud* 1 It is poorer than the north. 2 More. 3 A different history, different customs, a different climate, different terrain, the longer history of industrialization in the north, and being further away from the economic centre of Europe. 4 Less pollution, beautiful countryside and coastline and the human warmth of the people.

# Lesson 9

*Al ristorante* 1 Because it is light. 2 He says it is 'excellent, very good'. 3 Lombardy.

*Exercise 1* 1 Sì, mi piacciono, le prendo. 2 Sì, mi piace, la prendo. 3 Sì, mi piacciono, li prendo.

*Exercise 2* Dov'è la lettera di Mary? Non la trovo. E la rivista? Non la vedo. Dove sono i francobolli per le cartoline? Non li trovo. Vedi la penna? Non la trovo. E questo conto. Non lo capisco. Aiuto!

*Exercise 3* 1 ... mi scrive .. ... la leggo ... 2 ... ci conosce ... Ci dà ... 3 Le passo ... 4 ... ti va bene ... 5 La vedo ... 6 *Informal, singular* (tu): ... ti porta ... Ti lascia ... *Formal, singular* (lei): ... la porta ... La lascia ... *Plural* (voi): ... vi porta ... Vi lascia ...

*Exercise 4* 1 Il Signor Galli mi conosce bene. Lo vedo ogni settimana. Mi telefona spesso. 2 Conosci il Signor e la Signora Fabrizi? Ti piacciono? Li vedo ogni domenica. Gli parlo al telefono quasi ogni giorno. 3 Ti scrivo una lettera. Ti mando le foto di Gianni.

*La cucina italiana* 1 Because cooking is still very different from one region to another. 2 Because they grow it there. 3 Fruit and vegetables. 4 Because it is not produced there, there are no olives. 5 Butter, from the cows which are raised there.

*Una ricetta* 1 One for pasta – or at least, she implies that by saying she likes pasta. 2 Oil, garlic, broccoli, macaroni and parmesan cheese. 3 Chilli; you can also add anchovies or sardines, sultanas and pine nuts.

# Lesson 10

*Vacanze in Sicilia* 1 Because he has just come back from holiday. 2 Because he normally takes his holiday in August. 3 A holiday in Sicily; because there is so much to see, the countryside is wonderful and the coast spectacular. 4 He and his wife are going to the Gargano peninsula in July. 5 Marco is going to study English in Ireland and Maria is going on a sailing course in France.

*Exercise 1* 1 Sono stato (*assuming you are a man. For a woman:* Sono stata) 2 Sono andato/a 3 Sei andato/a 4 Sono andato/a 5 Siamo partiti 6 sono rimasti

*Exercise 2* 1 è arrivata 2 è andato 3 sono andati 4 è stato 5 siamo arrivati 6 sono venute

*Exercise 3* 1 il fratello 2 il nipote/il nipotino 3 la nipote 4 la figlia 5 il cognato 6 la zia 7 la moglie 8 lo zio 9 la sorella 10 il marito

*Exercise 4* If you have followed Carlo's model you can't have gone wrong.

*Exercise 5* 1 Sono i tuoi genitori? 2 E' la tua macchina? 3 Sono le tue sorelle? 4 Sono i tuoi figli? 5 E' il tuo ufficio? 6 E' tua moglie? *To the hotel acquaintance you would say:* 1 Sono i suoi genitori? 2 E' la sua macchina? 3 Sono le sue sorelle? 4 Sono i suoi figli? 5 E' il suo ufficio? 6 E' sua moglie?

*Exercise 6* Only you can answer this but don't forget you must use **avere** and you must either use **anni** or **ne**: **Ho quarant'anni/Ne ho quaranta.**

*Il tempo* 1 Yes, today. But not yesterday. 2 The weather is about to change. They hope the change will bring snow.

*Exercise 7* 1 Cloudy. 2 Rough. 3 Snow. 4 Rain. 5 (Thunder) storms.

*Il clima italiano* 1 Fog. 2 Because it is hot and humid. 3 The Adriatic Coast tends to be colder, the Tyrrhenian milder. 4 The south.

## Lesson 11

*Un giallo* 1 Her family. 2 To the market. 3 To put the perishable food she had bought in the fridge. 4 A white Volvo parked outside the house, with two men in it. 5 As she came out of the door, they turned away so that she did not see their faces. 6 Because they are on holiday abroad.

*Exercise 1* Sabato mattina *abbiamo fatto* la spesa e *abbiamo comprato* un vestito nuovo per me. Il pomeriggio *siamo andati* a una mostra interessante e poi la sera *siamo stati* a cena da vecchi amici. Domenica *abbiamo fatto* una gita con amici . . . *Siamo andati* in mare e *abbiamo pranzato* sulla barca con loro. *Abbiamo* anche *fatto* il bagno e *preso* il sole. Poi *abbiamo cenato* in un ristorante sul porto.

*Exercise 2* E' uscita . . . E' salita . . . E' andata . . . E' uscita . . . E' andata . . . Si è seduta . . . Ha ordinato . . . E' stata raggiunta . . . E' uscita . . . E' salita . . . E' andata . . . ha lasciato . . .

***Exercise 3*** 1 Non ho comprato niente. 2 Non ho letto niente. 3 Non ho finito niente/Non ho scritto niente. 4 Non ho mangiato niente. 5 Non ho fatto niente.

***La lettera di un'amica*** 1 Piero's marriage, the birth of her grandson and her own retirement. 2 Because it was her birthday and it was also the day her grandson was born. 3 She works as a consultant and as a writer and she looks after her grandson while her daughter is working. Her elderly parents also need help. 4 He has also retired and they were not used to being together so much. (This second point is implied rather than said.) Their house is big and each has a study of his/her own.

***Exercise 4*** (A) 1 Andando al lavoro, Sergio compra il giornale. Essendo di Firenze, compra La Nazione. Prendendo un espresso al bar, legge il giornale. (B) 1 Avendo una casa in campagna, i miei amici passano spesso il fine settimana lì. 2 Essendo grande il loro giardino, hanno sempre del lavoro da fare. 3 Avendo un orto, hanno sempre frutta e verdura fresca a tavola.

***Exercise 5*** 1 Suona il pianoforte da ventitrè anni. (He has played/been playing the piano for 23 years.) 2 Lavora ... da quattro anni. (He has been working as an engineer for 4 years.) 3 Conosce Antonio da sedici anni. (He has known A. for 16 years.) 4 Studia il francese da un po' più di un anno/da sedici mesi. (He has been studying French for a little more than a year/for sixteen months.) 5 Esce con Alessia da dieci anni. (He has been going out with Alessia for 10 years.) 6 Abita a Milano da due anni. (He has been living in Milan for two years.)

***Le poste lumache – La lettera dal lager tedesco*** 1 27 August 1944. 2 No, he was in a prisoner of war camp, a concentration camp. 3 He returned home. 4 His only son. 5 He was in hospital. 6 The excitement made him feel better and the doctors sent him home the next day.

***Exercise 6*** open

# Lesson 12

***La cugina italiana*** 1 The daughter of Angela's aunt, that is Angela's mother's elder sister, who married an Italian and who died some year's ago. 2 Because her mother had asked her to do so. 3 This is the first time she has done so. 4 A residential area on the outskirts of Turin.

*Exercise 1* 1 sposato 2 nel 3 maggiore 4 è nato 5 1975 6 figli 7 nata 8 è morto 9 minore 10 sposato

*Ecco il mio appartamento* 1 It faces west and gets the setting sun. 2 It's big enough for people to eat there. 3 Yes. (When asked if a door leads to a second bathroom she replies: Unfortunately not.) 4 Behind the building, in the courtyard. 5 A cellar.

*Exercise 2* 1 Ci abita da due anni. 2 Ci vado se ho tempo. 3 Ci sono stato due anni fa. 4 Ci traslocano a maggio.

*Exercise 3* 1 Ne abbiamo quattro. 2 Ne abbiamo tre. 3 Ne abbiamo sette in tutto. 4 Ne abbiamo uno (solo). 5 Ne abbiamo uno davanti e uno dietro. *Answer for your own home using these structures.*

*Exercise 4* 1 Ce ne sono tre. 2 Ce ne sono due. 3 Ce ne sono quattro. 4 Ce ne sono due. 5 Sì, ce n'è una (piccola).

*Exercise 5* 1 Vogliamo tornare l'anno prossimo ma non alla stessa villa. 2 L'anno prossimo vogliamo (vorremmo) un panorama sulla valle. 3 L'anno prossimo i nostri amici, i Simpson, vengono con noi, così abbiamo bisogno di quattro camere. 4 Preferiamo avere due stanze al pian terreno. 5 Vorremmo due o più bagni l'anno prossimo. 6 Soprattutto vogliamo una casa tranquilla (silenziosa), lontana dalla strada. Questa casa è (è stata) troppo rumorosa.

*Exercise 6* open

*Dove vivono gli Italiani* 1 Increasingly builders put in two, although sometimes the second one has a shower but no bathtub. 2 The dining room. 3 People want to get away from big cities, to the outskirts, to smaller towns or even to the country. 4 Often it is their grandparents' house. 5 They went to work in factories. 6 The fact that most families now have a car.

## Lesson 13

**Nel 1967** 1 Blocks of flats. 2 Countryside, fields, a farm with animals. 3 A farmhouse. 4 It wasn't made up; it was just mud. 5 By tram or by coach. 6 Because they use robots instead.

**Exercise 1** 1 era 2 faceva 3 aveva 4 avevano 5 erano 6 portava 7 andava 8 aveva 9 Sembrava 10 aveva 11 era

**Exercise 2** open

**Exercise 3** 1 erano 2 era 3 abitavamo 4 lavorava 5 guardavamo 6 avevamo 7 faceva 8 Eravamo 9 aveva 10 mangiavamo 11 portava 12 faceva 13 eravamo 14 ci divertivamo 15 Eravamo

**Exercise 4** open

**Exercise 5** 1 Leggevo 2 Ci parlavamo 3 ci guardavamo 4 Ero 5 Aspettavo 6 faceva 7 Aiutavo

**Exercise 6** 1 Sta facendo la doccia. 2 Sta facendo una besciamella. 3 Sta leggendo un racconto alla piccola Anna. 4 E' fuori. Sta facendo la spesa. 5 Sta dormendo.

**Album dei 50 anni: l'Italia 1945–1995** 1 A risky and difficult transition year. 2 Democracy. 3 Television, washing machines, plastic, motor cars, computers. 4 Electricity, drinking water and (flush) lavatory. 5 They left Italy to look for work in the Americas or in Europe. 6 People spoke dialects, Italian was not widely used. 7 The ethic of saving and of sacrifice. Today she sees (conspicuous) consumption and hedonism, the pursuit of (personal) happiness. 8 The political system has not developed in parallel to the standard of living.

## Lesson 14

**Una distorsione alla caviglia** 1 A bit better. 2 They didn't go to the cinema. Elena sprained her ankle and they went to the Casualty Department of the hospital. 3 Putting her foot to the ground.

*Exercise 1* 1 Viene spesso a trovarci. 2 Mi piacerebbe invitarlo a cena. 3 No, devo scrivergli oggi./Gli devo scrivere oggi. 4 Posso aiutarla?/La posso aiutare? 5 No, spero di andarci quest'anno.

*Exercise 2* 1 Eccoli. 2 Eccolo. 3 Eccomi. 4 Eccole.

*Exercise 3* (A) 1 Si diverta. 2 Mi faccia un favore. 3 Mi dia la chiave, per favore. 4 Gli dica di venire domani. (B) 1 Divertiti. 2 Fammi un favore. 3 Dammi la chiave, per piacere. 4 Digli di venire domani.

*Exercise 4* 1 Te lo faccio domani. 2 Glielo spiego. 3 Ce lo portano domani. 4 Sì, me ne ha parlato sabato.

*Dal medico* 1 Sore throat, headache and stomach ache, lack of appetite and a feeling of extreme tiredness. 2 Influenza. 3 Some pastilles and a syrup as well as bed rest, lots to drink (water, weak tea etc, no alcohol).

*Exercise 5* 1 Una volta, sì, fumavo, ma ora non fumo più. 2 Una volta, sì, bevevo molto, ma ora non bevo più. 3 Una volta, sì, mangiavo carne rossa, ma ora non ne mangio più. 4 Una volta, sì, dormivo male, ma ora non dormo più male, dormo bene.

*Exercise 6* 1 Non lo vedo più. *I don't see him any more.* 2 Non mi scrive più. *He doesn't write to me any more.* 3 Non lo aiuto più. *I don't help him any more.* 4 Non ci telefoniamo più. *We don't telephone each other any more.*

# Lesson 15

*La lotteria* 1 Rarely. 2 He would buy a new car and he would go on a world tour. 3 She would buy a house by the sea, install a grand piano, take piano lessons and spend her days playing the piano. She would also invite her friends to one long party.

*Exercise 1* 1 Cambierebbe casa. 2 Comprerebbe una casa con giardino. 3 Si sposerebbe con Anita. 4 Imparerebbero a giocare a golf. 5 Non smetterebbe di lavorare.

*Exercise 2* open

*Exercise 3* 1 Non fumo mai. 2 Non bevo mai vodka. 3 Non vado mai in discoteca. 4 Non compro mai cibi surgelati. 5 Non cammino mai a piedi nudi.

*Exercise 4* 1 Non vado mai al cinema. 2 Non vedo nessuno nella piazza. 3 A Maria non piace affatto la musica rock. 4 Carlo non ha nessun amico. 5 Non mangio mai al ristorante. 6 Il direttore non beve niente. (*Or:* Il direttore non beve affatto/mica.) 7 Non ho niente da fare. 8 Non è ancora arrivato il professore.

*Se fossi in te* 1 She doesn't know about it – Aldo hasn't dared tell her. 2 Because she is in her last year of high school and will be going to university in the autumn. 3 She might be able to get leave from her job and either work in the US or do some further study. They are in the lead in her field in the US. 4 Their English would benefit and good English is so important nowadays. They might also find interesting possibilities for their studies.

*Exercise 5* 1 Se andassimo a Roma, vedremmo Marco. 2 Se mi scrivesse, risponderei. 3 Se avessimo i soldi, lo aiuteremmo. 4 Se vincessi la lotteria, Anna, che cosa faresti? 5 Se vincesse la lotteria, Prof. Turco, che cosa farebbe? 6 Se sapessero, sarebbero contenti.

*Exercise 6* 1 Se mi avesse detto che era stanco, l'avrei aiutato. 2 Se non avesse bevuto tanto, non si sarebbe sentito male. 3 Se non fosse andato così veloce, non avrebbe avuto l'incidente. 4 Se non fossi andata alla festa da Giulia, non avrei incontrato Tommaso. 5 Se non avessi comprato un biglietto della lotteria, non avrei vinto un premio.

*Napoli oggi è tutta da scoprire* 1 Tourists are crowding into the hotels in Naples. 2 Because many museums etc. had been closed for years.

## Lesson 16

*Benissimo. Possiamo firmare* 1 Four. 2 15 per cent. 3 10 per cent. 4 A technician from Mr Rossi's firm. 5 Visit Angela's firm to see the robots in place.

*Exercise 1* 1 Il nostro tecnico arriverà all'aeroporto East Midlands alle 16.00 del 17 luglio/il 17 luglio alle 16. 2 Comincerà l'installazione il 18. 3 Finirà entro la fine del mese. 4 Avrà bisogno di una camera in un albergo. 5 Sarà possibile prenderlo all'aeroporto? 6 Vi sarà possibile dargli una macchina per questo periodo? 7 Spiegherà i robots ai vostri tecnici durante l'installazione.

*Exercise 2* 1 spedirò 2 finirò 3 telefonerò 4 ritirerò 5 aiuterò

*Business letters* *First letter:* 1 Ingegner Mancuso. 2 nostro, Vostro. (The capital letter is a courtesy.) 3 It accompanies a quotation. *Second letter:* 1 technical help. 2 Because Meccanica Panigale have already telephoned to ask for help. This is merely a confirmation.

*Un invito* 1 Gabriella and her husband will come and collect her from her hotel. 2 On Saturday morning at 8 a.m.

*Exercise 3* 1 vista. 2 smarriti. 3 mangiata? 4 assaggigato.

*Exercise 4* 1 si annoierà 2 inventerai 3 avrai 4 rafforzeranno 5 avrai 6 sarai 7 farai 8 prenderai 9 avrai 10 te la caverai 11 sarà 12 sarai

# Lesson 17

*Desidero che mi dia un consiglio* 1 The daughter of Angela's cousin Gabriella. 2 It must be smart but it must be suitable for important professional occasions as well as the wedding. She wants something simple, well cut and made of beautiful fabric.

*Exercise 1* 1 venga 2 sia partita 3 possa 4 arrivi 5 abbia comprata 6 sia andato

*Exercise 2* 1 faccia i letti. 2 pulisca la cucina. 3 lavi questi vestiti. 4 stiri la biancheria ... 5 prepari il pranzo ...

*Exercise 3* Vorrei: 1 una camicetta che sia facile da stirare. 2 una maglia che si possa lavare in (nella) lavatrice. 3 una borsa in cui ci sia spazio (posto) per un libro.

*Exercise 4* 1 capisca 2 abbia 3 sappia 4 sia

*Alla boutique* 1 Because he can then tell what fabric will be suitable. 2 The skirt is a bit too big. 3 She finds an outfit she likes and it doesn't take long to do so; she has the rest of the morning free to visit an art gallery (museum).

*Exercise 5* 1 andrebbe bene . . .; potrebbe prendere . . . 2 volevo. *Mi ero presa is a pluperfect, 'I had taken'.* 3 ha comprato; abbiamo risparmiato. 4 farà. 5 Venga; diamoci. 6 *la* può sostituire . . . (direct object); *le* sta molto bene . . . (indirect object); che *le* piaccia . . . (indirect object); *mi* piace; *mi* potete . . . (indirect object); *lo* prendo (direct object); diamo*ci* (indirect – reciprocal). *You may also have picked:* che *ne* dice? ('of it'). 7 *gliela* possiamo stringere . . . 8 *quello che* cerca; *quello che* volevo; qualcosa *che* le piaccia . . .; il vestito *che* ha comprato.

**Un weekend per due** 1 Quattro. 2 Venerdì e sabato; da Milano o da Roma. 3 In riva al mare, di fronte al Castel dell'Ovo. 4 Il Miramare. 5 Il Paradiso. 6,7 Risposta libera. *The choice is yours.*

# Italian–English glossary

The translations given are those applicable in this book. Where gender is not clear, i.e. in the case of nouns not ending in **-o** or **-a**, or not accompanied by an adjective, it is indicated. For verbs in **-ire**, those which work like **capire** – i.e. have **-isc-** in certain tenses – are indicated with *. Parts of speech (noun, adverb, etc.) are indicated only when there might be confusion. Words which are stressed on the antepenultimate syllable and those where the learner might be uncertain of stress, i.e. those ending in **-io, -ia**, have the vowel of the stressed syllable underlined.

*Abbreviations*: *n.* = noun; *sing.* = singular; *pl.* = plural; *m.* = masculine; *f.* = feminine; *inv.* = invariable; *fam.* = familiar, informal; *adj.* = adjective; *adv.* = adverb; *pp.* = past participle, *prep.* = preposition.

| | | | |
|---|---|---|---|
| **a, ad** | to, at | **abituato** | used to, accustomed |
| **abbandonare** | to abandon | | |
| **abbastanza** | fairly | **accadere** | to happen |
| **abbigliamento** | clothing | **accanto a** | next to, beside |
| **abbonato** | subscriber | | |
| **abbondante** | abundant | **accettare** | to accept |
| **abbraccio** | a hug; (*at end of letter*) love from | **accidenti!** | good heavens! |
| | | **acciuga** | anchovy |
| | | **accogliere** | to welcome, to |
| **abitare** | to live | (*pp.* **accolto**) | receive |
| **abito** | clothes, dress, suit, outfit – *can be used for men's and women's* | **accomodarsi** | to make onself comfortable |
| | | **accompagnare** | to accompany, to go with |
| | | **accordo** | agreement |
| **abituarsi** | to become accustomed to | **essere** | to agree |
| | | **d'accordo** | agreed, OK |

| | |
|---|---|
| accorgersi | to realize, to notice |
| aceto | vinegar |
| acqua | water |
| acqua minerale | spring water |
|   acqua minerale naturale | still spring water |
|   acqua minerale gassata | carbonated spring water |
| acquistare | to purchase |
| adattarsi | to adapt |
| adatto/a | suitable (for) |
| addirittura | even |
| addormentarsi | to fall asleep |
| adesso | now |
| adriatico/a | Adriatic |
| adulto/a | adult |
| aereo | aeroplane |
| aerobica | aerobics |
| aeroporto | airport |
| affari (m. pl.) | business |
| affatto | not at all |
| affetto | affection |
| affettuoso/a | affectionate |
| affollare | to crowd, to flock to |
| affollato/a | crowded |
| aggiornarsi | to get up to date, to do a refresher course |
| aggiungere (pp. aggiunto) | to add |
| aglio | garlic |
| agnello | lamb |
| agosto | August |
| agricoltura | agriculture |
| agrumi (m. pl.) | citrus fruits |
| aiutare | to help |
| aiuto | help |
| al di là di | beyond |
| albergatore, -trice | hotelier |
| albergo | hotel |
| albero | tree |
| albicocca | apricot |
| alcool (m.) | alcohol |
| alcuni/e | some |
| alimento | food |
| aliscafo | hydrofoil |
| allegro/a | happy |
| allenarsi | to train |
| allergia | allergy |
| alloggio | lodging, dwelling, place to live in |
| allora | then, well then |
| allungarsi | to stretch |
| almeno | at least |
| alpino/a | alpine |
| altare (m.) | altar |
| altitudine (f.) | altitude |
| alto/a | tall, high |
| altopiano | plateau |
| altro/a | other, another, more |
| alzarsi | to get up |
| amare | to love |
| ambasciata | embassy |
| ambasciatore (m.) | ambassador |
| ambiente (m.) | environment, surroundings |
| America | America |
| americano/a | American |
| amica | friend (f.) |
| amicizia | friendship |
| amico | friend (m.) |
| amministratore delegato | managing director |
| ammirare | to admire |
| amore (m.) | love |
| ampio/a | spacious |
| anche | also, too |

| | | | |
|---|---|---|---|
| **ancora** | still; again; more | **Appennini** | the Appennines |
| **non ...** | not yet | (*m. pl.*) | |
| **ancora** | | **appetito** | appetite |
| **andare** | to go; to suit | **appuntamento** | an appointment |
| **andare in** | to retire | **appunto** | precisely, exactly |
| **pensione** | | **aprile** (*m.*) | April |
| **andare via** | to go away | **aprire** (*pp.* | to open |
| **andarsene** | to go away, to | **aperto**) | |
| | leave | **arancia** | orange |
| **andata** | outward journey | **aranciata** | orangeade |
| **andata e ritorno** | a return ticket | **arancione** | orange |
| **anfiteatro** | amphitheatre | **architetto** | architect |
| **angolo** | corner | **architettura** | architecture |
| **animale** (*m.*) | animal | **arco** | arch, arc |
| **animazione** (*f.*) | animation | **aria** | air |
| **annata** | year (*see* | **arido** | arid |
| | *Lesson 14*) | **arma** | branch, corps, |
| **anniversario** | anniversary | | arm (*of a* |
| **anno** | year | | *service*) |
| **annoiarsi** | to be bored, to | **arrabbiarsi** | to get angry |
| | get bored | **arrivare** | to arrive |
| **annunciare** | to announce | **arrivederci** | goodbye |
| **anticipatamente** | in advance | **arrivederla** | goodbye |
| **anticipo** | advance | | (*formal, to* |
| **antico/a** | old, ancient, | | *one person* |
| | antique | | *only*) |
| **antipasto** | hors d'oeuvre, | **arrivo** | arrival |
| | starter | **arrosto** | roast |
| **anzi** | on the contrary, | **arte** (*f.*) | art |
| | indeed | **articolo** | article |
| **anziano/a** | elderly (*adj.*); | **ascensore** (*m.*) | lift, elevator |
| (*n. and adj.*) | elderly person | **ascoltare** | to listen to |
| | (*n.*) | **asfaltato/a** | covered with |
| **aperitivo** | aperitif | | asphalt |
| **aperto** | open | **aspettare** | to wait for |
| **appartamento** | apartment, flat | **aspettativa** | leave of absence |
| **appassionato/a** | very fond of, | **assaggiare** | to taste, try |
| | very keen on | | (*food, drink*) |
| **appena** | just, scarcely, | **assegno** | cheque |
| | hardly | **assenza** | absence |
| **appena** | as soon as | **assistere** | to be present |
| **possibile** | possible | | at |

| | | | |
|---|---|---|---|
| **assolutamente** | absolutely, at all costs | **azzurro** | blue, sky blue |
| **astrazione** (*f.*) | abstraction, abstract idea | **bacio** | kiss |
| | | **bacin(o)** | little kiss |
| **attenzione** (*f.*) | attention | **badare** | to take notice of, to look after |
| **attimo** | moment | | |
| **attirare** | attract | **bagaglio** | baggage, luggage |
| **attività** | activity | | |
| **attore, -ttrice** | actor, actress (*m.*) | **bagno** | bath, bathroom |
| **attraversare** | to cross | **balcone** (*m.*) | balcony |
| **attraverso** | across, through | **ballare** | to dance |
| **attuale** | current, present | **bambino** | child, baby |
| **attualmente** | at the moment, at the present time | **banca** | bank |
| | | **bancarella** | stall |
| | | **banco** | bank |
| **augurio** | (good) wish | **bar** (*m.*) | bar, café |
| **auguri** (*pl.*) | best wishes | **barca** | boat |
| **Australia** | Australia | **barca a vela** | sailing boat |
| **australiano/a** | Australian | **barista** (*m.*) | barman |
| **autenticamente** | authentically | **basare** | to base |
| **autoambulanza** | ambulance | **base** (*f.*) | basis |
| **autobus** (*m.*) | bus | **a base di** | based on |
| **automatico/a** | automatic | **basilica** | basilica |
| **automobile** (*f.*) | motor, car | **basilico** | basil |
| **automobilista** | motorist (*m.* or *f.*) | **basso/a** | low |
| | | **bastare** | to be enough, sufficient |
| **automobilistico/a** | motor (*as adj.*), to do with the motor car | **battere** | to beat |
| | | **battistero** | baptistry |
| **autostrada** | motorway | **bellezza** | beauty |
| **autunno** | autumn, fall | **bellico/a** | relating to war |
| **avanguardia** | forefront, lead, vanguard | **bello/a** | lovely, beautiful |
| | | **benché** | although |
| **avanti!** | come in! | **bene** | well |
| **avere** | to have | **benissimo** | very well (*adv.*) |
| **avvenimento** | event | **benessere** (*m.*) | wellbeing, prosperity |
| **avvocatessa** | (female) lawyer (*but see text*) | | |
| | | **benvenuto** | welcome |
| **avvocato** | lawyer | **dare il benvenuto** | to welcome |
| **azienda** | business, firm | | |
| **azienda per il turismo** | tourist office | **bere** (*pp.* **bevuto**) | to drink |

| | | | |
|---|---|---|---|
| **bestiame** (*m.*) | cattle | **breve** | short, brief |
| **biancheria** | linen | **brioche** (*f.*) | bun |
| **bianco/a** | white | **britannico/a** | British |
| **biblioteca** | library | **broccoli** (*m.*) | broccoli |
| **biglietteria** | ticket office | **brutto/a** | ugly, bad (*of* |
| **biglietto** | ticket | | *weather*), |
| **binario** | platform | | nasty |
| **biondo/a** | fair-haired | **buonanotte** | good night |
| **birra** | beer | **buonasera** | good evening |
| **bisognare** | to be necessary | **buongiorno** | good morning, |
|   **bisogna** |   it is necessary | |   good day |
| **bisogno** | need | **buono/a** | good |
|   **avere** |   to need | **burro** | butter |
|   **bisogno di** | | **busta** | envelope |
| **bistecca** | steak | **buttare** | to throw |
| **blocchetto** | little block | **cabina telefonica** | telephone box |
| **blu** | navy blue, dark | **cadere** | to fall |
| |   blue | **caffè** (*m.*) | coffee (black); |
| **bocca** | mouth | |   café, bar |
|   **in bocca** |   good luck! | **calamaro** | squid |
|   **al lupo!** | | **calcio** | football, soccer |
| **bollente** | boiling | **calcistico/a** | related to |
| **bollire** | to boil | |   football, |
| **bollito** | stewed | |   soccer |
| **bolognese** | in the style of | **caldo/a** | hot |
| |   Bologna | **calmo/a** | calm |
| **boom** (*m.*) | economic boom | **calore** (*m.*) | warmth |
| **borsa** | bag | **calza** | stocking |
|   **borsa da spesa** |   shopping bag | **calzino** | sock |
| **bosco** | wood | **cambiare** | to change |
| **bottiglia** | bottle |   **cambiare aria** |   to have a |
| **box** (*m.*) | garage | |   change of |
| |   (*integrated* | |   scene |
| |   *into building* | **cambio** | change, |
| |   *of house*) | |   exchange |
| **braccio,** (*pl.* | arm | **camera** | room, bedroom |
|   **le braccia**) | | **cameriere** | waiter |
| **Brasile** (*m.*) | Brazil | **camicetta** | blouse |
| **brasiliano/a** | Brazilian | **camicia** | shirt |
| **bravo/a** | skilful, expert, | **camminare** | to walk |
| |   good (*at doing* | **campagna** | country, |
| |   *something*) | |   countryside |

| | | | |
|---|---|---|---|
| **campanile** (*m.*) | bell tower | **carta di credito** | credit card |
| **campeggio** | camp site | **carta d'identità** | identity card |
| **campo** | field, (*mil.*) camp | **carta telefonica** | phone card |
| **campo di concentramento** | concentration camp | **cartello** | sign, notice |
| **Canada** (*m.*) | Canada | **cartolina** | postcard |
| **canadese** | Canadian | **casa** | house, home |
| **canale** (*m.*) | canal, channel | **casalinga** | housewife, home-maker |
| **cancello** | gate | **cascina** | farm, dairy, dairy farm |
| **Cancro** | Cancer | **casetta** | little house, cottage |
| **candela** | candle | **cassa** | cash desk, till |
| **cantare** | to sing | **cassiere/a** | cashier |
| **cantina** | cellar | **castello** | castle, palace |
| **caotico/a** | chaotic | **catena** | chain |
| **capace** | capable | **cattedrale** (*f.*) | cathedral |
| **capelli** (*m. pl.*) | hair | **cattivo/a** | bad, naughty |
| **capire*** | to understand | **cattolico/a** | (Roman) Catholic |
| **capitale** (*f.*) | capital | **causa** | cause |
| **cappello** | hat | **a causa di** | because of |
| **cappotto** | overcoat | **cavarsela** | to get by, to manage |
| **cappuccino** | white coffee | **caviglia** | ankle |
| **carabiniere** (*m.*) | carabiniere, member of the military force with police responsibilities | **celeste** | blue, light blue |
| | | **cellulare** (*m.*) | cellular, portable telephone |
| **carattere** (*m.*) | character | **cena** | supper, evening meal |
| **caratteristico/a** | characteristic, typical (of a place) | **centimetro** | centimetre |
| | | **cento** | a hundred |
| **carciofo** | globe artichoke | **centrale** | central, middle |
| **carie** (*f.*) | caries, tooth decay | **centralino** | exchange, switchboard |
| **carino/a** | pretty, cute, sweet | **centro** | centre |
| **carne** (*f.*) | meat | **cercare** | to look for, to seek, to try |
| **caro/a** | expensive, dear; (*n.*) loved one | **cerimonia** | ceremony |
| **carota** | carrot | **certo** | certainly; yes, of course |
| **carta** | paper, card, menu | | |

**certo/a** — certain, some
  **certe persone** — some people
**che** — that, which, who, whom
**che!** — what!
**che? che cosa?** — what?
**chi?** — who?
**chiacchierare** — to chat, chatter
**chiamare** — to call
**chiamarsi** — to be called
**chiarimento** — clarification
**chiaro/a** — clear
**chiave** (*f.*) — key
**chiedere** — to ask
  (*pp.* **chiesto**)
**chiesa** — church
**chilo** — kilo
**chilometro** — kilometre
**chissà (chi sa?)** — I wonder, maybe, who knows?
**chiudere** — to close
  (*pp.* **chiuso**)
**ciao** — hello, hi (*informal*); goodbye (*informal*)
**cibo** — food
**cielo** — sky
**ciliegia** — cherry
**cima** — summit
**Cina** — China
**cinema** (*m.*) — cinema
**cinese** — Chinese
**cinque** — five
**ciò** — that
**cioccolata** — chocolate
**cioè** — that is, i.e.
**cipolla** — onion
**circa** — about, approximately
**circondare** — to surround

**circostante** — surrounding
**circumvesuviana,** — which goes
  **la ferrovia ...** — round Vesuvius, the railway ...
**città** — city, town
**cittadina** — small town
**civiltà** — civilization
**classe** (*f.*) — class
**classico/a** — classic, classical
**cliente** (*m.* or *f.*) — customer, client
**clima** (*m.*) — climate
**coda** — tail, queue
**cogliere** — to pick, pluck
  (*pp.* **colto**)
**cognato/a** — brother/sister-in-law
**colazione, prima** — breakfast
  **colazione**
**collaborazione** — collaboration
  (*f.*)
**collant** (*m.*) — tights (a pair of)
**collega** (*m.* or *f.*; — colleague
  *pl.* **-ghi, -ghe**)
**collettivo/a** — collective
**collina** — hill
**collo** — neck
**colore** (*m.*) — colour
**coltivare** — to cultivate
**colto/a** — educated
**come** — like, as
**come?** — how? what?
**cominciare** — to begin
**commerciale** — commercial
  (*adj.*)
**commercialista** — accountant
  (*m.* or *f.*)
**commesso/a** — shop assistant
**comodo/a** — comfortable, convenient
**compagnia** — company
**compleanno** — birthday

| | | | |
|---|---|---|---|
| **complesso/a** | complex | **considerare** | to consider |
| **comprare** | to buy | **considerarsi** | to consider |
| **comprendere** | to include, | | oneself |
| (*pp.* **compreso**) | comprise | **consiglio** | (piece of) |
| **computer** (*m.*) | computer | | advice |
| **comunale** | municipal | **consistere** | to consist |
| **comune** | common | **consolato** | consulate |
| **comune** (*m.*) | municipality, | **consulente** | |
| | town council | (*m.* or *f.*) | consultant |
| **comunicare** | to communicate | **consumo** | consumption |
| **comunque** | however, | **contadino** | peasant, farmer, |
| | anyway | | country |
| **con** | with | | dweller |
| **concordare** | to reach an | **contatto** | contact |
| | agreement | **contento/a** | pleased, happy |
| **condizionale** | conditional | **continentale** | continental |
| (*m.*) | (*mood of* | (*adj.*) | |
| | *verb*) | **continuare** | to continue |
| **conducente** (*m.*) | driver | **continuo/a** | continuous, |
| **conferenza** | lecture | | continual |
| **confermare** | to confirm | **conto** | bill, account |
| **confessare** | to confess | **per conto loro** | on their own |
| **confessarsi** | to make | **contorno** | vegetables |
| | confession (to | | served with |
| | confess | | the meat |
| | oneself) | | course |
| **confinante** | having a shared | **contratto** | contract |
| | border, | **contro** | against |
| | neighbouring | **controllo** | check, control |
| **congratulazioni** | congratulations | **convincere** | to convince |
| (*f. pl.*) | | (*pp.* **convinto**) | |
| **congresso** | conference | **coperto** | cover (*in* |
| **conoscere** (*pp.* | to know, to be | | *restaurant*) |
| **conosciuto**) | acquainted | **coppia** | couple |
| | with, to get to | **coprire** (*pp.* | to cover |
| | know | **coperto**) | |
| **consegna** | delivery, | **coraggio** | courage |
| | consignment | **coraggioso** | brave |
| **consegnare** | to deliver, to | **cordiale** | cordial |
| | hand over | **coricarsi** | to go to bed, to |
| **conservare** | to conserve, to | | lie down |
| | preserve | **corpo** | body |

**corrente** (*f.*)    current
**corridoio**    corridor
**corrispondere**    to correspond
   (*pp.*
    **corrisposto**)
**corso**    boulevard, wide
    street; course
**cortese**    courteous, kind
**cortesia**    courtesy
   **per cortesia**    please
**cortile** (*m.*)    courtyard
**corto/a**    short
**cosa**    thing
**così**    thus, so, like
    this, in this
    way
**così via**    and so on
**costa**    coast
**costare**    to cost
**costiero/a**    coastal
**costituire***    to constitute
**costo**    cost
   **a tutti i costi**    at all costs
**costruire***    to construct, to
    build
**costruttore,**    builder
   **-ttrice**
**costume** (*m.*)    custom
**cotoletta**    cutlet
**cotone** (*m.*)    cotton
**credere**    to believe, think
**crescere**    to grow
**cronaca**    news
**cucina**    kitchen, cooking
**cugino/a**    cousin
**cui**    which, whom
**culturale**    cultural
**cuocere**    to cook
   (*pp.* **cotto**)
**cuoco/a**    cook
**cuore** (*m.*)    heart
**cura**    treatment, care

**curare**    to take care of,
    to treat
    (*medically*)
**cuscino**    cushion
**da**    from, since,
    to/at the
    house of
**dappertutto**    everywhere
**dare** (*pp.* **dato**)    to give
**data**    date
**dato**    datum, *pl.* data
**davanti (a)**    in front of
**davvero**    really
**debole**    weak
**decidere**    to decide
   (*pp.* **deciso**)
**decimo/a**    tenth
**decisione** (*f.*)    decision
**delegazione** (*f.*)    delegation
**delicato/a**    delicate
**democrazia**    democracy
**denaro**    money
**densità**    density
**dente** (*m.*)    tooth
**dentista**    dentist
   (*m.* or *f.*)
**dentro**    inside, within
**deportato**    deportee
**descrivere**    to describe
   (*pp.* **descritto**)
**desiderare**    to want, desire,
    wish
**destinazione** (*f.*)    destination
**destro/a**    right
**di**    of, from,
**diagonale**    diagonal
**diagonalmente**    diagonally
**dialetto**    dialect
**dicembre** (*m.*)    December
**dieci**    ten
**dietro** (adv.)    behind
**differenza**    difference

| | | | |
|---|---|---|---|
| **diffìcile** | difficult | **dolce** (*m.*) | pudding |
| **difficoltà** | difficulty | **dolce** (*adj.*) | sweet |
| **di fronte** | opposite | **dolore** (*m.*) | pain |
| **diffuso/a** | widespread | **domanda** | question |
| **dimenticare** | to forget | **domani** | tomorrow |
| **diminuire*** | to decrease | **domenica** | Sunday |
| **di nuovo** | again | **dominante** | dominant |
| **diocesano/a** | diocesan | **dominare** | to dominate, |
| **dipendere** | to depend | | overlook |
| **dipinto** | painting | **donna** | woman |
| **dire** (*pp.* **detto**) | to say | **donna d'affari** | businesswoman |
| **diretto** | direct, directed | **dopo** | after |
| **direttore** (*m.*), | director | **dopodomani** | the day after |
| **-ttrice** (*f.*) | | | tomorrow |
| **diritto** | right; law | **doppio/a** | double |
| **discoteca** | discotheque | **dormire** | to sleep |
| **disoccupazione** | unemployment | **dottore,** | doctor |
| (*f.*) | | **dottoressa** | |
| **dispiacere** | to displease | **dove** | where |
| **mi dispiace** | I am sorry | **dovere** | to have to, |
| **disporre** | to have at one's | | must |
| (*pp.* **disposto**) | disposal, to | **dritto/a**, (also) | straight |
| | arrange | **diritto/a** | |
| **disposizione** (*f.*) | disposition | **ducale** | belonging to a |
| **a disposizione** | available | | duke or (*in* |
| **disposto/a** | arranged | | *Venice*) doge |
| **distanza** | distance | **due** | two |
| **distorsione** (*f.*) | sprain | **dunque** | so, therefore |
| **disturbare** | to disturb, bother | **duomo** | cathedral |
| **ditta** | firm, company | **durante** | during |
| **diventare** | to become | **duro/a** | hard |
| **diverso/a** | different | **e, ed** | and |
| **divertente** | amusing, | **eccetera, ecc.** | et cetera, etc. |
| | enjoyable, fun | **eccezionale** | exceptional |
| **divertimento** | amusement, | **ecco** | here is/are; there |
| | entertainment | | is/are (*pointing* |
| **divertirsi** | to enjoy oneself | | *out*); well then |
| **doccia** | shower | | (*starting to* |
| **documento** | document, *used* | | *explain* |
| | *to mean* | | *something*) |
| | proof of | **economia** | economy, |
| | identity | | economics |

| | | | |
|---|---|---|---|
| **economico/a** | economical/ economic | **esercizio** | exercise |
| **edonismo** | hedonism, pursuit of happiness | **esistere** | to exist |
| | | **esodo** | exodus, mass departure |
| **educato/a** | polite, well brought up | **espresso** | black coffee, express (train, letter) |
| **egregio/a** | distinguished | **essere** (*pp.* **stato**) | to be |
| **Egregio Signore** | Dear Sir | **essere in giro** | to be going around |
| **elefante** (*m.*) | elephant | **est** (*m.*) | east |
| **elegante** | elegant | **estate** (*f.*) | summer |
| **elementare** | elementary | **estendersi** | to extend |
| **elementari (le classi)** | elementary school | **estero/a** | foreign |
| | | **all'estero** | abroad |
| **elenco** | list, directory | **età** | age |
| **elettricità** | electricity | **etica** | ethic |
| **elettronica** | electronics | **etichetta** | label, sticker |
| **elettronico/a** | electronic | **etrusco/a** | Etruscan |
| **eliminare** | to eliminate | **ettaro** | hectare |
| **emergenza** | emergency | **etto** | 100 grammes |
| **emigrare** | to emigrate | **Europa** | Europe |
| **emotivamente** | emotionally | **evacuare** | to evacuate |
| **emozione** (*f.*) | emotion | **evitare** | to avoid |
| **entrarci** | to be to do with | **evoluzione** (*f.*) | evolution |
| **non c'entra** | he/it is nothing to with it | **ex-deportato** | ex-deportee |
| | | **fa** | ago |
| | | **fabbrica** | factory |
| **entrare** | to enter | **faccia** | face |
| **entrata** | entrance | **facile** | easy |
| **entro** | by (*a point in or period of time*) | **fagiolino** | French, green bean |
| **epoca** | age, period, era | **fagiolo** | bean |
| **all'epoca** | at the time | **fai-da-te** | do-it-yourself |
| **errore** (*m.*) | error, mistake | **falso/a** | false |
| **esame** (*m.*) | examination | **fame** (*f.*) | hunger |
| **esattamente** | exactly | **avere fame** | to be hungry |
| **esatto/a** | exact | **famiglia** | family |
| **esclusivamente** | exclusively | **familiari** | family members, relations |
| **escursione** (*f.*) | excursion | | |
| **esempio** | example | **famoso/a** | famous |
| **ad esempio** | for example | **fango** | mud |

**farcela** — to succeed, to manage, to make it, to cope

**fare** (*pp.* **fatto**) — to do, to make

  **fare il biglietto** — to buy a ticket

**farmacia** — chemist's

**fatica** — drudgery, effort, physically hard work

**fatto** — fact

**fattoria** — farm

**favore** (*m.*) — favour

  **per favore** — please

**fax** (*m.*) — fax

**febbraio** — February

**febbre** (*f.*) — fever, high temperature

**fegato** — liver

**felice** — happy

**ferie** (*f. pl.*) — holidays (paid)

**fermare** — to stop

**fermata** — stop

**fermo/a** — still, not moving

**feroce** — fierce

**ferrovia** — railway

**festa** — party

**fidanzato/a** — fiancé(e)

**figlio/a** — son/daughter

  **figlio unico** — only son

**film** (*m.*) — film

**finale** — final

**finalmente** — at last, finally

**finanziamento** — financing

**finanziario/a** — financial

**fine** (*f.*) — end

**fine settimana** (*m.* or *f.*) — weekend

**finestra** — window

**finire*** — to end, to finish

**fino a** — as far as, until

**fiore** (*m.*) — flower

  **nervi a fior di pelle** — nerves on edge

**fiorente** — flourishing

**firma** — signature

**firmare** — to sign

**fiscale** — fiscal, relating to tax

**fissare** — to fix, to arrange

**fiume** (*m.*) — river

**fondo** — bottom

**fontana** — fountain

**forma** — shape, form

**formaggio** — cheese

**formale** — formal

**formare** — to form

**formula** — formula

**fornire*** — to provide

**forno** — oven

**foro** — forum

**forse** — perhaps

**forte** — strong

**fortezza** — fortress

**fortuna** — fortune, luck

**fortunato/a** — fortunate, lucky

**foto** (*f.*) — photo

**fra** — between, among

  **fra un mese** — in a month's time

**fragola** — strawberry

**francese** — French

**Francia** — France

**francobollo** — (postage) stamp

**fratello** — brother

**frattempo** — meanwhile

  **nel frattempo** — in the meanwhile

**frazione** (*f.*) — outlying village

**freddo/a** — cold

**frequentare** — to frequent; to attend (school)

| | | | |
|---|---|---|---|
| **frequente** | frequent | **genitori** (*m. pl.*) | parents |
| **fresco/a** | fresh, cool | **gennaio** | January |
| **fretta** | haste | **gente** (*f. sing.*) | people |
| **avere fretta** | to be in a hurry | **gentile** | kind |
| | | **Gentile** | Dear Madam |
| **frigorifero, frigo** | refrigerator, fridge | **Signora** | |
| | | **geografia** | geography |
| **frizzante** | sparkling (*of wine*) | **gerundio** | gerund |
| | | **gestire\*** | to manage |
| **fronte** (*f.*) | forehead | **gettare** | to throw |
| **di fronte a** | opposite | **getto** | a jet, a spout |
| **frontiera** | frontier | **a getto** | without |
| **frutta** | fruit | **continuo** | stopping |
| **fruttivendolo** | greengrocer, fruitseller | **gettone** (*m.*) | telephone token |
| | | **già** | already |
| **fuggire** | to flee | **giacca** | jacket |
| **fumare** | to smoke | **giallo/a** | yellow |
| **fungo** | mushroom | **Giappone** (*m.*) | Japan |
| **funzionare** | to work, function | **giapponese** | Japanese |
| | | **giardino** | garden |
| **fuoco** | fire | **ginnasio** | high school (*the first two years of the classical liceo*) |
| **fuori** | outside | | |
| **furto** | theft, burglary | | |
| **futuro** | future | | |
| **gabinetto** | lavatory; surgery (*of a doctor or dentist*) | **giocare** | to play (*a game*) |
| | | **giornalaio/a** | newspaper seller |
| | | **giornale** (*m.*) | newspaper |
| **galleria** | art gallery | **giornata** | day (*see Lesson 14*) |
| **Galles** (*m.*) | Wales | | |
| **gallese** | Welsh | **giorno** | day |
| **gamba** | leg | **giovane** | young |
| **gara** | race, competition | **giovedì** (*m.*) | Thursday |
| **garage** (*m.*) | garage | **girare** | to turn, to go around, to circulate |
| **gelateria** | icecream parlour | | |
| **gelato** | icecream | | |
| **genealogico/a** | genealogical | **giro** | circuit, circle, tour |
| **albero** | family tree | | |
| **genealogico** | | **andare in giro** | to go around, |
| **generalmente** | generally, usually | **gita** | excursion, trip, outing |
| **genere** (*m.*) | kind, sort | | |
| **in genere** | generally | **gitante** (*m. or f.*) | tripper, person on an outing |
| **genero** | son-in-law | | |

| | | | |
|---|---|---|---|
| **giù** | down | **identità** | identity |
| **giugno** | June | **ieri** | yesterday |
| **giungere** | arrive, reach | **illustrato/a** | illustrated |
| (*pp.* **giunto**) | | **immaginare** | to imagine |
| **giusto/a** | right, correct, | **immagine** (*f.*) | image |
| | just | **immensamente** | immensely, |
| **gnocchi** (*m. pl.*) | gnocchi, | | enormously |
| | dumplings | **imparare** | to learn |
| **godere** | to enjoy | **impegnativo/a** | exacting, |
| **gola** | throat | | demanding; |
| **golf** (*m.*) | golf; cardigan | | (*of price*) high |
| **golfo** | gulf, bay | **impegnato/a** | engaged, busy, |
| **gondola** | gondola | | committed |
| **gonna** | skirt | **impegno** | commitment, |
| **governo** | government | | pledge |
| **grammo** | gramme | **imperfetto** | imperfect |
| **Gran Bretagna** | Great Britain | **imperiale** | imperial |
| **granché** | a lot (*usually* | **impermeabile** | raincoat |
| | *used in* | (*m.*) | |
| | *negative* | **impianto** | plant, machinery, |
| | *sentences*) | | equipment |
| **grande** | big, large | **impiegato** | employee |
| **grandine** (*f.*) | hail | **importante** | important |
| **grattare** | to scratch | **importare** | to matter, to be |
| **gratuito/a** | free | | important |
| **grazie** | thanks, thank | **non importa** | it doesn't |
| | you | | matter |
| **greco/a** | Greek | **impossibile** | impossible |
| **grigio/a** | grey | **impresa** | enterprise, |
| **griglia** | grill | | business |
| **grosso/a** | big | **in effetti** | in fact |
| **guardare** | to look, to watch | **in realtà** | in fact |
| **Guardia di** | tax police | **inattivo/a** | inactive, dormant |
| **Finanza** | | | (*of volcano*) |
| **guarire\*** | to cure, to heal, | **incantevole** | enchanting, |
| | to get better | | delightful, |
| **guerra** | war | | charming |
| **guida** (*f.* even | guide, guidebook | **incendio** | fire |
| if male) | | **incertezza** | uncertainty |
| **guidare** | to guide, to drive | **incidente** (*m.*) | accident |
| | (*a vehicle*) | **includere** | to include |
| **idea** | idea | (*pp.* **incluso**) | |

| | |
|---|---|
| **incontro** | meeting |
| **indicatore** | indicator |
| **indietro** | back; (*of clock, watch*) slow |
| **indirizzo** | address |
| **indiscutibile** | unquestionable, undisputable |
| **indomani** | the next day |
| **industria** | industry |
| **industriale** | industrial |
| **industrializza-zione** | industrialization |
| **infatti** | yes, indeed |
| **infelice** | unhappy |
| **infermiere/a** | nurse |
| **infine** | finally |
| **infinito/a**; (*n.*) **infinito** | infinite, innumerable; (*n.*) infinitive |
| **influenza** | influence; influenza |
| **influire*** | to influence |
| **informare** | to inform |
| **informarsi** | to inform oneself |
| **informazione** (*m.*) | information |
| **ingegnere** (*m.*) | engineer |
| **Inghilterra** | England |
| **ingiallito/a** | yellowed |
| **inglese** | English |
| **iniziativa** | initiative |
| **inizio** | start, beginning |
| **innamorato/a** | in love |
| **inoltre** | besides, furthermore, moreover |
| **inquinamento** | pollution |
| **insalata** | salad |
| **insegnante** (*m.* or *f.*) | teacher |
| **inserire*** | to insert, to settle, to fit in |
| **insieme** | together |
| **insistere** | to insist |
| **insolitamente** | unusually |
| **insolito/a** | unusual |
| **insomma** | in short |
| **installare** | to install |
| **installazione** (*f.*) | installation |
| **intanto** | meanwhile |
| **intensamente** | intensively, strongly |
| **interamente** | entirely |
| **interessante** | interesting |
| **interessarsi** | to be interested in |
| **interesse** (*m.*) | interest |
| **interno** | interior; (*telephone*) extension |
| **interno/a** | internal |
| **intero/a** | whole |
| **interrogativo** | question, problem |
| **interrompere** (*pp.* **interrotto**) | to interrupt |
| **intervallo** | interval, break |
| **intervento** | intervention |
| **inteso** | understood, agreed |
| **intimità** | intimacy |
| **intorno** (*adv.*) | around |
| **intorno a** (*prep.*) | round, around |
| **intuizione** (*f.*) | intuition |
| **inutile** | useless |
| **invece** | instead, on the other hand |
| **inventare** | to invent |
| **inverno** | winter |
| **investigatore** (*m.*) | investigator, detective |
| **invitare** | to invite |
| **invito** | invitation |
| **io** | I |

| | | | |
|---|---|---|---|
| **Irlanda** | Ireland | **lì** | there |
| **irlandese** | Irish | **libero/a** | free |
| **irrigare** | to irrigate | **libertà** | freedom, liberty |
| **iscriversi** | to enrol | **libreria** | bookshop |
| **isola** | island | **libro** | book |
| **isolare** | to isolate | **liceo** | high school |
| **istruito/a** | educated | **lieto/a** | happy |
| **italiano/a** | Italian | **limone** (*m.*) | lemon |
| **là** | there | **linea** | line |
| **lago** | lake | **lingua** | tongue, |
| **lamentarsi** | to complain | | language |
| **lampadario** | chandelier, | **linguaggio** | language |
| | candleholder | **lira** | lira (*Italian unit* |
| **lana** | wool | | *of currency*) |
| **largo** | wide | **lirico/a** | lyric |
| **lasagne** (*f. pl.*) | pasta in flat | **musica lirica** | opera |
| | sheets | **litro** | litre |
| **lasciare** | to leave | **locale** (*m.*) | room, |
| **latitudine** (*f.*) | latitude | | establishment, |
| **lato** | side | | premises |
| **latte** (*m.*) | milk | **locale** | local |
| **lavanderia** | utility room, | **lombardo/a** | Lombard, of |
| | laundry | | Lombardy |
| **lavarsi** | to wash | **lontano/a** | far |
| | (oneself) | (*adj.* and *adv.*) | |
| **lavatrice** (*f.*) | washing machine | **lotteria** | lottery |
| **lavorare** | to work | **luglio** | July |
| **lavoro** | work, job | **lui** | he, him |
| **legge**(*f.*) | law | **lumaca** | snail, slug |
| **leggere** | to read | **lume** (*m.*) | light |
| (*pp.* **letto**) | | **luminoso/a** | light |
| **leggero/a** | light | **lunedì** (*m.*) | Monday |
| **legno** | wood | **lungo/a** | long |
| **lei** | she, her; you | **lungo** | along |
| | (*formal*) | **luogo** | place |
| **lentamente** | slowly | **lupo** | wolf |
| **lento/a** | slow | **in bocca** | good luck! |
| **leone** (*m.*) | lion | **al lupo!** | |
| **lettera** | letter | **ma** | but |
| **letto** | bed | **macché** | you're joking! |
| **lettura** | reading | | what |
| **lezione** (*f.*) | lesson | | nonsense! |

| | |
|---|---|
| **maccheroni** (*m. pl.*) | maccheroni, macaroni, (*short pasta tubes*) |
| **macchina** | car, automobile |
| **macchinetta** | little machine |
| **macellaio** | butcher |
| **macerie** (*f. pl.*) | rubble, ruins |
| **madre** (*f.*) | mother |
| **madre-lingua** (*f.*) | mother tongue |
| **magari** | perhaps; would that it were so! |
| **maggio** | May |
| **maggiorana** | marjoram |
| **maggiore** | bigger, major |
|   **fratello maggiore** | elder brother |
| **maglia** | sweater |
| **magnifico/a** | magnificent, wonderful, splendid |
| **magro/a** | thin, lean, non-oily (*of fish*) |
| **mai** | never |
| **maiale** (*m.*) | pig, pork |
| **malattia** | illness |
| **male** | bad |
|   **meno male** | fortunately, luckily |
|   **fare male** | to hurt |
| **malessere** (*m.*) | malaise, indisposition; bad condition financially |
| **malsano/a** | unhealthy, morbid |
| **maltempo** | bad weather |
| **mamma** | mummy, mom |
| **mancare** | to be missing |
| **mangiare** | to eat |
| **mano** (*f.*) (*pl.* **mani**) | hand |
| **mantenere** | to maintain |
| **manzo** | beef |
| **mare** (*m.*) | sea |
| **marito** | husband |
| **marrone** | brown |
| **marsala** | dessert wine from Marsala in Sicily |
| **martedì** (*m.*) | Tuesday |
| **marzo** | March |
| **massa** | mass |
|   **di massa** | for the masses |
| **massimo/a** | greatest, biggest |
| **master** (*m.*) | a master's degree, particularly MBA |
| **matrimoniale** | matrimonial, (*of bed*) double |
| **matrimonio** | wedding |
| **mattinata** | morning (*see Lesson 14*) |
| **mattino/mattina** | morning |
| **maturità** | maturity; high school diploma |
| **medicina** | medicine |
| **medico** | doctor |
| **medievale** | mediaeval |
| **medio/a** | medium(-sized), middle, average |
| **meglio** (*adv.*) | better |
| **mela** | apple |
| **melanzana** | aubergine, eggplant |
| **melone** (*m.*) | melon |
| **membro** | member |
| **meno** | less, minus |
| **mentre** | while |
| **meraviglia** | wonder, marvel |
| **meraviglioso/a** | marvellous |

| | | | |
|---|---|---|---|
| mercato | market | | paltry |
| mercoledì (*m.*) | Wednesday | misteriosamente | mysteriously |
| merenda | snack (*in the afternoon, for children*) | mistero | mystery |
| | | misura | size |
| | | mite | mild |
| meridionale | southern | modello | model |
| mescolare | to mix | modernizzare | to modernize |
| mese (*m.*) | month | moderno/a | modern |
| messaggio | message | modo | way; mood |
| Messico | Mexico | in ogni modo | anyway, in any case |
| messicano/a | Mexican | | |
| meta | destination | modulo | form |
| metà | half | moglie (*f.*) | wife |
| metro | metre | molto (*adv.*) | very, very much |
| metterci | (*of time*) to take | molto/a (*adj.*) | many, much |
| mettere (pp. **messo**) | to put | momento | moment, time |
| | | mondiale (*adj.*) | world |
| mezzanotte (*m.*) | midnight | la seconda guerra mondiale | the Second World War |
| mezzo | half, middle | | |
| in mezzo a | in the middle of | mondo | world |
| | | moneta | coin |
| mezzogiorno | noon, midday; south; Southern Italy | montagna | mountain |
| | | monte (*m.*) | mount, mountain |
| | | monumento | monument |
| mica | not at all | morbido/a | soft |
| migliorare | to improve | morboso/a | morbid |
| migliore, il/la | the best | morire (*pp.* **morto**) | to die |
| migliore (*adj.*) | better | | |
| milione (*m.*) | million | mosaico | mosaic |
| milite ignoto | unknown soldier | mosso/a | (*of sea*) rough |
| mille (*m.*) | a thousand | mostra | exhibition |
| millimetro | millimetre | mostrare | to show |
| minestra | soup; the pasta course | motivo | reason |
| | | mucca | cow |
| minimo/a | least | multa | fine |
| ministro | minister | municipio | town hall |
| minore | smaller, minor | muscolo | muscle |
| il/la minore | the smallest | museo | museum, gallery |
| minuto | minute | | |
| mio/a | my | musica | music |
| miracolo | miracle | | |
| misero/a | poor, wretched, | | |

| | | | |
|---|---|---|---|
| **nascere** | to be born | **nord** (*m.*) | north |
| (*pp.* **nato**) | | **normale** | normal |
| **nascita** | birth | **nostrano/a** | local, locally |
| **naso** | nose | | produced |
| **Natale** (*m.*) | Christmas | **nostro/a** | our |
| **naturale** | natural | **notare** | to note, notice |
| **naturalmente** | naturally, of | **notevole** | notable, |
| | course | | significant, |
| **nazionale** | national | | considerable |
| **neanche** | not even | **notizia** | piece of news |
| **nebbia** | fog | **noto** | known, |
| **necessario/a** | necessary | | well-known |
| **negoziante** (*m.*) | shopkeeper, | **notte** (*f.*) | night |
| | tradesman | **nove** | nine |
| **negozio** | shop | **novembre** (*m.*) | November |
| **nemmeno** | not even | **novità** | innovation, |
| **neozelandese** | New Zealander, | | novelty, |
| | from New | | newness |
| | Zealand | **nudo/a** | naked, bare |
| **neppure** | not even | **nulla** | nothing |
| **nero/a** | black | **numero** | number |
| **nervi** (*m. pl.*) | nerves | **numeroso/a** | numerous, many |
| **nessuno/a** | none, not one | **nuora** | daughter-in-law |
| **neve** (*f.*) | snow | **Nuova Zelanda** | New Zealand |
| **nevicare** | to snow | **nuovo/a** | new |
| **nevralgia** | neuralgia | **di nuovo** | again |
| **niente** | nothing | **nuvoloso/a** | cloudy |
| **nipote** (*m.* or *f.*) | nephew, niece; | **o** | or |
| | grandson, | **obliterare** | obliterate, punch |
| | granddaughter | | (*a ticket*) |
| **nipotino/a** | little nephew/ | **occasione** (*f.*) | opportunity, |
| | niece; grand- | | bargain; |
| | son/grand- | | occasion |
| | daughter | **occhio** | eye |
| **no** | no | (*pl.* **occhi**) | |
| **noce** (*f.*) | walnut | **occidentale** | western |
| **noi** | we | **occorrere** | to be necessary |
| **nome** (*m.*) | name | **occorre** | it is necessary |
| **non** | not | **occupare** | to occupy |
| **nonna** | grandmother | **occuparsi (di)** | to look after, |
| **nonno** | grandfather | | take care of |
| **nono/a** | ninth | **occupato/a** | occupied, busy |

| | | | |
|---|---|---|---|
| **odierno/a** | of today | **oscillazione** (*f.*) | oscillation |
| **odori** (*m. pl.*) | herbs | **ospedale** (*m.*) | hospital |
| **offerta** | offer | **ospitalità** | hospitality |
| **offrire** | to offer | **ottavo/a** | eighth |
| (*pp.* **offerto**) | | **ottimo/a** | very good, |
| **oggetto** | object, purpose; | | excellent |
| | (*at head of* | **otto** | eight |
| | *letter*) re | **ottobre** (*m.*) | October |
| **oggi** | today | **ovest** (*m.*) | west |
| **ogni** | every, each | **pace** (*f.*) | peace |
| **ognuno/a** | everyone, each | **padre** (*m.*) | father |
| | person | **paesaggio** | scenery, |
| **Olanda** | Holland (*more* | | countryside |
| | *correctly:* | **paese** (*m.*) | country; village |
| | ***Paesi Bassi***) | **pagamento** | payment |
| **olandese** | Dutch | **pagare** | to pay |
| **olio** | oil | **paio** (*m.*; *pl.* | pair |
| **oliva** | olive | **paia** – *f.*) | |
| **oltre** | beyond | **palazzo** | palace, large |
| **opera** | work; opera | | building, block |
| **operaio/a** | workman, worker | | of flats/ |
| **opinione** (*f.*) | opinion | | apartments |
| **opportunità** | opportunity | **palestra** | gymnasium |
| **oppure** | or, or else | **pane** (*m.*) | bread |
| **ora** (*adv.*) | now | **panino** | bread roll |
| **ora** (*n.*) | hour, time | **panna** | cream |
| **orario** | timetable, | **panorama** | view |
| | schedule | (*m. inv.*) | |
| **orchestrina** | small orchestra | **pantaloni** | trousers |
| | (*as in a café* | (*m. pl.*) | |
| | *or restaurant*) | **parcheggiare** | to park |
| **ordinare** | to order | **parcheggio** | a parking space, |
| **ordine** (*m.*) | order | | a car park |
| **orecchio** | ear | **parco** | park |
| **organizzare** | to organize | **parecchio/a** | a lot, a good |
| **orientale** | eastern | | deal, (*pl.*) |
| **ormai** | now | | several |
| **oro** | gold | **parente** | relation |
| **orologio** | clock, watch | (*m.* or *f.*) | |
| **orto** | kitchen garden, | **parere** | to seem |
| | vegetable | (*pp.* **parso**) | |
| | garden | **pari a** | equal to |

| | | | |
|---|---|---|---|
| **parlare** | to talk, to speak | **pazienza!** | never mind! |
| **parmigiano** | Parmesan cheese | **peccato (che peccato)** | what a pity |
| **parola** | word | **pecora** | sheep, ewe |
| **parte** (*f.*) | part, side | **pecorino** | cheese made from ewe's milk |
| **la maggior parte** | the majority | | |
| **partenza** | departure | **pedonale** | reserved for pedestrians |
| **participio** | participle | | |
| **particolare** | particular | **peggio** (*adv.*) | worse |
| **particolarmente** | particularly | **peggiore** (*adj.*) | worse |
| **partire** | to set off, leave, depart | **pelle** (*f.*) | leather, skin |
| | | **a fior di pelle** | skin deep |
| **partita** | match (*sport*) | **pendente** | leaning, hanging |
| **Pasqua** | Easter | **pendice** (*f.*) | slope |
| **passaporto** | passport | **penisola** | peninsula |
| **passare** | to pass | **penna** | pen |
| **passato** | sieved or liquidized soup | **pensare** | to think |
| | | **pensiero** | thought |
| | | **pensione** (*f.*) | pension |
| **passato/a** | past | **pepe** (*m.*) | pepper |
| **passato prossimo** | near past (*tense*), past perfect | **peperoncino** | chilli |
| | | **peperone** (*m.*) | (green or red) pepper |
| **passato remoto** | remote past (*tense*), past absolute, past historic | **per** | for |
| | | **per cortesia** | please |
| | | **per favore** | please |
| | | **per piacere** | please |
| **passeggiare** | to go for a walk | **pera** | pear |
| **passeggiata** | walk, stroll | **perchè** | why; because; so that (+ *subjunctive*) |
| **passo** | step | | |
| **pasta** | pastry, pasta (*spaghetti, etc.*) | | |
| | | **perciò** | therefore |
| **pastiglia** | pastille | **percorso** | journey, distance travelled |
| **pasto** | meal | | |
| **patata** | potato | | |
| **patria** | native land, fatherland | **perdere** (*pp.* **perduto** or **perso**) | to lose |
| **patrimonio** | heritage | | |
| **pausa** | pause, break | **perfetto/a** | perfect |
| **paziente** | patient | **perfino** (*adv.*) | even |
| **pazienza** | patience | **pericoloso/a** | dangerous |
| **avere pazienza** | to be patient | **periferia** | suburbs, outskirts |

| | | | |
|---|---|---|---|
| **periodo** | period | **piccante** | sharp tasting, piquant |
| **permettere** (*pp.* **permesso**) | to allow, permit | **piccolo/a** | small, little |
| **però** | however, but | **piede** (*m.*) | foot |
| **persona** | person | **a piedi** | on foot |
| **personaggio** | personage, character | **pieno/a** | full |
| | | **pilota** | pilot |
| **personale** (*n.* and *adj.*) | personnel (*n.*); personal (*adj.*) | **pinolo** | pine nut |
| | | **pioggia** | rain |
| **pesante** | heavy | **piovere** | to rain |
| **pesca** | peach | **pipa** | pipe |
| **pescatore** (*m.*) | fisherman | **pisello** | pea |
| **pesce** (*m.*) | fish | **pittore, -ttrice** | painter |
| **Pesci** (*pl.*) | Pisces (*zodiac*) | **pittoresco/a** | picturesque |
| **pessimo** | very bad | **più** | more, most, plus |
| **pettinarsi** | to comb, do one's hair | **non ... più** | no longer |
| | | **piuttosto** | rather |
| **pezzo** | piece | **pizzeria** | pizzeria, pizza restaurant |
| **piacere** (*m.*) | pleasure | | |
| **per piacere** | please | **plastica** | plastic |
| **piacere** | to be pleasing | **poco, un po'** | a little bit |
| **mi piace** | I like, it is pleasing to me | **poi** | next, then |
| | | **poiché** | since, as |
| **piacevole** | pleasant, pleasing | **polenta** | maize flour porridge, polenta |
| **piangere** (*pp.* **pianto**) | to weep, to cry | | |
| | | **politica** | politics |
| **piano** (*adv.*) | slowly, carefully, softly | **politico/a** | political |
| | | **polizia** | police |
| **piano** | floor | **pollo** | chicken |
| **al secondo piano** | on the second floor | **polmone** (*m.*) | lung |
| | | **polso** | wrist |
| **pianoforte** (*m.*) | piano | **pomeriggio** | afternoon |
| **pianoforte a coda** | grand piano | **pomodoro** | tomato |
| | | **pompelmo** | grapefruit |
| **pianta** | plan | **ponte** (*m.*) | bridge |
| **pian terreno** | ground floor | **popolare** | popular, belonging to the people |
| **pianura** | plain | | |
| **piatto** | dish, plate | | |
| **piazza** | square | | |
| **piazzale** (*m.*) | square | **popolazione** (*f.*) | population |
| **piazzetta** | little square | **popolo** | the people |

| | | | |
|---|---|---|---|
| **porcino** | cèpe (*type of mushroom*) | **prenotazione** (*m.*) | booking |
| **porgere (saluti)** | to offer (greetings) *in a formal letter* | **preoccuparsi** | to worry |
| | | **preparare** | to prepare |
| | | **prepararsi** | to get (oneself) ready |
| **porta** | door; (*in airport*) gate | **presentare** | to present, introduce |
| **porta-finestra** | French window | **presente** | present; *in formal letter* this letter |
| **portare** | carry, take, bring, wear | | |
| **portico** | portico, arcade | **presidente** | presidente |
| **posizione** (*f.*) | position | **presidente del consiglio** | prime minister |
| **possedere** | to possess | | |
| **possibile** | possible | **pressione** (*f.*) | pressure |
| **possibilità** | possibility | **presto** (*adv.*) | soon, early, quickly |
| **posta** | post, mail | | |
| **posto** | place; space, room | **preventivo/a** | preventive |
| | | **preventivo** | estimate, (price) quotation |
| **potabile** | potable, drinkable | | |
| | | **previsione** (*f.*) | forecast |
| **potere** | to be able to | **prezzemolo** | parsley |
| **povero/a** | poor | **prezzo** | price |
| **pranzo** | lunch, midday meal | **prigioniero/a** | prisoner |
| | | **prima (di)** (*prep.*) | before |
| **pratica** | practice | | |
| **praticante** | practising | **prima** (*adv.*) | before, earlier |
| **pratico/a** | practical | **prima colazione** | breakfast |
| **prato** | meadow, grassy field | **primavera** | spring |
| | | **primo/a** | first |
| **preciso/a** | precise | **primo** | (*in meal*) the first (pasta) course |
| **preferire\*** | to prefer | | |
| **preferito/a** | favourite | | |
| **prefisso** | telephone area/ country code | **principale** | principal |
| | | **privato/a** | private |
| **pregare** | to pray, ask | **probabile** | probable |
| **prego** | go ahead; don't mention it | **probabilmente** | probably |
| | | **problema** (*m.; pl.* **-i**) | problem |
| **premio** | prize | | |
| **prendere** (*pp.* **preso**) | to take, to have (*coffee*) | **prodotto** | product, produce |
| | | **produrre** (*pp.* **prodotto**) | to produce |
| **prenotare** | to book, reserve | | |

| | | | |
|---|---|---|---|
| **professionale** | professional | **pullman** (*m.*) | motor coach |
| **professore** | teacher (*secondary school or university*) | **punto** | point |
| | | **può darsi** | maybe, perhaps |
| | | **pure** | by all means, also; even, yet |
| **professoressa** | (female) teacher | **purtroppo** | unfortunately |
| **profumo** | perfume, scent | **qua** | here |
| **progetto** | project, plan | **quadrato/a** | squared |
| **promettere** (*pp.* **promesso**) | to promise | **qualche cosa, qualcosa** | something |
| **pronto** | hello (*answering the telephone*) | **qualche** | some |
| | | **qualcuno/a** | someone |
| | | **quale** | which |
| **pronto soccorso** | emergency (hospital), first aid | **qualsiasi** | any (it doesn't matter which) |
| **pronto/a** | ready | **qualunque** | any (it doesn't matter which) |
| **pronunciare** | to pronounce | **quando** | when |
| **proporre** | to propose | **quanto/a** | how much, how many |
| **proprietario/a** | owner | | |
| **proprio** (*adv.*) | really, right, precisely | **quartiere** (*m.*) | district |
| **proprio/a** | own | **quarto/a** | fourth |
| **prosciutto** | ham | **quarto** | quarter |
| **prosciutto cotto** | cooked ham | **quasi** | almost |
| **prosciutto crudo** | cured ham, Parma ham | **quattro** | four |
| | | **quello/a** | that, that one |
| **proseguire** | to continue | **questione** (*f.*) | question |
| **prospero/a** | prosperous | **questo/a** | this |
| **prossimo/a** | next | **qui** | here |
| **provare** | to try | **quinto/a** | fifth |
| **proverbio** | proverb | **quotidiano/a** | daily |
| **provincia** | province | **raccontare** | to tell, relate |
| **provvedere** | to see to, to take care of, make provision for | **racconto** | story |
| | | **radio** (*f.*) | radio |
| | | **radiografia** | X-ray |
| | | **radiolina** | little, portable radio |
| **prugna** | plum | | |
| **pubblicità** | advertising, publicity | **rafforzare** | to strengthen |
| | | **raffreddore** (*m.*) | cold |
| **pubblico/a** | public | **ragazza** | girl, girlfriend |
| **pulire*** | to clean | | |
| **pulito/a** | clean | **ragazzo** | boy, boyfriend |

| | | | |
|---|---|---|---|
| **raggiungere** | to reach, to join | **ricevere** | receive |
| (*pp.* **raggiunto**) | | **ricevuta** | receipt |
| **ragione** (*f.*) | reason | **richiamare** | call back, call |
| **avere ragione** | to be right | | again |
| **rallentare** | to slow down, to | **richiedere** (*pp.* | to request |
| | reduce speed | **richiesto**) | |
| **rapidamente** | fast, quickly | **richiesta** | request |
| **rapido** | express, fast train | **ricordare** | to remember, |
| **rapido/a** | fast | | recall |
| **raramente** | rarely | **ricoverare** | to admit to |
| **re** (*m.*) | king | | hospital |
| **reale** | royal | **ridere** (*pp.* **riso**) | to laugh |
| **realtà** | reality | **riempire** | to fill |
| **in realtà** | in fact | **riforma** | reform |
| **recente** | recent | **rilassarsi** | to relax |
| **reddito pro** | per capita | **rimandare** | to send back |
| **capite** | income | **rimanere** | to remain |
| **regalo** | present | (*pp.* **rimasto**) | |
| **regione** (*f.*) | region | **ringraziare** | to thank |
| **regolare** | regular | **riparare** | to repair |
| **regolarità** | regularity | **riparazione** (*f.*) | repair |
| **regolarmente** | regularly | **riposante** | restful |
| **relativamente** | relatively | **riposarsi** | to rest |
| **religioso/a** | religious | **ripostiglio** | box room, |
| **rendersi conto** | to realize | | lumber room |
| **rene** (*m.*) | kidney | **riprendersi** | to recover |
| **residenza** | residence | (*pp.* **ripreso**) | |
| **residenziale** | residential | **risaia** | rice field, |
| **resistere** | to resist | | paddy-field |
| **respirare** | to breathe | **risata** | laughter |
| **responsabile** | responsible | **rischio** | risk |
| **restante** (*m.*) | remainder | **rischioso/a** | risky |
| **restare** | to remain | **riso** | rice |
| **restauro** | restoration | **risolvere** (*pp.* | to resolve |
| **resti** (*m. pl.*) | remains | **risolto**) | |
| **restituire**\* | to give back | **Risorgimento** | revival, |
| **resto** | remainder | | Risorgimento |
| **riaprire** | to reopen | **risparmiare** | to save |
| **ricchezza** | wealth | **risparmio** | saving, thrift |
| **ricco/a** | rich | **rispondere** | to answer |
| **ricetta** | recipe; | (*pp.* **risposto**) | |
| | prescription | **risposta** | answer |

| | | | |
|---|---|---|---|
| **ristorante** (*m.*) | restaurant | **salmone** (*m.*) | salmon |
| **ristoratore/trice** | restorative | **salone** (*m.*) | hall, large room |
| **ritardo** | lateness, delay | **saltare** | to jump |
| **ritirare** | to withdraw; to collect | **salutare** | to say hello to, to greet |
| **ritorno** | return | **salute** (*f.*) | health |
| **ritrovarsi** | to meet | **saluto** | greeting |
| **riunione** (*f.*) | meeting |   **distinti saluti** | yours faithfully |
| **riuscire** | to succeed | | |
| **riva** | shore, bank | **salvia** | sage |
| **rivedere** | to see again | **sandalo** | sandal |
| **rivelare** | to reveal | **sangue** (*m.*) | blood |
| **rivista** | magazine | **sanitario/a** | related to health |
| **robot** (*m.*) | robot |   **servizio** | health service |
| **robotizzato/a** | robotized, automated |   **sanitario** | |
| **romanico/a** | romanesque | **sano/a** | healthy |
| **romano/a** | Roman | **santo (san, sant')** | saint |
| **romantico/a** | romantic | **sapere** | to know |
| **rosa** (*inv.*) | pink | **saporito/a** | tasty |
| **rosmarino** | rosemary | **Sardegna** | Sardinia |
| **rosso/a** | red | **sardina** | sardine |
| **rudere** (*m.*) | ruin | **sbagliare** | to make a mistake |
| **rumore** (*m.*) | noise | | |
| **rumoroso/a** | noisy | **sbarrato** | blocked, barricaded |
| **rurale** | rural | | |
| **russo/a** | Russian | **scala** | staircase |
| **sabato** | Saturday | **scaloppina** | escalope |
| **sacrificio** | sacrifice | **scappare** | to dash (away), to escape, to run away |
| **sala** | hall, room | | |
| **sala da ballo** | dance hall | | |
| **sala d'attesa** | waiting room | **scarpa** | shoe |
| **sala operatoria** | operating theatre | **scavo** | excavation |
| | | **scegliere** | |
| **salario** | salary |   (*pp.* **scelto**) | to choose |
| **salato/a** | salty, salted | **scelta** | choice |
| **saldatura** | welding | **scemo/a** | silly |
| **sale** (*m.*) | salt | **scendere** | to go down, to come down, to get off, out of (*vehicle*) |
| **saletta** | small room |   (*pp.* **sceso**) | |
| **salire** | to go up, to get on/into (*vehicle*) | | |
| | | **schiena** | back |
| | | **sci** (*m.*) | skiing, ski |

| | | | |
|---|---|---|---|
| **sciare** | to ski | **semaforo** | traffic light |
| **sciatore, sciatrice** | skier | **sembrare** | to seem |
| **sciroppo** | syrup, linctus | **seminterrato** | basement, semi-basement |
| **scolare** | to strain, drain | | |
| **scontato/a** | discounted, with a discount | **semplice** | simple |
| | | **semplicemente** | simply |
| **sconto** | discount | **sempre** | always |
| **scontrino** | till receipt, check | **sempre dritto** | straight on |
| | | **sensato** | sensible |
| **scoperta** | discovery | **sensibile** | sensitive |
| **scoprire** (*pp.* **scoperto**) | to discover, uncover | **senso** | sense, feeling, meaning |
| **scorso/a** | last | **sentimentale** | sentimental, related to the feelings |
| **Scozia** | Scotland | | |
| **scozzese** | Scottish | | |
| **scrittore, -ttrice** | writer | **sentire** | to feel, to hear, to listen |
| **scrivere** (*pp.* **scritto**) | to write | | |
| | | **senza** | without |
| **scultura** | sculpture | **senz'altro** | of course, without fail |
| **scuola** | school | | |
| **scuro/a** | dark | **separare** | to separate |
| **scusare** | to excuse | **sera** | evening |
| **scusarsi** | to excuse oneself, to apologize | **serata** | evening (*see Lesson 14*) |
| | | **sereno/a** | cloudless, clear |
| **sdraiarsi** | to lie down | **serie** (*f.*) | division |
| **se** | if | (*pl.* **le serie**) | |
| **secolo** | century | **servire** | to serve |
| **secondo** | second (*in a meal*) the main (*fish/meat*) course | **servizio** | service |
| | | **doppi servizi** | two bathrooms |
| | | **sesso** | sex |
| **secondo/a** | second | **sesto/a** | sixth |
| **secondo me, te, lui ecc.** | according to me, you, him etc. | **seta** | silk |
| | | **sete** (*f.*) | thirst |
| **sedersi** | to sit | **sette** | seven |
| **segretario/a** | secretary | **settembre** (*m.*) | September |
| **segreteria telefonica** | telephone answering machine | **settentrionale** | northern |
| | | **settimana** | week |
| | | **settimo/a** | seventh |
| **seguire** | to follow | **settore** (*m.*) | sector |
| **sei** | six | **sgabello** | stool |

| | | | |
|---|---|---|---|
| **si** | (*indef. pr.*) one, people, they; (*refl. pr.*) himself, herself, themselves | **solito/a** | usual |
| | | **di solito** | usually |
| | | **solo** (*adv.*) | only |
| | | **solo/a** (*adj.*) | alone, single, only one |
| **sì** | yes | **soltanto** (*adv.*) | only |
| **siccome** | since, for the reason that | **soluzione** (*f.*) | solution |
| | | **sondaggio** | sounding, survey, opinion poll |
| **Sicilia** | Sicily | **sonno** | sleep |
| **siciliano/a** | Sicilian | **sopra** | above |
| **sicuro/a** | safe, certain, sure, secure | **soprattutto** | especially, above all |
| **signora** | Mrs, madam, lady | **sorella** | sister |
| | | **sorprendente** | surprising |
| **signore** | Mr, sir, gentle-man, man | **sorprendere** (*pp.* **sorpreso**) | to surprise |
| **signorina** | Miss, young lady | **sorridere** | to smile |
| **silenzio** | silence | **sorseggiare** | to sip |
| **simile** | similar | **sosta** | pause, stop |
| **simpatico/a** | likeable, nice | **sostituire*** | to substitute, to put something in place of |
| **sindacato** | trade union | | |
| **sindaco** | mayor | | |
| **singolo/a** | single | **sotto** | under |
| **sinistra** | left | **sottoporre** (*pp.* **sottoposto**) | to submit |
| **sintomo** | symptom | | |
| **sistema** (*m.; pl.* **-i**) | system | **sottosviluppato/a** | underdeveloped |
| | | **spaghetti** (*m. pl.*) | spaghetti |
| **smarrire*** | to mislay, lose | | |
| **smettere** | to stop | **Spagna** | Spain |
| **soccorso** | help, aid, assistance | **spagnolo/a** | Spanish |
| | | **spago** | string |
| **sociale** | social | **spalla** | shoulder |
| **società** | society, company | **spasso** | recreation |
| **soggiorno** | living room | **andare a spasso** | to go for a walk |
| **sogliola** | sole (*fish*) | | |
| **sognare** | to dream | **spazio** | space |
| **sogno** | dream | **spazioso/a** | spacious |
| **neanche per sogno** | never in 1000 years | **spazzare** | to sweep |
| | | **speciale** | special |
| **soldi** (*m. pl.*) | money | **specifico/a** | specific |
| **sole** (*m.*) | sun | **spedire*** | to send |

| | | | |
|---|---|---|---|
| **spendere** (*pp.* **speso**) | to spend | **stanco/a** | tired |
| **speranza** | hope | **stanotte** (**questa notte**) | tonight, this night, last night |
| **sperare** | to hope | | |
| **spesa** | expense, shopping | **stanza** | room |
| **fare la spesa** | to go shopping | **stare** | to stay, to remain, + *infinitive* to be about to |
| **spesso** | often | | |
| **spettabile** | Messrs (*formal way of addressing firm in letters*) | **stasera (questa sera)** | this evening |
| | | **stato** | state |
| | | **Stati Uniti** (*m. pl.*) | United States |
| **spettacolare** | spectacular | **stavolta (questa volta)** | this time |
| **spettacolo** | show | | |
| **spiaggia** | beach | **stazione** (*f.*) | station |
| **spiegare** | to explain | **stella** | star |
| **spinaci** (*m. pl.*) | spinach | **stesso/a** | same |
| **spirito** | spirit | **stile** (*m.*) | style |
| **spogliatoio** | changing room | **stimolante** | stimulating |
| **sporco/a** | dirty | **stimolare** | to stimulate |
| **sport** (*m.*) | sport | **stivale** (*m.*) | boot |
| **sportivo/a** | sporting, fond of sports | **stomaco** | stomach |
| | | **storia** | history |
| **sposare** | to marry | **storico/a** | historical |
| **sposarsi** | to get married | **strada** | street, road |
| **sposato/a** | married | **stradale** | related to the roads |
| **spostare** | to move, displace | | |
| **spremuta** | freshly squeezed citrus fruit squash | **incidente stradale** | road accident |
| | | **stradina** | little street, lane |
| **spumante** (*m.*) | sparkling (*of wine*), champagne-type | **straniero/a** | foreigner |
| | | **strano/a** | strange |
| | | **stretto/a** | narrow |
| **spuntino** | snack | **stringere** (*pp.* **stretto**) | to squeeze, take in (*clothing*) |
| **squadra** | team | | |
| **stabile** | stable (*adj.*) | **studente** (*m.*) | student |
| **stadio** | stadium | **studentessa** | female student |
| **stagione** (*f.*) | season | **studiare** | to study |
| **stamattina** (**questa mattina**) | this morning | **studio** (*pl.* **gli studî**) | study |

| | | | |
|---|---|---|---|
| **stufato** | stew | **tardare** | to be late |
| **su** | on, upon, up | **tariffa** | tariff, fare |
| **subito** | immediately, suddenly | **tartufo** | truffle |
| | | **tasca** | pocket |
| **succedere** | to happen | **tascabile** | pocket (*adj.*) |
| (*pp.* **successo**) | | **tassa** | tax |
| **successo** | success | **tasso** | rate, level |
| **succo** | juice | **tavernetta** | party room (*in basement of modern house*) |
| **sud** (*m.*) | south | | |
| **Sud Africa** | South Africa | | |
| **sudafricano/a** | South African | **tavola, tavolo** | table |
| **suggerimento** | suggestion | **tavola calda** | snack bar |
| **suggerire***  | to suggest | **tavolino** | small table |
| **sugo** | gravy, sauce, juice | **taxi** (*also:* **tassì**) | taxi |
| **suo/a** | his, her, your | **tè/the** (*m.*) | tea |
| **suocero/a** | father/mother-in-law | **teatro** | theatre |
| | | **tecnico** | technician |
| **suonare** | to play (*a musical instrument*); to ring | **tecnico/a** | technical |
| | | **tedesco/a** | German |
| | | **telefonare** | to telephone |
| **superficie** (*f.*) | surface | **telefonata** | telephone call |
| **supermercato** | supermarket | **telefonicamente** | by telephone |
| **superscontato** | with a big discount | **telefonino** | portable telephone |
| **supplemento** | supplement | **telefono** | telephone |
| **surgelato/a** | (deep) frozen | **teleselezione** (*f.*) | direct dialling (long distance) |
| **susina** | plum | | |
| **sveglia** | alarm clock | **televisione** (*f.*) | television |
| **svegliarsi** | to wake up | **temperatura** | temperature |
| **sviluppo** | development | **tempio** | temple |
| **Svizzera** | Switzerland | **tempo** | time, weather |
| **svizzero/a** | Swiss | **tempo libero** | free, spare time |
| **tabaccaio/a** | tobacconist | **temporale** (*m.*) | storm |
| **tacchino** | turkey | **tenere** | to hold, to keep |
| **tagliatelle** (*f. pl.*) | pasta in flat ribbons | **tennis** (*m.*) | tennis |
| | | **terra** | earth, land, ground |
| **taglio** | cut | **terrazzo** | terrace, balcony |
| **tailleur** (*m.*) | (woman's) suit | **terreno** | land, ground |
| **tanto/a** | so much, (*pl.*) so many, (+ *adj.*) so | **territorio** | territory |
| | | **terzo/a** | third |
| | | **tessuto** | fabric, cloth |

| | | | |
|---|---|---|---|
| **testa** | head | **tuono** | thunder |
| **tifoso/a** | fan (*sport*) | **turismo** | tourism |
| **tilt (in tilt)** | upside down, in confusion | **turista** (*m.* or *f.*) | tourist |
| | | **turistico/a** | touristic |
| **timo** | thyme | **tutto/a** | all |
| **tinello** | small dining room; kitchen-diner; scullery | **TV, tivù** (*f.*) | TV |
| | | **uccidere** (*pp.* **ucciso**) | to kill |
| **tipico/a** | typical | **ufficio** | office |
| **toast** (*m.*) | toasted sandwich | **ufficio postale** | post office |
| **togliere** (*pp.* **tolto**) | to remove | **ultimo/a** | last (*in a series*) |
| | | **umano/a** | human |
| **tomba** | tomb | **umidità** | damp, humidity |
| **tornare** | to return, to come back | **umido/a** | damp, wet |
| | | **un, un', uno, una** | a, an, one |
| **torre** (*f.*) | tower | **unico/a** | unique, only |
| **torta** | cake | **unificazione** (*f.*) | unification |
| **tortellini** (*m. pl.*) | pasta with meat stuffing | **università** | university |
| | | **universitario/a** | university |
| **torto, avere** | to be wrong | **uomo** (*pl.* **uomini**) | man |
| **tra** | between, among | | |
| **traduzione** (*f.*) | translation | **uomo d'affari** | businessman |
| **traffico** | traffic | **uovo** (*m.; pl.* **le uova** *f.*) | egg |
| **tram** (*m.*) | tram | | |
| **tramonto** | sunset | **urbano/a** | urban |
| **tranquillo/a** | quiet | **vigile urbano** | town policeman |
| **transizione** (*f.*) | transition | | |
| **traslocare** | to move house | **urgenza** | emergency |
| **trattoria** | restaurant | **d'urgenza** | urgently, as an emergency |
| **travellers cheque** (*m. inv.*) | travellers' cheque | | |
| | | **usare** | to use |
| **tre** | three | **uscire** | to go out |
| **treno** | train | **uscita** | exit |
| **triste** | sad | **utile** | useful |
| **troppo** | too | **uva** | grapes |
| **trota** | trout | **uva passa** | raisins |
| **trovare** | to find | **va bene** | OK, good, that's fine |
| **andare a trovare** | to go and see (*a person*) | | |
| | | **vacanza** | holiday |
| **trovarsi** | to be situated | **valido/a** | valid |
| **tu** | you (*fam.*) | **valigia** | suitcase |
| **tuo/a** | your | **valle** (*f.*) | valley |

| | | | |
|---|---|---|---|
| **valuta** | currency | **viaggiare** | to travel |
| **vantaggio** | advantage | **viaggiatore,** | traveller |
| **variare** | to vary | **-trice** | |
| **vario/a** | various | **viaggio** | travel, journey |
| **vasca (da bagno)** | bath tub | **viale** | avenue |
| **vecchio/a** | old | **vicino** (*adj.* | near, close |
| **vedere** (*pp.* **visto** | to see | and *adv.*) | |
| or **veduto**) | | **vicino/a** (*n.*) | neighbour |
| **veicolo** | vehicle | **vigile (urbano)** | policeman |
| **vela** | sail, sailing | **vigile del fuoco** | fireman |
| **veloce** | fast | **vigore** (*m.*) | vigour |
| **velocemente** | rapidly | **in vigore** | in force |
| **vena** | vein | **villaggio** | village |
| **vendere** | to sell | **vincere** (*pp.* | to win |
| **vendita** | sale | **vinto**) | |
| **venditore, -trice** | seller | **vino** | wine |
| **venerdì** (*m.*) | Friday | **viola** | violet |
| **venire** (*pp.* | to come | **visione** (*f.*) | vision |
| **venuto**) | | **visita** | visit, medical |
| **venire fuori** | to come out | | examination |
| **vento** | wind | **visitare** | to visit (*place*); |
| **veramente** | actually, truly, | | to examine |
| | really | | (*patient*) |
| **verbo** | verb | **viso** | face |
| **verde** | green | **vita** | life |
| **verdura** | (green) vegetable | **vitello** | veal |
| **vero/a** | true | **vivace** | lively |
| **versare** | to remit, to pay | **vivere** (*pp.* | to live |
| | in, to pay (*a* | **vissuto**) | |
| | *cheque*) | **vivo/a** | alive |
| **verso** | towards; at | **vocabolario** | vocabulary |
| | about | **voce** (*f.*) | voice |
| **vestiario** | clothing, | **voi** | you (*pl.*) |
| | wardrobe | **volante** | driving wheel |
| **vestirsi** | to get dressed, | **volare** | to fly |
| | to dress | **volentieri** | willingly, with |
| **vestito** | clothing, dress | | pleasure |
| **via** | street | **volere** | to want |
| **via** (*adv.*) | away with . . . , | **volere bene a** | to be fond of, |
| | be off! go | **qualcuno** | love, someone |
| | away! | **volere dire** | to mean |
| **via aerea** | by air mail | **volo** | flight |

| | | | |
|---|---|---|---|
| **volta** | time, occasion | **zitto/a** | quiet, |
| **vostro/a** | your | | silent |
| **vulcanico/a** | volcanic | **sta' zitto** | be quiet! |
| **vulcano** | volcano | **zona** | zone, area |
| **vuoto/a** | empty | **zucchero** | sugar |
| **zero** | zero | **zucchino** | baby marrow, |
| **zia** | aunt | | zucchino |
| **zio** | uncle | **zuppiera** | soup tureen |

# English–Italian glossary

This list is selective. Words to be found in the lessons indicated under *Topics* in the index are not normally included. Many words which are similar in Italian will be located easily in the Italian–English glossary. The gender of nouns not ending in **-o** or **-a** has been included. The feminine of adjectives is given when it is different from the masculine.

| | | | |
|---|---|---|---|
| a, an | **un, una** | also | **anche** |
| above | **sopra** | although | **benchè** |
| to accept | **accettare** | among | **fra, tra** |
| accident | **incidente** (*m.*) | amusement | **divertimento** |
| according to | **secondo** | amusing | **divertente** |
| across | **attraverso** | answer | **risposta** |
| advance | **anticipo** | to answer | **rispondere** |
| advice | **consiglio** | any (it doesn't | **qualsiasi** |
| aeroplane | **aereo** | matter which) | |
| after | **dopo** | apartment, flat | **appartamento** |
| afternoon | **pomeriggio** | to apologize | **scusare** |
| again | **ancora, di nuovo** | appointment | **appuntamento** |
| against | **contro** | arrival | **arrivo** |
| age | **età** | art gallery | **museo, galleria** |
| ago | **fa** | | **d'arte** |
| agreement | **accordo** | at | **a** |
| airport | **aeroporto** | at least | **almeno** |
| all | **tutto/a** | to attend | **frequentare** |
| to allow | **permettere** | (school) | |
| almost | **quasi** | average | **medio/a** |
| alone | **solo/a** | bad | **cattivo/a** |
| along | **lungo/a** | badly | **male** |
| a lot | **parecchio, molto** | bag | **borsa** |
| already | **già** | bank | **banca** |

| | | | |
|---|---|---|---|
| to be | **essere** | car | **macchina, auto (-mobile)** (*f.*) |
| to be able to | **potere** | | |
| to be bored | **annoiarsi** | car park | **parcheggio** |
| to be born | **nascere** | cash desk | **cassa** |
| to be called | **chiamarsi** | cathedral | **duomo,** |
| to be fond of | **volere bene a** | | **cattedrale** (*f.*) |
| beautiful | **bello/a** | cellar | **cantina** |
| because | **perchè** | centre | **centro** |
| to become | **diventare** | century | **secolo** |
| before | **prima (di)** | to change | **cambiare** |
| to begin | **cominciare** | change (after paying) | **resto** |
| beginning | **inizio** | | |
| behind | **dietro (a/di)** | chemist's shop | **farmacia** |
| to believe | **credere** | cheque | **assegno** |
| besides | **inoltre** | child | **bambino/a** |
| better (*adv.*) | **meglio** | to choose | **scegliere** |
| better (*adj.*) | **migliore** | city | **città** |
| between | **fra, tra** | to clean | **pulire** |
| beyond | **oltre** | clean | **pulito/a** |
| big | **grande, grosso/a** | climate | **clima** (*m.*) |
| bigger | **maggiore** | coin | **moneta** |
| biggest | **massimo/a, più grande** | cold (*adj.*) | **freddo/a** |
| | | cold (*n.*) | **raffreddore** (*m.*) |
| bill | **conto** | colour | **colore** (*m.*) |
| birthday | **compleanno** | to come | **venire** |
| block of flats | **palazzo** | comfortable | **comodo/a** |
| book | **libro** | comfortable, to make oneself | **accomodarsi** |
| to book | **prenotare** | | |
| booking | **prenotazione** (*f.*) | common | **comune** |
| boy | **ragazzo** | consulate | **consolato** |
| brave | **coraggioso/a** | to continue | **continuare** |
| bread | **pane** (*m.*) | cooking | **cucina** |
| bread roll | **panino** | cool | **fresco/a** |
| breakfast | **(prima) colazione** (*f.*) | corner | **angolo** |
| | | correct | **giusto/a** |
| bus | **autobus** (*m.*) | to cost | **costare** |
| business | **affari** (*pl.*) | cotton | **cotone** (*m.*) |
| but | **ma** | country | **paese** (*m.*) |
| to buy | **comprare** | currency | **valuta** |
| by ('by Sunday') | **entro** | current | **attuale** |
| by | **da, per** | daily | **quotidiano/a** |
| to call | **chiamare** | damp | **umido/a** |

| | | | |
|---|---|---|---|
| date | **data** | even | **pure** |
| day | **giorno, giornata** | every | **ogni** |
| dear | **caro/a** | everyone | **ognuno, tutti** |
| to decide | **decidere** | everywhere | **dappertutto** |
| to decrease | **diminuire** | example | **esempio** |
| to deliver | **consegnare** | excellent | **ottimo/a** |
| to depart | **partire** | to excuse | **scusare** |
| departure | **partenza** | exit | **uscita** |
| dialling code | **prefisso** | expense | **spesa** |
| to die | **morire** | expensive | **caro/a** |
| difference | **differenza** | to explain | **spiegare** |
| different | **diverso/a,** | factory | **fabbrica** |
| | **differente** | fairly | **abbastanza** |
| difficult | **difficile** | to fall | **cadere** |
| directory | **elenco** | family | **famiglia** |
| dirty | **sporco/a** | far | **lontano** |
| discount | **sconto** | farmer | **contadino** |
| to displease | **dispiacere** | fast | **rapido/a,** |
| to do | **fare** | | **veloce** |
| doctor | **dottore, -essa;** | field | **campo** |
| | **medico** | firm | **ditta** |
| door | **porta** | first | **primo/a** |
| double | **doppio/a** | fish | **pesce** (*m.*) |
| down | **giù** | flat (*n.*) | **appartamento** |
| to drive | **guidare** | flight | **volo** |
| during | **durante** | follow | **seguire** |
| each | **ogni** | football | **calcio** |
| early | **presto, in** | for | **per** |
| | **anticipo** | foreigner | **straniero/a** |
| earth | **terra** | free | **libero/a** |
| egg | **uovo** (*m.; pl.* | French | **francese** |
| | **uova,** *f.*) | fresh | **fresco/a** |
| electricity | **elettricità, luce** | friend | **amico/a** |
| | (*f.*) | from | **da, di** |
| embassy | **ambasciata** | fruit | **frutta** |
| engaged | **occupato/a** | full | **pieno** |
| (not free) | | garden | **giardino** |
| to enjoy oneself | **divertirsi** | generally | **in genere,** |
| entrance | **entrata** | | **generalmente** |
| envelope | **busta** | to get by | **cavarsela** |
| environment | **ambiente** (*m.*) | to get in/on | **salire su** |
| et cetera | **eccetera, ecc.** | (*vehicle*) | |

| | | | |
|---|---|---|---|
| to get off/out of (*vehicle*) | scendere da | hospital | ospedale (*m.*) |
| | | hot | caldo/a |
| to get up | alzarsi | hotel | albergo |
| girl | ragazza | hour | ora |
| to give | dare | house | casa |
| to go | andare | how? | come? |
| to go down | scendere | how many? | quanti? |
| to go out | uscire | how much? | quanto? |
| to go up | salire | however | comunque, però |
| gold | oro | hunger | fame (la) |
| good wishes | auguri | ice cream | gelato |
| good heavens! | accidenti! | if | se |
| goodbye | arrivederci, arrivederla | illness | malattia |
| | | immediately | subito |
| government | governo | impossible | impossibile |
| to greet | salutare | in | a, in |
| greeting | saluto | in fact | in effetti, in realtà |
| to grow | crescere | | |
| guide | guida (f.) (*even if male*) | in front of | davanti a |
| | | in short | insomma |
| guidebook | guida (f.) | indeed | infatti |
| half | metà, mezzo | to injure | ferire |
| ham | prosciutto | inside | dentro |
| hand | mano (f.) | instead | invece |
| happy | felice, contento/a | interesting | interessante |
| to have | avere | to introduce | presentare |
| he | lui | to kill | uccidere |
| to heal | guarire | kind | gentile |
| health | salute | kitchen | cucina |
| healthy | sano/a | to know | sapere (*fact*), conoscere (*person/place*) |
| heavy | pesante | | |
| hello (*on telephone*) | pronto | | |
| | | language | lingua |
| to help | aiutare | last (most recent) | scorso/a |
| help | aiuto | last (in series) | ultimo/a |
| here | qua, qui | lateness | ritardo |
| here is, are | ecco | lavatory | gabinetto, toilette (f.) |
| high | alto/a | | |
| hill | collina | to learn | imparare |
| history | storia | leather | pelle (f.) |
| to hold | tenere | left | sinistro/a |
| holiday | vacanza | less | meno |

| | | | |
|---|---|---|---|
| letter | **lettera** | mouth | **bocca** |
| lift | **ascensore** (*m.*) | Mr | **signor(e)** |
| light (*n.*) | **luce** (*f.*) | Mrs | **signora** |
| light (*adj.*) | **leggero/a** | much | **molto/a** |
| like | **come** | museum | **museo** |
| to like | **piacere a** (*see* | name | **nome** (*m.*) |
| | Lessons 2, 3 8) | near | **vicino/a** |
| to listen | **ascoltare** | to need | **avere bisogno di** |
| little bit | **un poco, un po'** | never | **mai** |
| to live | **abitare, vivere** | never mind! | **pazienza!** |
| long | **lungo/a** | new | **nuovo/a** |
| to look at | **guardare** | news | **notizia** |
| to look for | **cercare** | newspaper | **giornale** (*m.*) |
| to lose | **perdere** | next | **poi** |
| to love | **amare** | next (*in order*) | **prossimo/a** |
| lovely | **bello/a** | next to | **accanto a** |
| luckily | **meno male** | night | **notte** (*f.*) |
| lucky | **fortunato/a** | no | **no** |
| lunch | **pranzo** | no one | **nessuno/a** |
| magazine | **rivista** | noise | **rumore** (*m.*) |
| to make | **fare** | not at all | **mica** |
| to make a | **sbagliare** | not even | **neanche,** |
| mistake | | | **nemmeno,** |
| man | **uomo** (*pl.* | | **neppure** |
| | **uomini**) | nothing | **niente, nulla** |
| many | **molti** | to notice | **notare** |
| market | **mercato** | now | **adesso, ora** |
| married | **sposato/a** | number | **numero** |
| match (*sport*) | **partita** | of | **di** |
| to matter | **importare** | office | **ufficio** |
| to mean | **volere dire** | often | **spesso** |
| meanwhile | **intanto** | old | **vecchio/a** |
| meat | **carne** (*f.*) | on | **su** |
| mild | **mite** | on the contrary | **anzi** |
| minute | **minuto** | on the other | **invece** |
| Miss | **signorina** | hand | |
| money | **denaro** (*sing.*), | only | **solo** |
| | **soldi** (*pl.*) | open | **aperto/a** |
| month | **mese** | to open | **aprire** |
| more | **più** | opposite | **di fronte a** |
| motorway | **autostrada** | to order | **ordinare** |
| mountain | **montagna** | other | **altro/a** |

| | | | |
|---|---|---|---|
| our | **nostro/a** | reason | **motivo, ragione** |
| outside | **fuori** | | **(f.)** |
| own | **proprio/a** | receipt | **ricevuta** |
| to own | **possedere** | to receive | **ricevere** |
| pain | **dolore** (*m.*) | region | **regione** (*f.*) |
| pair | **paio**, *pl.* **paia** (*f.*) | to remain | **rimanere** |
| paper | **carta** | to rest | **riposarsi** |
| passport | **passaporto** | restaurant | **ristorante** (*m.*) |
| to pay | **pagare** | to return | **tornare** |
| peace | **pace** (*f.*) | rich | **ricco/a** |
| pen | **penna** | right (not left) | **destro/a** |
| people | **gente** (*f. sing.*) | right (*v.* duty) | **diritto** |
| pepper | **pepe** (*m.*) | room | **stanza** |
| perhaps | **forse, può darsi, magari** | same | **stesso/a** |
| | | to say | **dire** |
| piece | **pezzo** | scarcely | **appena** |
| place | **posto, luogo** | schedule | **orario** |
| plan | **pianta, progetto** | sea | **mare** (*m.*) |
| platform | **binario** (*lit.* track) | to see | **vedere** |
| | | to seem | **sembrare, parere** |
| to play | **giocare** | to sell | **vendere** |
| to play (*musical instrument*) | **suonare** | several | **parecchi** |
| | | she | **lei** |
| please | **per favore, per piacere, per cortesia** | shopping, to do the | **fare la spesa** |
| | | short | **breve, corto/a** |
| pleased | **contento/a** | to show | **mostrare** |
| poor | **povero/a** | silk | **seta** |
| possible | **possibile** | similar | **simile** |
| postcard | **cartolina** | since (*reason*) | **siccome, poichè** |
| to prefer | **preferire** | since (*time*) | **da** |
| price | **prezzo** | sister | **sorella** |
| project | **progetto** | to sit down | **accomodarsi, sedersi** |
| to put | **mettere** | | |
| question | **domanda** | size | **misura** |
| rain | **pioggia** | skilful | **bravo/a** |
| to rain | **piovere** | skin | **pelle** (*f.*) |
| rather | **piuttosto** | to sleep | **dormire** |
| to read | **leggere** | slow | **lento/a** |
| ready | **pronto/a** | slowly | **piano, lentamente** |
| to realize | **rendersi conto di** | | |
| really | **davvero, proprio** | small | **piccolo/a** |

| | | | |
|---|---|---|---|
| to smoke | **fumare** | therefore | **perciò** |
| so | **così, dunque** | thing | **cosa** |
| so many | **tanti** | this | **questo/a** |
| so much | **tanto/a** | this evening | **stasera** |
| so that | **perchè** (+ | this morning | **stamattina** |
| | *subjunctive*) | through | **attraverso, per** |
| softly | **piano** | thus | **così** |
| some | **alcuni/e** (*with* | ticket | **biglietto** |
| | *pl.*); **qualche** | time | **ora** (*by clock*), |
| | (*with sing.*) | | **tempo, volta** |
| someone | **qualcuno/a** | | (*occasion*) |
| something | **qualche cosa,** | timetable | **orario** |
| | **qualcosa** | tired | **stanco/a** |
| space | **posto, spazio** | to | **a** |
| to speak | **parlare** | today | **oggi** |
| square | **piazza**; (*adj.*) | together | **insieme** |
| | **quadrato/a** | tomorrow | **domani** |
| stamp | **francobollo** | tongue | **lingua** |
| state | **stato** | tonight | **stanotte** |
| station | **stazione** (*f.*) | too | **troppo** |
| still (not moving) | **fermo/a** | towards | **verso** |
| still (*adv.*) | **ancora** | town | **città** |
| stop (bus-) | **fermata** | town hall | **municipio,** |
| to stop | **fermare** | | **palazzo** |
| straight | **dritto/a** | | **comunale** |
| strange | **strano/a** | traffic light | **semaforo** |
| street | **strada, via** | train | **treno** |
| sun | **sole** (*m.*) | travel | **viaggiare** |
| supermarket | **supermercato** | tree | **albero** |
| supper | **cena** | trip | **gita, escursione** |
| sweet (*adj.*) | **dolce** | | (*f.*) |
| to take | **prendere** | true | **vero/a** |
| to take care of | **curare** | to try | **provare** |
| tall | **alto/a** | to turn | **girare** |
| telephone | **telefono** | ugly | **brutto/a** |
| to thank | **ringraziare** | under | **sotto** |
| thank you | **grazie** | to understand | **capire** |
| that | **quello/a, ciò** | unemployment | **disoccupazione** |
| that is, i.e. | **cioè** | | (*f.*) |
| theft | **furto** | unfortunately | **purtroppo** |
| then | **allora, poi** | unhappy | **infelice,** |
| there | **là, lì** | | **scontento/a** |

| | | | |
|---|---|---|---|
| up | **su** | who? | **chi?** |
| to use | **usare** | why? | **perchè?** |
| used to | **abituato/a a** | to win | **vincere** |
| useful | **utile** | wine | **vino** |
| usual | **solito/a** | wish | **augurio** |
| very | **molto** | with | **con** |
| village | **paese** (*m.*) | with pleasure | **volentieri** |
| to wait for | **aspettare** | woman | **donna** |
| to wake up | **svegliarsi** | wool | **lana** |
| walk | **passeggiata** | word | **parola** |
| to walk | **camminare** | work | **lavoro** |
| to want | **volere,** | to work | **funzionare** |
| | **desiderare** | (to function) | |
| war | **guerra** | to work | **lavorare** |
| to wash (oneself) | **lavarsi** | (*opposite:* play) | |
| washing machine | **lavatrice** (*f.*) | worker | **operaio** |
| water | **acqua** | world | **mondo** |
| weak | **debole** | worse | **peggiore** |
| week | **settimana** | to write | **scrivere** |
| to weep | **piangere** | year | **anno** |
| well (*adv.*) | **bene** | yesterday | **ieri** |
| what? | **che cosa?** | you (*formal*) | **lei** |
| when? | **quando?** | you (*fam.*) | **tu** |
| where? | **dove?** | young | **giovane** |
| while | **mentre** | your | **vostro, tuo, suo** |

# Index

## Grammar

## *Words and expressions*

## Topics